IN THE SHADE OF THE JUNIPER TREE

Other Books by Ed Ainsworth

POT LUCK
EAGLES FLY WEST
CALIFORNIA JUBILEE
BILL MAGEE'S WESTERN BARBECUE COOKBOOK
DEATH CUES THE PAGEANT
PAINTERS OF THE DESERT
THE CALIFORNIA I LOVE
    (By Leo Carrillo with Ed Ainsworth)
BECKONING DESERT
GOLDEN CHECKERBOARD
ERNIE PYLE'S SOUTHWEST
    (Editor)
MAVERICK MAYOR
THE COWBOY IN ART

Fr Junípero Serra

"He always brought it about
that his subordinates were well
satisfied . . . resting under this
leafy shade so happily that we
may say of them what the holy text
says of the Prophet Elijah; namely, that 'he lay down and slept beneath the shade of a Juniper tree'
— For although it was a tree of no
great height and we were all
stretched out over this region of
more than two hundred leagues,
in spite of the fact that the shade
is supposedly small in comparison
with the size of the tree, it covered
us all with its continuous and
efficacious counsels which were
ever being sent out by his well-cut
pen. And these counsels not only
served to direct us but also to comfort and inspire us, and others with
us, in the work of the Conversion
of the gentiles and in the spiritual
and temporal development of the
Missions."

Palóu—*Vida*
(*Williams translation*)

In the Shade of the Juniper Tree

A LIFE OF FRAY JUNÍPERO SERRA

KATHERINE AINSWORTH AND
EDWARD M. AINSWORTH

With a Preface by Salvador Garcia, O.F.M.

GARDEN CITY, NEW YORK

DOUBLEDAY & COMPANY, INC.

1970

PREFACE

"Glory to the Lord, by His Saints
and by those who sing His deeds."

Edward Ainsworth and his wife Katherine have written *In the Shade of the Juniper Tree,* singing the beautiful heroic deeds of this saintly wanderer, Fray Junípero Serra, a resident of this Parish of San Fernando, who, with the support of his brothers, took it upon himself to achieve the spiritual conquest of Upper California, territory that he made to lie under the shade of the Cross of Christ.

Fray Junípero was a marvelous example of a spiritual conqueror, glory of Franciscanism, and a member of this ancient apostolic College of San Fernando, now transformed into a parish.

Don Edward Ainsworth, R.I.P., and his wife, marvels of Christianity, who have achieved this work so completely, may they be remembered and imitated for their Christianity, as those who bravely sing the glories of Fray Junípero. Oh, may it be and truly, that all who may find pleasure in the reading of their book, follow in their footsteps.

May God bless and keep in His holy peace, the beginner of this work, and give his lady the courage to continue delving into the life and history of great men. To her go our warm congratulations and Franciscan blessing, which we give her with all our heart for completing the work of her husband.

The Parish Priest
R.P. Fr. Salvador Garcia, O.F.M.
Parish of San Fernando
Mexico 3, D.F.

Translated from the Spanish by
Ignacio Soto, Jr.
Mexico City, D.F.

PREFACIO

"Alabado sea el Señor por sus Santos y
por aquellos que cantan sus proezasi."

EDUARDO AINSWORTH y su SRA. ESPOSA KATHERINE
han escrito *En la Sombra del Arbol de Junípero,* cantando las hermosas
epopeyas de este santo andariego, Fray Junípero Serra, morador de
esta Parroquia de San Fernando, quien juntamente con sus hermanos
y al frente des los mismos, se echó a cuestas la conquista espiritual
de la Alta California, a la que hizo reposar bajo la sombra de la Cruz
de Cristo.

Fray Junípero, ejemplo maravilloso de conquistador espiritual, gloria
del franciscanismo y de este antiguo Colegio Apostólico de San Fernando
que hoy día se ha transformado en parroquia.

Don Eduardo Ainsworth (R.I.P.) y su esposa, maravillas de la
cristiandad que han logrado tan plenamente esta obra, sean recordados
e imitados por su cristianismo, quienes valientemente cantan las glorias
de Fray Junípero. Ojalá y de veras, sigan los pasos de éstos señores
todos los que se recreen con la lectura de su libro.

Dios bendiga y tenga en su Santa Paz al iniciador de esta obra y a su
Sra. esposa le dé el valor de seguir escudriñando la historia de los
grandes hombres. A ella vaya nuestra felicitación más cordial y la
bendición franciscana que le mandamos de todo corazón por llevar a
cabo la obra de su esposo.

El Párroco
R.P. Fr. Salvador Garcia, O.F.M.
Parroguía de San Fernando
Mexico 3, D.F.

ACKNOWLEDGMENTS

This book was conceived and begun by Edward M. Ainsworth. It was the first of what we hoped would be a series of works we would develop together following our mutual retirements, Ed's from over four decades of journalism and mine as librarian of the city of Monrovia, California. The manuscript was well under way when suddenly, after writing all day, Ed quietly and gently, like the man he was writing about, slipped off into unknown territory to make his "Gran Entrada."

The task of completing this book thus fell upon me—an inexperienced historian and untried writer. That a book has emerged is greatly due to the encouragement and assistance of many people to whom thanks are due.

A special word of gratitude must go to Father Maynard Geiger, O.F.M., whose generosity in permitting me to lean so heavily upon his great work *The Life and Times of Fr. Junípero Serra* and his permission to quote therefrom are greatly appreciated. Father Geiger's letters of wise information were of inestimable value as was the generous sharing of vast knowledge of the expulsion of the Jesuits by Dr. Alberto F. Pradeau.

Don Meadows and Burr Belden, authorities on Baja California and Dr. William Stewart, director of Los Angeles County and State Arboretum were of great help as were the staffs of the Monrovia Public Library, Pasadena Public Library, the State Library of Jalisco, Mexico, the California State Library, the Indio Public Library, the San Diego Library, and especially the Riverside Public Library, which extended its entire resources to me including the loan of exceedingly rare volumes.

A debt of gratitude is acknowledged to my attorney, Don Lake, ably assisted by Ernest E. Sanchez, for taking care of pressing worldly problems which permitted me to have a free mind to devote to this book. Then, of course, heartfelt thanks must go to Lori Kielty, amanuensis, relentless critic, and faithful friend; and to Richard Laugharn, my editor, whose understanding and wise guidance made this book possible.

May I be forgiven for calling once again upon Palóu and quote his closing words of the *Vida:*

> Wilt thou not in meantime, beloved reader, pray for me, and if thou findest any error, attribute it not to malice, but rather excuse my weakness which I am willing to correct.

Katherine Ainsworth
Mecca, California
August, 1969

CONTENTS

IN THE SHADE OF THE JUNIPER TREE

PROLOGUE

PORTENTS AND AUGURIES

Portents hovered over the world.

It was a moment of threatening changes.

The long shadow of westering mankind was pointing, like the presaging finger of a prophet, at a savage land known as Alta California. On this primitive shore, laved by the Pacific, the rays of unfolding events in this summer of A.D. 1767 were concentrating as if the sun itself were guiding the chariot of history to a momentous rendezvous.

Alta California was being singled out as a vital way station on the new road stretching beyond the horizon.

Even in its isolation, it was exerting an enormous magnetic force. Toward it, drawn by an irresistible attraction, moved men who were to shape not only its future but that of the earth itself. Although it was as yet unsettled, except by native tribes, it was coveted by many nations. Russia was creeping toward it from the north. Great Britain, from the day in 1579 when Sir Francis Drake landed on California shores and called it New Albion, had yearned to own it. France had cast glances that way. Prussia was inciting Russia to move faster to acquire it.

Spain, already the owner of all Mexico and of the long peninsula of Baja California, had been apathetic. But there were indications she, too, was showing more interest in Alta California because of apprehension over the threats from other quarters.

At this instant, history hung suspended, awaiting developments.

These developments came in a strange way, affecting not only Alta California but the whole North American continent, from ocean to ocean, and indeed many other continents likewise. Involved were the English colonies of the East Coast, the immense savannahs and the billowing prairies and towering mountains, the endless sands of Arizona and New Mexico, and the serpentine Río Colorado emptying into the fearsome Sea of Cortés in a realm of gargantuan red tides.

Onto this monster stage came the figures of destiny. They were not great armies with banners flying, not doughty generals in crimson uniforms.

Instead, they were two former shepherd boys from Spain, one the envoy of the King and the other a simple priest intent only upon saving souls, and between them they altered the course of the earth. . . .

CHAPTER I

THE NIGHT THAT CHANGED THE WORLD,

JUNE 25, 1767

In sleeping Mexico City only the muffled footfalls of the advancing soldiers and the small flinty percussions of the cavalry horses' hoofs on the cobblestones intruded upon the sinister silence. Blackness shrouded the streets. It was the dark of the moon and, although it was after three o'clock, no hint of dawn yet was to be seen. While the three thousand soldiers, foot and horse, made their way stealthily forward, more than eighty thousand residents of the city slept in their shuttered houses behind the iron grills, unaware of any reason for a military movement in the night. Now was the normal time for church bells to begin their predawn clamor, but none sounded.

Fifty columns of troops spread out to surround their assigned areas. They marched, under orders of total silence, along the routes of old Aztec causeways, on the site of the Emperor Montezuma's palace, in the very street where the defeated Cortés and his conquistadores had fled on *La Noche de Triste*, or The Night of Sorrow, by the Palace of the Viceroy out in all directions from the brooding cathedral.

At the head of the largest column of three hundred men walked Joseph de Gálvez, the Visitador-General of the King of Spain, his head bowed, placing his feet carefully with each step to avoid stumbling on the uneven stones. In his hand he carried the King's order.

Its content was graven in his heart, and the events of the past few days leading up to this night of horror were indelibly impressed upon his tired mind. He knew that for all the rest of his life he could never forget what he was proceeding to do at this moment, June 25, 1767.

As was his custom, he had knelt and prayed before stepping out into the still blackness of this night. By praying, he always believed that somehow his burden of responsibility was shared and he could more readily face whatever task lay before him.

Beside him, almost invisible in the darkness, moved the commander of the troops. No words passed between them. Familiar as he was with Mexico City after having been in and around it for two years, Gálvez found it impossible to be sure exactly where they were. The blank walls of the houses, flush with the street, were indistinguishable from the unlighted sky. Gálvez held the royal decree tightly with one hand, groped with the other for his large gold watch, found it secure with the small key he had used to wind it at midnight before starting into the dark streets.

He felt a warning touch on his sleeve, heard a muffled order to the soldiers to halt. From his pocket he drew the watch, glanced quickly at it when the commander struck a spark. The hands showed three minutes to four. He must wait 180 seconds more. The King's order had been explicit.

At the appointed moment, he whispered a word to the commander. A doorbell sounded. The voice of a porter, thick with drowsiness, called out a question.

"Open in the name of the King," said the commander.

Inside, there was a delay while the porter apparently sought instructions from someone in authority.

"Open!" repeated the officer. "The inhabitants are under arrest in the name of the King."

The door swung on its hinges. A faint light from a taper showed inside.

"To the bell tower!" ordered the commander.

Soldiers raced through the doorway and up the stairs to prevent the bell of the Colegio Máximo de San Pedro y San Pablo, of the Society of Jesus, from sounding an alarm.

Visitador-General Gálvez stepped inside. Before him stood the rector of the college. Quietly, Gálvez issued orders to the soldiers, through their commander, to guard the ninety rooms of the Jesuits in the college and to require each to report to the chapel immediately. Then he motioned to the rector that they should consult privately. The rector bowed, moved toward his room amid some of the puzzled Jesuits who had been aroused by the entry of the soldiers.

A subdued murmur sounded as the disheveled priests were herded toward the chapel, asking one another what was happening. The soldiers' hurried steps sounded on stairways and in corridors as they moved to guard the rooms as a preliminary to a search for treasure. The rumor of hidden gold, vast stores of priceless pearls, and silver, supposedly secreted in all religious edifices, had long persisted despite constant denials by the Jesuits. Outside, the guards stood motionless as the first gray tinge of dawn began to penetrate the street.

Gálvez hastened the procedure. He informed the rector of the royal decree and asked for the keys. They were given to him. He and the rector walked to the chapel. With him Gálvez absently carried one of the huge keys after having handed the King's decree to a royal secre-

tary from the Viceroy's palace. Every eye followed the figures of Gálvez, the rector, and the secretary to the foot of the altar. The rector
held up his hands. Absolute silence enveloped the room.

The roll was called. Thirty-one fathers, forty-three scholastics, and
sixteen lay brothers answered. Ninety. Gálvez nodded. The count tal-
lied. Gálvez motioned to the secretary who began, in a trembling
voice, to read the King's decree.

As the fatal words were spoken the Jesuits at first appeared in-
credulous, then stunned.

Some bowed their heads. Others fell to their knees. Many resorted
to their rosaries, their lips moving silently.

As the secretary read the words:

> I invest you with my whole authority and royal power that you
> shall forthwith repair with an armed force—a mano armada—to
> the houses of the Jesuits. You will seize the persons of all of
> them, and dispatch them within twenty-four hours as prisoners
> to the port of Vera Cruz, where they will be embarked on vessels
> provided for that purpose. At the moment of such arrest you
> will cause to be sealed the records of said houses, and the papers
> of such persons, without allowing them to remove anything but
> their breviaries and such garments as are absolutely necessary
> for the journey.

one father raised his hands imploringly to heaven, turned his face
upward, screamed, and began to tear at his head, bereft of his reason.
Another foamed at the mouth and fell in a fit of apoplexy. The
others, aside from a few who attended the two victims, continued to
stand quietly and listen.

With the phrases: "If after the embarkation there should be found
in that district a single Jesuit, even if ill or dying, you shall suffer the
penalty of death. Yo, el Rey." the secretary concluded.

Gálvez, nervously twisting the giant key in his hands, faced the
rector and asked:

"How do you answer?"

The rector quietly replied:

"We shall obey the King."

Gálvez grew apprehensive during that long night of making preparations for the surprise raids upon the Jesuits. When he stood by the
Viceroy's side and watched him break the seals on the closely guarded
royal dispatches at eight o'clock in the evening and heard him sol-
emnly read the ominous message to the stunned assemblage, his
anxiety increased. As he looked upon the shocked faces of the archbishop of Mexico and other high officials, who had ostensibly been

summoned to a meeting for the consideration of an important and confidential affair of state, he steeled himself for the resistance he was sure they would encounter.

The rector's submission, therefore, caught him by surprise. Gálvez began to weep.

The rector took the King's order, kissed it, and asked the priests to sign it.

Gálvez, wiping his eyes, issued final orders for the searching of the rooms, the feeding of the prisoners, and the guarding of the college during the day. Then he started for the four other Jesuit colleges.

He stepped out into the sickly light in the midst of a bewildered and silent city. All church bells were stifled. The wonted clamor for early Mass was lacking. A stillness hovered over churches, businesses, and homes. The street cleaners worked with frightened faces, pushing their brooms of twigs mechanically. The reek of horse dung was in the air. A few early carts and wagons loaded with watermelons, papayas, beans, and vegetables made their way toward the markets, the drivers appearing frozen in their seats. Burros with firewood clopped dejectedly on their way. Worshipers began gathering in front of the churches, staring at the soldiers surrounding every religious house in the city. Twenty-five communities of priests and twenty of nuns were surrounded in addition to the five Jesuit residences.

Soldiers stood elbow to elbow in front of the Viceroy's palace across the zócalo from the Cathedral. Forty cannon were placed in all the surrounding avenues to cover every approach. Cavalry patrolled the whole region near the palace. Soldiers compelled everyone who entered the streets to walk by himself.

A shot sounded when one man failed to move away from another, and the victim fell bleeding and dead.

"He is deaf, he could not hear you!" cried his companion.

Women, informed they could not go to Confession, burst into tears. More than fifty thousand inhabitants were accustomed to visit the Jesuits for spiritual consolation; it began to dawn upon them that their priests were in custody. An order was issued from the Viceroy's office that no one—not even children who often put on replicas of Jesuit habits in their play—could wear any such garb.

Rumors, later borne out in actuality, swept from mouth to mouth—that death was to be the penalty for anyone caught speaking to a Jesuit, that carriages were to be seized for transporting the imprisoned priests from the capital to some unspecified destination, that the money being offered by compassionate parishioners to the Jesuits was being refused by the government officials.

Muttering crowds began to gather at the churches, crying out for administration of the sacraments. No priests were available anywhere for the purpose—Franciscans, Dominicans, or any other order. All were under precautionary detention. Shouts from the crowds grew louder and louder. The soldiers prepared for a riot.

At this moment, Gálvez hastened back to the Viceroy's palace, entering through the door and going immediately into consultation with the King's representative, Viceroy de Croix. Hasty orders were sent to the soldiers at the Franciscan and Dominican residences for the Fathers to be permitted to go to the churches to conduct Masses, in the hope of averting violence. In the meantime, soldiers were told to disperse the largest crowds demanding the Masses, until the services could be arranged.

Worse tension, Gálvez and the Viceroy learned from reports pouring in from all over the city, was developing at the Professed House of the Jesuits close to the Cathedral. This was the residence where thirty priests who had taken special vows and made such professions as direct obedience to the Pope were housed. They were regarded by the people with unusual veneration. The crowds at some of the churches, learning that the Jesuits in the Professed House and the church which faced Avenida Isabella Católica were under guard of a hundred soldiers, began to move through the streets and to talk of rescue.

Don Antonio José Areche, fiscal of the *audiencia*, the King's all-powerful court in the province of Mexico, rushed to the Viceroy's palace in a distraught state after having carried out the Professed House visitation at four in the morning. He reported in amazement that there had been total submission and the Jesuits had knelt before him, recited the "Te Deum" and then received the Sacrament. Similar reports came from the other three houses.

Already racked with emotion and suffering from extreme exhaustion, Gálvez was compelled to plunge at once into arranging transportation out of the city for the Jesuits, while at the same time preparing with the Viceroy and the military commanders to control the rioting which every moment appeared more inevitable. The commandeering of carriages was the first necessity. Gálvez and the Viceroy were certain that, despite their best efforts, it was inevitable the secret of the destination of the Jesuits would become known. The port of Vera Cruz having been specifically mentioned in the King's decree, which had been read to the Jesuits in the presence of soldiers and government officials, they feared that armed resistance would be organized along the way, and in Jalapa, the principal city on the route. The order that no one could speak to the Jesuits was more a gesture than a genuine protection of the intention to take them to Vera Cruz for exile.

Gálvez was impatiently awaiting the first reports from the other cities in Mexico where the imprisonment of the Jesuits was to be carried out. The suddenness of the King's command had made it impossible to accomplish the seizure until couriers could alert the various military leaders and civil officials who would carry out the instructions. Twenty-four colleges and five residences of the Society of Jesus were scattered throughout the provinces in addition to individual missionaries in faraway Baja California and the mountain fastnesses of the Tarahumara country. Gálvez studied again the list of Jesuit residences: in Chihuahua, Parral, Campeche, Puerto del Principe, and Parras. He expected that first reports on the colleges might come from Puebla and Valladolid. He shook his head when he speculated on how long it would take for execution of the orders in the other cities where colleges or seminaries were located: Guadalajara, Tepotzotlán, Guatemala, Querétero, Zacatecas, Oaxaca, León, Durango, Guanajuato, San Luis Potosí, Celaya, Patzcuaro, Mérida, Chiapas, San Luis de la Paz, and Vera Cruz itself.

Couriers kept coming and going every few minutes. From the Professed House came word that the soldiers had been forced to drive away the crowd, which had momentarily become more menacing. At some of the churches, the Franciscans and Dominicans were conducting Masses in an atmosphere of tension and talk of rebellion.

By midmorning the seriousness of the people's anger was made apparent in the failure of the effort to obtain carriages to take the Jesuits away. Rumors had carried the message all over the city that the priests were to be taken to Vera Cruz for shipment to Spain. Immediately, the wealthy owners of carriages—there were four thousand vehicles within a few minutes drive of the Viceroy's palace—began to drive them out of Mexico City or to hide them in barns or in the woods. A few carriages were dismembered, and the wheels rolled away and secreted.

In the crisis, every available soldier was put on duty, both to prevent rioting and to seek carriages.

Gálvez decided to attempt to restore order before risking a general insurrection by attempting the removal of the Jesuits during the daylight hours or even during the coming night.

The Visitador-General and the Viceroy went into private consultation.

They set 2 A.M. June 27—one night hence—for an experimental attempt to spirit away the Fathers at the Professed House, the center of the greatest danger, and at the small Colegio de San Gregorio with only twelve members.

Until then, they prepared to put the city under total martial rule.

Joseph de Gálvez, supreme agent of Charles III, the Bourbon King of Spain, slumped in his chair. He put his hands over his eyes. He was trying vainly to blot out his thoughts. He knew he was performing a deed for which, loyal as he was, he could never forgive himself.

"*Yo, el Rey.*"

He could see the immutable signature.

"I, the King."

Where would it all lead? Despite his unwavering loyalty to the King, Gálvez found himself pondering the question: What had turned a great monarch, a fine administrator, and a benevolent King such as Charles III into this unreasoning despot capable of such a heinous act? What forces were being unleashed? How could it end?

As a former shepherd boy in the wild mountains of his native region near Málaga, and later as a lawyer, and still later as a trusted adviser to the King, Gálvez was trained in obedience. It was a part of him. Even now, repelled as he was, he could not disobey. He gave obedience, and he exacted it, in the King's name.

Wearily, but with reverence, he crossed himself and prepared to complete the prescribed expulsion of the Jesuits. He was unable to know amid the general misery of the royal edict that he was changing the destiny not only of the unhappy members of the Society of Jesus but also that of a small priest, a fellow countryman, a follower of gentle St. Francis, whose portentous life henceforth was to be entwined with his own.

CHAPTER II

INVISIBLE ACTIVATIONS:

THE YEARS OF INTRIGUE

Invisible activations, like ghostly couriers in the dark of that moonless night, spread from the high valley of Mexico across mountains, chasms, and seas to alter the conduct of men and change the fate of distant countrysides. In whispered conversations, by letters and in official dispatches the news of the seizure of the Jesuits in Spain began to emanate in all directions. By word of mouth on lonely jungle paths the intelligence was carried from one lonely hut to another. It penetrated to villages and towns and pushed toward the ports where ships set sail to carry it across the ocean. These activations swept toward teeming capitals and savage villages. They moved to envelop emperors and kings, priests and Indians, statesmen and sailors, royal harlots and soldiers, Christians and heathen, traitors and patriots, ancient kingdoms and unborn nations.

They entered into the cauldron of human affairs where seething elements already were engendering mighty changes on the face of the earth.

On many continents men and women on this night of June 25, 1767, were engaged in activities in which the expulsion of the Jesuits was to provide a dominating element, in some cases observable with electrifying effect at once, in others forming a creeping catalyst for a slowly unfolding future.

It was the night that changed the world.

*   *   *

Years of plotting and intrigue preceded the surprising and tyrannical acts of that fateful night.

The Jesuits, at the height of their influence and dominance, were struck down by the act of an angry, indignant, and apprehensive King who had formerly looked with favor upon them.

Accused of cupidity and greed in the acquisition of wealth and subsequent refusal to pay taxes to the crown; of using the missions of the New World for their own aggrandizement; and of threatening to set up independent control of various countries where their missions had been established, they had been expelled from the dominions of King José I of Portugal in 1759 by a royal decree declaring the Jesuits to be traitors and rebels, and the estates of the society were confiscated. On the same day, a year previous, the King had been shot at and the responsibility for this crime was placed upon the Jesuits, several of their members being imprisoned. The iniquitous Marqués de Pombal, minister of state, desiring to reform the church and bring it under the strict control of the government, effected the decree as of September 2, 1759.

Following the expulsion from Portugal came the suppression of the order in France. As long as the Jesuits concerned themselves with the morals of the lower classes there was no difficulty, but when a member of the Order "interfered with the domestic arrangements" of the King of France and his mistress, the notorious Madame Pompadour, refusing to administer Holy Communion to the King until he changed his immoral ways, trouble ensued. The wrathful Pompadour brought her influence to bear upon the King, his minister, duc de Choiseul, and other men of the new philosophical school of Encyclopedists dominated by the thinking of Voltaire.

On August 6, 1762, the French parliament declared the Jesuit order to be inadmissible in any civilized state, because of its hostility to natural rights, as well as to spiritual and temporal authority. King Louis XV finally extinguished the order in November 1764. The royal harlot had won her victory. Her baleful influence did not stop in France.

Aranda, prime minister of Spain and a pupil of the same Choiseul so helpful to Pompadour in her persecution of the Jesuits, presented to King Charles III letters, forged it was later claimed, at the instigation of Choiseul, which literally drove the King to the point of insanity over the "treachery of the Jesuits." So powerful were these letters in their effect, the King refused to appoint an investigating agency, nor would he divulge their contents, but signed the Decree of Expulsion on April 2, 1767.

When Pope Clement XIII asked to have the expulsion of the Jesuits be thoroughly investigated and inquired the reasons of Charles's action, the King replied, "I shall ever keep secret in my own heart the infamous plot which has made this rigor necessary. I do so to spare the world a great scandal. Your Holiness must believe me on my word. The safety of my life requires from me a profound silence on this matter."

Subsequently the reasons for his ruthless action came to light and were never denied. The King had surrounded himself with foreign ministers with close ties to the French court and who were imbued with the spirit of the French philosophical thinking. The imperious and contemptuous Aranda shared in this thinking. Born in Aragón, he had served under Ferdinand VI as director general of artillery and introduced the Prussian system of drill to the Spanish army, which he commanded in Portugal. He was named captain general of Valencia in 1764 and later of Aragón and then became President of the Council of Castile. Entering politics two years later, he soon became a powerful figure at court. Playing both ends against the middle was easy for him and he became a grand master of Spanish Freemasonry while remaining a Catholic.

It was Aranda who privately presented the King a forged letter purporting to be from the general of the Jesuits to the superior of the central Jesuit house in Madrid. It bore a Roman postmark and other signs of authenticity. The letter stated that the author had in his possession absolute proof of the King's illegitimacy and contained threats of publication at a fitting time. With Aranda's insistence that the letter was authentic, the King accepted it as genuine and was maniacally angry, both at the slander against his family and the danger of someone else claiming the right to the throne. He signed the decree ending the order both in Spain and the New World.

The malevolent Aranda, to make certain the impact of this act would be felt by Jesuits everywhere on the same day, had maps spread before the irate King and his councilors. Careful calculations of distances were made and extreme care taken to plan so carefully that nothing was overlooked which could possibly keep the plot from succeeding. Several regiments of Spanish soldiers were hastily sent to Mexico to quell any possible riots.

Utmost secrecy prevailed, and the haste with which the act was put into effect took the people as well as the victims by shocked surprise. Later, when the people had time to ponder, a story was whispered about that in his need for secrecy, Aranda had brought children from all corners of Spain and each was given a scrap of writing to copy. The fragment made no sense until joined with other pieces and in this manner, so it was rumored, the fateful decree was copied.

In reality the first draft was written in the penmanship of his secretary and signed by the King on February 27, 1767. The transcription, dated March 1, 1767, and signed by the secretary of state, the Count of Aranda, was printed and issued at Madrid. The Decree of Expulsion, planned to be put into effect June 25, 1767, simultaneously in Spain and all its possessions, had to be sent overseas and sufficient time allowed for its execution. It is not known for sure where and when the notices were printed, but it is known that certain secret documents were being printed at the printing establishment of the "Cazeta" (a government publication) and the employees, all of them, were held in the shop, with soldiers guarding all exits, day and night for several days.

The order for the expulsion of the Jesuits reached Carlos Francisco de Croix, forty-fifth viceroy of New Spain on May 30 and was dated March 14, 1767, and consisted of several pages of instructions given in minute detail. These had to be reprinted in Mexico City to be distributed among the official couriers in order that the decree could be placed in the hands of the officers who were to carry it out. It is not a matter of historical record just how this reproduction was done, but it was rumored that the Viceroy called in José Antonio Hogal, owner of a printing shop, and threatened him with death if he divulged the contents of the royal order.*

De Croix had served his King well as a lieutenant-general of the royal army and as a colonel of the Walloon guards. King Charles regarded him highly as a man of fine character, bravery, and above all of absolute fealty to the monarch, and one who would comply with the demands of the Visitador-General. De Croix, having replaced the recalcitrant Viceroy Cruíllas at Gálvez's request, took one look at the reprinted orders and realized their portentous implications and sent for his own nephew, Teodoro de Croix, and the Visitador-General.

Once the three were sequestered in the palace, they acted with all the secrecy of the original framing of the decree dictated by Aranda and its promulgation. De Croix told them of the awesome contents of the message. They sat stunned with the realization of what the implications would be.

De Croix spoke softly, "As all the inhabitants are worthy pupils and zealous partisans of that company, I have taken good care to trust none of them with the execution of the decree of the King. The secret would surely have gotten out, which would by no means have been convenient."

Gálvez nodded in agreement, his eyes staring fixedly upon the pale face of the Viceroy.

"For this reason," continued the hoarse whisper of De Croix, "I have decided to confide in none but you Señor Gálvez, who is here in the service of the King, and to you, my trusted nephew. We three, therefore, shall make all the arrangements ourselves, writing with our own hands all the orders necessary."

Wordlessly they sat around a table and began to copy dispatches to be sent with the King's orders. They worked silently and, as the hours

* Alberto Francisco Pradeau. *La Expulsión de los Jesuítas de las Provincias de Sonora, Ostimuri, y Sinaloa.* Mexico, 1959.

of the night dragged on, their ink-stained fingers cramped and ached. In their haste they occasionally misspelled important names.

Finally the task was completed, De Croix rose and stretched his aching arms and said, "Gentlemen, these will immediately be dispatched by special messenger, that they may be carried out simultaneously to the most remote places of this vast empire."

The greatest care was exercised in the choice of officers sent to the outlying provinces for the purpose of delivering the letters. Among them were some members of the Visitador's official family, going out supposedly as subdelegates of the visitation, but all secretly carrying the orders for the expulsion. Army officers were also sent, but the public believed them to be on military assignment. This was done, wrote Gálvez later, because it was deemed absolutely necessary, as, once the secret was out, "New Spain would have become the bloody theatre of the gravest tragedies, for there was in fact no other authority recognized than that of the regulars of the Company."

The messages having been copied and safely put into the hands of trusted messengers taking them into the far regions, De Croix waited until early in the evening of June 24, 1767, to summon the audiencia, the archbishop of Mexico, and the rest of the high officials to the palace, and then staged one of history's greatest bits of play-acting. They had been called together supposedly for the consideration of an important and confidential affair of state. De Croix, with a flourish, produced a sealed package that he had received from the supreme government. He removed the carefully resealed outer envelope revealing another enclosed within upon which was written the words: "*So pena de la vida, no abrireis este; hasta, que llege el 24 de junio a la caída de la tarde.*" (Under penalty of death, you will not open this wrapper till June 24 at nightfall.)

This cover was removed and instructions were found giving explicit directions concerning the measures to be taken in the arrest of the Jesuits, naming those who were to do the task and directions on how they were to proceed. After removing another wrapper, the last, De Croix read to the stunned group the words of the King ordering the expulsion of the Jesuits ending with the ominous words: "*Yo, el Rey.*"

Just before sunrise the next morning of June 25, 1767, was the time for the execution of the royal decree. Gálvez, uneasy as he was about the assured revolt of the people to such a decree, nevertheless prepared to obey his King. He selected the Colegio Máximo de San Pedro y San Pablo, of the Society of Jesus, as his responsibility.

Glancing at the Viceroy and receiving a brief nod of approval, Gálvez left the palace and welcomed the darkness of the moonless night. It was as though for a brief moment he could draw back the cloak of anonymity about him in the blackness. He smiled grimly as he recalled the look of horror upon the faces of those assembled to hear the reading of the King's orders. The archbishop had taken comfort in his beads while the others had shrunk into a state of agitation and shock. By this time, De Croix undoubtedly had explained that they were to remain within the palace until the surprise move upon the Jesuits had taken place. Hot chocolate and sweet bread would be served, but no one would be permitted to leave. There must be no opportunity for an alarm to be sounded.

The hours of the fateful night wearily dragged on. There was still much to be done. Joseph de Gálvez braced himself for the rigors dawn would bring.

*   *   *

This night that changed the world was to have a marked influence upon two former shepherd boys from Spain. At this moment of travail, Joseph de Gálvez, representative of the King of Spain and an active participant in the night's events, was unaware even of the existence of the other, Fr. Junípero Serra of Majorca. In a crude Indian village thirty leagues from Mexico City the small Franciscan priest, rising in the dark as was his custom, watched the dawn begin to outline the mighty buttresses and massive tower of the church at Ixmiquilpan, once the capital of the Otomí Indians. His mind turned to his next sermon in the mission he was preaching to these natives. He dwelt in his thoughts upon the imagery he sought to use to convey to his listeners the glory of the Faith and the meaning of the Christian mysteries. He knew nothing of the King's expulsion order for the Jesuits and was unaware that this action was creating for him a challenging new pathway into the future.

CHAPTER III

FIRST SHEPHERD BOY:

MIGUEL JOSÉ (JUNÍPERO) SERRA

He was born in a small stone house of almost biblical primitiveness in the village of Petra on the island of Majorca at one o'clock in the morning of November 24, 1713. The third child born to Antonio and Margarita Serra, his father hurried him to the parish Church of San Pedro where he was christened Miguel José that same day. The first two children having died in infancy, the adoring parents were taking no chances with this child.

The little home on Calle Barracar radiated religion, and parental piety was infused into the boy as he grew. He said his catechism as naturally as he ate the simple fare prepared by his loving mother, and made his devotions quite as matter-of-factly as he took the livestock to pasture or carried water home from the town pump. He soon became familiar with farm work, for on Majorca children at an early age joined with their parents and grandparents in going out to the fields they cultivated. Usually the Majorcan peasants lived some distance from the land they farmed and left their homes early in the morning with carts drawn by gentle donkeys and filled with small children and farm implements, or they walked afoot and joined with other relatives and friends chatting and gossiping as they went to the fields.

The day's work was done industriously and in an unhurried manner, for the serenity and calmness, particular to the native-born Majorcan seldom ever left him. The constant burden of the hoeing and tilling of the land, which had been carried on for generations in order to wrest a living from the rocky soil, was made bearable by the beauty of the island terrain. On Majorca, amid the blue and purple seas, with ancient stone-walled terraces upon which grew pomegranates, figs, plums, melons, olives, almonds, and oranges, life was pleasant and contentment was a way of life.

Dominating the plain of Petra, and plainly to be seen from the fields of grain below, was the hill of Bon Any. Crowning this hill the chapel of the patron saint of Petra, Nuestra Señora de Bon Any or

Our Lady of the Good Year, was then as now a place of pilgrimage dear to the hearts of the people.

A small boy lying on the grass on this hilltop, which stretched heavenward for over a thousand feet, could look out over most of the island of Majorca and catch glimpses of the glistening blue waters of the Mediterranean. The constant breezes, wafting the fragrance of wild flowers blooming midst the fields of grain, with here and there the blaze of a poppy making an intense burst of color, forced the arms of the giant windmills, Petra's main source of water supply, to turn patiently in endless motion.

A boy's daydreams might have reached out to those faraway lands out beyond the waters of the Mediterranean. That sea had played a dominant role in his heritage. For twenty centuries the islanders had experienced the impact of both Romans and Greeks sailing to their shores. It is claimed that it was from the island of Majorca that Hannibal recruited his regiment of powerfully accurate stone throwers who won many battles for him. They had traded with the Greeks during the age of Pericles and had sent their athletes to compete in the Olympic games. And mythical history tells that Hercules found the golden apples of the Hesperides on the island. Dominated successively by Carthage, Rome, the Barbarians, and the Moors, the doughty Majorcans had set up their own independent kingdom in 1229, only to be forced to surrender to the King of Aragón, and then in 1479 they had been united with the crown of Spain.

The rocky coast line with its hidden coves and inlets was the hiding place of marauding pirates. A system of watchtowers was built around the perimeter of the island with huge piles of straw and wood ready to communicate alarms, by smoke during the day and fire by night, and each had a watchman with a conch shell ready to sound warnings to the farmers of approaching danger from the sea. By 1590 this warning system had been perfected by the efforts of the physician, astronomer, and chronicler of Majorca, Dr. don Juan Binimelis, until every cove and stretch of the coast line was protected by a tower.

But the imagination of the boy Serra was not primarily stirred to such romantic things. He thought of those distant lands with their heathen waiting the word of the Faith and he longed to imitate the lives of the saints he read about and to go forth to save souls.

From the hilltop of Bon Any, the town of Petra with its two thousand inhabitants could plainly be seen. Even from the hilltop could be sensed the air of hushed quietude that pervaded the little town. One could almost feel the gentle stamp of serenity which seemed to rest upon the small stone houses with their tiny walled gardens. The frail lad, gazing down upon the rooftops of variegated colored tiles—some

beige, some dark brown, and others amber in color—and all quivering
with the heat waves of the sun, could single out the top of his own
snug home. The Serra home consisted of two stories. On the first floor
there was a parlor, a kitchen, and a small adjoining stable for the
family donkey. An arched front door led directly from the street into
the parlor with its rough cement floor and walls painted a stark white.
The upper story was mainly a large room used for drying and storage
purposes. Off this was a tiny room with a sloping roof, and it was in
this room that the boy had been born.

On the Calle Mayor, two blocks from the house where he was born
on Calle Barracar, the imposing Gothic tower of the Church of San
Pedro, the parish church of his Baptism, and the Moorish tower of
San Bernardino, the convent church attached to the Franciscan monastery, rose up as sentinels protecting the faithful. On a warm sunny
day the sound of church bells tolling, the tones softly muted by distance, must have had a special meaning and beauty to the sensitive
lad standing on the hill of Bon Any.

Such a boy, comforted by the closeness of the Patroness Virgin
Mary, who was affectionately called Our Lady of Good Harvests,
would store up such impressions and memories. Sixty years later in his
life, while in those far-off lands of his childhood dreams, he would
recall the serene, ample figure of this beloved image as she sat in the
chapel holding her rotund infant son upon her knee. He would then
record in the baptismal book of the Mission San Carlos that he baptized an Indian girl and "gave her the name of Buen Año. This is
the title by which Most Holy Mary is known in my beloved homeland."

Spanish became the language he used in his daily apostolic work,
but when he recalled the gentle days of his childhood, he often
reverted to the native patois of Majorca. The language of the Majorcans is more predominately Catalán than Spanish and Catalonian
is a sturdy, vigorous language—not French, and not completely Spanish. Serra was to reserve the Catalán of his youth for letters to his
family and he would come to use phrases from both languages inter-
changeably.

From his earliest childhood the boy Serra walked down the narrow
cobblestoned Calle Mayor with his parents to the Church and Friary
of San Bernardino, where he was greatly loved and admired by the
friars for his quick intellect and devout nature. He studied Latin at
the primary school for boys and became perfect in it. He also became
skilled in chants and sang in the choir all the while nursing the
fervent desire to wear the habit of the Franciscan Order. As soon as
his parents realized the intensity of their son's wishes for a religious
vocation they took him to the capital city of Palma.

The twenty-five-mile journey from his native Petra through the terraced farmlands, past the orchards of almonds and the olives, gnarled and tortured into grotesque shapes by the passage of time, plunged the boy into a maelstrom of sound and activity. So that he would not forget the childhood teachings of good morals and religious doctrine, his parents placed him in the charge of a canon of the Cathedral. This devout priest, seeing how the boy applied himself to the study of philosophy and realizing the seriousness of his purpose, taught him to recite the Divine Office.

The shy country boy must have looked upon the massive strength of the Cathedral of Palma and trembled with wonder at the severely impressive edifice which had dominated the shores of the fifteen-mile-long bay since the thirteenth century. Built upon the site of a former mosque, it had been dedicated to the Blessed Virgin by King Jaime I. The light coming in through the brilliant-colored glass of the round windows, only dimly piercing the gloom of the Cathedral's vastness, would have pressed down upon the boy who could not possibly have known that one day in 1743 he would stand upon the altar and deliver a Corpus Christi sermon which would win him great renown. To preach this sermon in the Cathedral was an honor granted only to orators of proven outstanding ability.

Nearby the Cathedral stood the Lonja, or formal commercial exchange and the architectural treasure of the city. Guillermo Sagrera, the great architect of Perpignan, built the Lonja, taking twelve years to do so and at his own expense. Did the boy Serra passing by this building going to and fro from the Cathedral take any interest in the excitement and noisy confusion which went on as the merchants gathered daily to harangue and carry on the financial affairs of the city?

During this year Serra applied to the Provincial of Majorca for admission to the Franciscan Order and was rejected because of his small stature and frail, youthful appearance. It was not until his teachers earnestly presented his cause that he was permitted to enter the Convent of Jesus, outside the walls of Palma.

The year of probation passed quickly and Serra made his religious profession in the Convent of Jesus on September 15, 1731. He considered this day to be the most beautiful in his life and thereafter renewed his vows each anniversary date because, as he frequently said, "All good things came to me with it." He even credited his improvement in health and growth to the blessings he received from taking the vows of chastity, poverty, and obedience. "When I was a novice I was always sickly and very small of body, so small I could not reach the choir rack, nor could I help my companions in the little labors of our service, and for that reason the Master of Novices employed me to serve at all the saying of Masses; but after making the vows I began to grow in strength and health and succeeded in reaching a medium stature. All this I attribute to my Profession, for which I ever gave thanks to God." He made a further secret vow that he would strive all the days of his life toward saintliness.

As he donned the rough habit of his chosen order, an undergarment of coarsely woven cloth next to the skin, a loosely fitting monk's robe with a cowl, tied about the waist with a belt made of a white cord with three knots, and sandals upon bare feet, the time had come for him to decide whether he would retain his own name or if he would take one of a religious nature. In Serra's mind there was but one choice.

In all his reading about the venerable men of the seraphic order founded by his beloved St. Francis, one humble soul touched his heart with great tenderness. This was Brother Junípero, the constant companion and helper of the Founder, whose holy phrases and graces delighted Serra.

This Brother Junípero was a delightfully simple soul with disarming ways of always taking everything in its most literal sense. He was a cobbler, with a childlike, warm, and impulsive nature, and so selfless he had to be watched lest he give the gold altar cloth to the poor. St. Clare called him "God's toy" and he became known as the "Jester of God." Once, after being instructed he must refrain from giving everything to the poor, he said to a beggar, "The guardian has ordered me not to give away my tunic. But, of course, if you would like to take it from me . . ."

It has been said that Brother Junípero feigned insanity and stupidity to humble himself in the eyes of his fellows and in the eyes of God. Actually he was far more than a quaint old fool and possessed a ready wit and was of high intelligence, often speaking in an epigrammatic speech. He was highly regarded by St. Francis who said of him, after receiving complaints from other members of the Order, "Would that I had a forest of such trees."

Miguel José Serra became Fr. Junípero Serra on that day and vowed to be one of the trees in the forest of St. Francis. He would strive for the hardiness and resilience of the juniper tree, undaunted by any winds of adversity; and forever, as long as breath lasted in him, wield a persistent saw (Serra) to cut down all the works of the devil.

From that moment on he would lead the life demanded by the rules of the Franciscan Order and daily spend from six to seven hours in prayer and reciting the breviary, or Divine Office, for the day—matins, lauds, prime, tierce, sext, nones, vespers, and compline. The rigorous daily schedule customarily began at midnight and lasted until 2 A.M.

with the recitation of matins and lauds in chorus, followed by a period devoted to silent prayer. Rising at 6 A.M. prayer, prime and tierce were recited with Mass being followed by breakfast. At 11 A.M. came sext and nones and an examination of conscience, the noontime meal recreation period and siesta lasted until 4 P.M. Vespers, compline, and prayer preceded the seven-o'clock meal, then evening prayer and bed. The lay brothers spent the remaining time in manual labor while the clerics studied, taught, or preached.

Leaving the Convent of Jesus, Junípero returned to the center of the town and spent the next seventeen years at San Francisco, both as a student and as a teacher of philosophy. This church, the second largest on the island, was started two hundred and eleven years before Columbus obstinately followed his vision and sailed forth against great odds to discover the New World. The church of San Francisco, with its twenty-three side chapels would always remain dear to Serra and in his memory he would recall the beauty of its cloistered gardens enclosed by arches of wondrous beauty and symmetry. He enjoyed walking along the wide ambulatories and meditating as the light patterns made by sunlight playing upon the Moorish style arches, cast shadows upon the monastery walls, making a lovely picture of ageless tranquillity. In the center of this garden was the old well supplying water to the Order and bearing the date of 1658 carved upon it.

Because of his brilliant success as a student, his superiors suggested to Junípero that he take the competitive examination for professor of philosophy which he successfully passed, and thus was permitted to teach philosophy and theology before taking his final vows. He lectured for three years and was exceedingly popular with his students. He had as many as sixty pupils, religious as well as secular at one time, many of whom under his inspiration went on to earn their doctorates. Among his students were Francisco Palóu and Juan Crespí, who became his devoted disciples and lifetime friends, following him wherever his apostolic work called.

Both were natives of Palma and were destined to gain fame, but in a quieter, less dramatic manner than their instructor. Palóu was born January 26, 1723, and was baptized at the Cathedral the next day, being given the name of Francisco Miguel José Joachim. He entered the Franciscan novitiate November 1, 1739. After serving with Serra faithfully and subserviently, Palóu in the year before his retirement undertook to write a biography of his venerable teacher. This rates as one of the finest biographies ever written and it is to his work that all researchers first turn when beginning the study of Serra's life. Subsequent investigation has brought to light additional documentation, most of which actually bears out Palóu's account.

Crespí, on the other hand, was to become known as a diarist, explorer, and naturalist with the Portolá expedition in the distant land of California. He was born March 1, 1721, and became a Franciscan novice on January 2, 1738.

Serra became a priest just before Christmas 1737 and was made doctor of theology in 1743. At the University of Palma he taught higher dogmatics according to the philosophical and theological teachings of Duns Scotus (1266–1308), considered by many authorities to have been the most profound and original philosopher of the Middle Ages. Serra occupied the most distinguished chain in the university of Palma, which had been founded by Ramón Llull during the Middle Ages. Majorcans look with reverence upon Blessed Ramón Llull (1235–1315) and consider him to be the greatest man ever born upon their island.

"Llull stands forth as so splendid a pioneer and initiator in so many fields that we can well understand the enthusiastic verdict of those who declare that he is the most remarkable figure of the Middle Ages. For the philologist he is the first of Catalán poets. In philosophy he is the great thinker. In religion he is on the spiritual side of the founder of Spanish mysticism, the father of all the Spanish and many other later European mystics, and on the practical side the finest type of the modern missionary, admiring and learning from those he seeks to convert, even though he dies for his own faith."*

The Majorcans love to tell the story of the dashing medieval figure, once a troubadour and cavalier born into a royal family, who loved so ardently that his songs and name were known throughout the land. He passionately pursued a lady of great beauty and followed her into the Church of Santa Eulalia on horseback, to the horror of the other worshipers. One day, seeing no other way to quell the impetuosity of the young man, the lady uncovered her bosom and revealed to him the cancerous growth which was ravishing her beauty. Ramón was so repelled he lost all desire for carnal pleasures. He claimed that an inner voice called to him and he sought spiritual guidance in a pilgrimage to the shrines of Roque d' Amadour and Compostella. Ramón Llull became a Franciscan friar after renouncing his wealth and social position. He withdrew to the mountaintops where he became an *iluminado*. Through this inner illumination he was led into scholastic philosophy. He wrote an extraordinary work, the *Arbor Vitae*, which was the compendium of all human knowledge and thus is recognized as the world's first encyclopedia. His years as a missionary among the Moslems in Arabia and his deep philosophical beliefs influenced countless scholars and had a lasting impression upon Junípero

* Havelock Ellis. *The Soul of Spain*. London, 1911.

Serra who occupied the chair at the University named in Llull's honor for so many years. "In it," Palóu was to write, "he did his work with great fame as a man of profound learning to the satisfaction of both his Province as well as of the University."

Serra gained fame as a preacher and became greatly in demand during his vacations from the university. Because of the melodious quality of his voice and the fluency and gracefulness of his language as well as the fervor of his religious convictions, he was given the honor of delivering the annual lecture honoring Ramón Llull.

It was during the fifth year of his professorship at the university that Serra was invited to give this sermon honoring Llull. This annual event honored the patron saint of the university and was given in the Church of San Francisco, which contained the remains of the great man. Serra must have gazed up at the sarcophagus with the reclining figure representing the Blessed Ramón, which was tilted rather than placed horizontal so that the viewers below could have full view, many times and derived inspiration from it. Privately believing this to be the last sermon he would preach at Palma, Junípero devoted many hours to its preparation as it was to be preached before the most elite members of society and the most learned of religious scholars. His sonorous voice filled the vast caverns of the church. So lofty was the message he preached and so melodious the words, Palóu overheard one member of the audience state that the sermon "deserved to be printed in gold."

Despite all the honor and fame coming to him as a noted lecturer, and the satisfaction gained by teaching such outstanding pupils as Palóu and Crespí, who were to be his lifelong friends and companions, Junípero deep in his heart knew anguish and remorse because he was being thwarted in his ardent yearning to be among the heathen. He dreamed of following in the footsteps of the great missionary St. Francis Solano who had traveled alone throughout Peru, Chile, and northern Argentina, playing the violin and singlehandedly baptizing several hundred thousand natives.

At last, a way out of this dilemma presented itself.

Word came to the university that a special representative from the apostolic college of San Fernando of Mexico had arrived in Spain. This college in Spanish America was especially dedicated to the conversion of savage Indians and sent a recruitment representative to Spain every ten or fifteen years to obtain new recruits for this dangerous work. Father Mezquía, the representative, sent word to the university that he had reliably been informed that one of their friars wished to join with the other thirty-three missionaries he had orders to bring back with him.

Palóu, upon hearing about this from Father Rafael Verger, a professor on the faculty, decided to apply for one of these vacancies but could not bring himself to do so without confiding in his beloved master. Serra intercepted him as Palóu was about to open the door. He had come to confide in Palóu that he was the friar being mentioned. They wept with joy and agreed immediately and secretly to begin the preparatory steps. In January Serra wrote to the all-powerful Father Velasco, commissioner of the Indies, whose decision as to whom would be chosen would be final. One month later a discouraging response was received and the letter informed the two conspirators that the delegate from San Fernando had made up the contingent and no places for them were available. Their letter was to be kept on file in the off chance any of the applicants failed to take the trip.

Fortune favored them, for when Father Mezquía and his thirty-three recruits arrived at Cádiz, the port of embarkation, five of them who had never looked upon the mighty sweep of the sea cringed with fright and returned to their homes. Mezquía hurriedly sent Junípero the two authorizations he had requested.

Junípero was preaching Lenten sermons in the church of his youth when Palóu rushed to Petra and brought him the diploma making him a member of the College of San Fernando. He finished his duties and preached before his parents on Easter Sunday for the last time. The following Thursday he knelt before them and asked for their blessing and then, choking back the tears, departed without telling them he was leaving them forever. The two friends sailed from Palma on an English cargo ship on April 13.

The excitement of their first sea voyage was immediately marred by the actions of the captain of the vessel. He was "an obstinate heretic" according to Palóu and during the first part of the voyage refused to leave them long enough for them to recite the Divine Office. He had a musty Bible which had been translated into English and kept challenging the two priests about dogmas. Besides English he spoke a little Portuguese in which he could barely make himself understood.

He plagued them by reading a passage of scripture and then placing his own interpretation upon it. Serra, the Bible student, easily perceived the errors of his statements and quoted the correct passage and then quoted another which upset the irate man's arguments. The captain, resorting once again to his tattered Bible and then unable to find a way out of his mistake, would proclaim that a leaf must have been torn from his Book. "He was," said Palóu, "left in confusion and ashamed, but would never give up, but remained obstinate."

The captain's irritation grew to such proportions he daily threatened to throw them overboard, but Serra, quietly and as obstinate in his own gentle way, continued to defend the scriptures until the captain wrathily drew his knife and pointed it at the friar's throat. At last the burly Palóu bravely interceded and threatened to prefer charges against the captain, which would have meant his head in a court of Spanish law, if he failed to put them ashore at Málaga. The angry captain threw himself upon his bed consumed with wrath, and all the night the two priests kept a watchful eye on the "perverse heretic," who managed to restrain his anger and did not bother them for the rest of the two-week voyage to Málaga. Palóu recalled Serra's words to him that night: "I can comfort myself by the thought that I never provoked him to conversation or to dispute, as it seemed to me that was time lost, but that in conscience it was my duty to make a reply for the credit of our Catholic Religion."

They rested at the Convent of San Francisco in the province of Granada for five days and then departed for Cádiz, reaching that port on May 7.

Before embarking from Cádiz, Junípero wrote in his native tongue a tender, loving, and compassionate letter of farewell to his adored parents sending it to his father's cousin, because neither of his parents could read, and asked that he read it aloud to them:

Long Live Jesus, Mary, Joseph!
Most dear Friend in Jesus Christ, Father Francisco Serra:
Dear, intimate friend: Words cannot express the feelings of my heart as I bid you farewell nor can I properly repeat to you my request that you be the consolation of my parents to sustain them in their sorrow. I wish I could communicate to them the great joy that fills my heart. If I could do this, then surely they would always encourage me to go forward and never turn back. Let them remember that the office of an apostolic preacher, especially in its actual exercise is the greatest calling to which they could wish me to be chosen. . . .
Tell them that I shall ever feel the loss of not being able to be near them as theretofore to console them, but since first things must come first and before all else, the first thing to do is to fulfill the will of God. It was for the love of God that I left them and if I, for the love of God and with the aid of His grace, had the strength of will to do so, it will be to the point that they too, for the love of God be content to be deprived of my company. . . .
Let them rejoice that they have a son who is a priest, though

an unworthy one and a sinner, who daily in the holy sacrifice
of the Mass prays for them with all the fervor in his soul
and on many days applies the Mass for them alone, so that the
Lord may aid them; that they may not lack their daily bread,
that He may give them patience in their trials, resignation to
His holy will, peace and union with everyone, courage to fight
the temptations of the evil one and last of all, when it is God's
will, a tranquil death in His holy grace. If I, by the grace of
God, succeed in becoming a good religious, my prayers will
become more efficacious, and they in consequence will be gain-
ers. . . .
Finally, may the Lord bring us together in heaven and for the
present may He guard Your Reverence for many years as I
beseech Him to do.
From this house of the Holy Mission in this city of Cádiz,
August 20, 1749.

> Your cordial friend in Christ,
> Fray Junípero Serra,
> Most unworthy priest.

Once this letter was written, Junípero wholeheartedly turned his
thoughts westward and entered into the preparations for the voyage.
The ship *Villasota*, formerly *Nuestra Señora de Guadalupe*, and cap-
tained by Juan Manuel de Bonilla, with twenty Franciscans and seven
unnamed Dominicans aboard, departed from Cádiz on August 30
or 31, 1749 (the records are confusing). The voyage was one of great
deprivations, the worst being the lack of drinking water, the rations
having been reduced to about one half pint every twenty-four hours.
Junípero later wrote, "There were moments when my throat was burning so I would have drunk slime." However, he must have given no
indication of discomfiture to his shipmates for we find Palóu stating,
"One would have said he was the only person who was not suffering
from thirst." To those who marveled at his fortitude and commented
upon it, Serra wryly answered, "I have observed the best way of
saving one's saliva is to eat little and talk less." Humble though he was,
Junípero justifiably took satisfaction in being the sole member of
the expedition who did not succumb to seasickness.

The harried voyagers welcomed a stopover at Puerto Rico from
October 18 to 31. While on the island they preached a mission because
they learned that most of the inhabitants had not gone to Confession
during the nine years since a previous group of Franciscan missionaries
had passed through. They "scattered themselves all over the city in
order to take it by storm with homilies and pious ejaculations, and

then marched into the Cathedral." By the time of their departure not a single person was left without having confessed, so fervent was the zeal of Father Junípero Serra.

They sailed for Vera Cruz the second of November and had almost arrived at that port when a tremendous storm struck, driving their vessel with such fury they sought intercession of the Saints for protection. They arrived at Vera Cruz on December 9, 1749.

After a brief rest, he preached a mission to the people of Vera Cruz at the Church of Santo Domingo and was well received by them. Serra was now ready to begin his long journey along El Camino Real, or The King's Highway, to save the heathen and bring them to God.

Small of stature, large of heart, he staunchly set out to accomplish his task.

CHAPTER IV

SECOND SHEPHERD BOY:

JOSEPH DE GÁLVEZ

When young Serra was seven years of age and attending school at the Convent of San Bernardino in Petra, a boy was born in an obscure village in the rocky foothills in Andalusian Spain near Vélez-Málaga. Joseph Bernardo Gálvez Gallardo,* second son of Antonio Gálvez y Carbajal and Ana Gallardo Jurado, was born on January 2, 1720. The small hamlet of his birth consisted of some two hundred whitewashed little houses. The cobblestone streets were narrow and the town of Macharavialla had several little plazas. A rocky ridge connected Monte de las Piedras, the exact site of the Gálvez home, to an adjoining ridge upon which rested the village.

The Gálvez family was poor—poorer than most of the residents, the father having died before Joseph was born—and the boy spent his early years tending animals on the hillsides. From the crest on the steep, stony elevation the boy could look down the winding arroyo through the outcroppings of gray slate to an indentation between the hills and catch a glimpse of the glistening sea. The sea would beckon to such a lad as this with his restless energy and driving ambition. Phoenician boats had plied their way some three thousand years ago upon those very waters, and later on pirates had lurked in the quiet bays near Málaga waiting to pounce upon unsuspecting victims. Along the coast line ruins of Moorish castles and old fortresses stood as silent, ghostly sentinels of another era. Midst the twisted olive trees and fragrant lemon groves, growing upon the rounded hill-

* A word of explanation about this name is in order. Born Joseph Bernardo Gálvez Gallardo; never signing his name in any other manner but Joseph, except for several occasions when he used Josef; designated Joseph in his commission as Visitador-General from King Charles III of Spain, by some inexplicable fate he is always mentioned as José de Gálvez by historians. Herbert Ingram Priestley in 1911 wrote what is still the definitive biography of Gálvez and began his prefatory biographical sketch by using the name Joseph and then made the somewhat puzzling statement that he was going to modernize the first name . . . thus "Joseph Gálvez becomes José Gálvez," and every writer from that time has done the same. We have chosen to use the form preferred by the man himself and, therefore, have called him Joseph de Gálvez.

sides of brick-red clay and stretching out on both sides of the dusty arroyo with its tracing of rutted wagon tracks, the boy Joseph Gálvez dreamed of fame and of those far-off places.

His family had a noble though modest ancient lineage and could claim the rank of *hijodalgo,* or hidalgo. One ancestor, having fought valiantly against the Moors, was granted the privilege of sepulture and a permanent sitting place in the village church. They were known as "Old Christians" and certified as not having heathen or foreign blood; nor had they ever engaged in any low or mechanical employment. All this was documented at a later date when one of the brothers sought an honor from the crown.

Joseph's quick, agile mind soon came to the attention of the local priest, as the boy managed to catch infrequent moments of schooling. The priest made him an acolyte of the little church of San Jacinto de Macharavialla and when he was about fourteen, Joseph was brought to the attention of the Bishop of Málaga. The bishop obtained a scholarship, or *beca,* in the Colegio Seminario de San Sebastian de Málaga and there he began his studies for the priesthood. When this bishop died, Joseph evidently had a change of mind about a religious vocation and the new bishop assisted him in obtaining entrance in the famous old University of Salamanca where he began the study of law.

Details of his life are vague during this period and the official records of the university do not list his name. However, he somehow obtained a law degree and then spent the next twenty years of his life as a struggling lawyer in Madrid. He managed to obtain an appointment in 1750 to the office of governor of Zamboanga, Mindanao, in the Philippine Islands for a period of five years. There is no record of his ever having gone to the Philippines to fulfill the duties of this appointment and he may have obtained it merely for the purpose of selling it.

It was on August 2, 1750, that he married his second wife, Lucía Romet y Pichelin, a Frenchwoman. Little is known of his first wife, María Magdalena Grimaldo, who died without giving him a child. It was undoubtedly through the influence of his second wife that he obtained a knowledge of the French language and a place of influence in the social life dominated at the time by representatives of France. He became legal counselor for the French ambassador and made capital of this advantageous position to capture the attention of Grimaldi, first minister of state to Charles III, who made him one of his secretaries.

It was also about this time that a noted lawsuit between a foreign house of business and the state occurred with Gálvez representing the foreigners. His brilliance won the case to the astonishment of all the ablest legal minds and he came to the attention of the King. The youthful attorney was granted the honor of a private interview with Charles III. When the King commented upon his boldness in defending a case against the state, Gálvez is rumored to have answered, "Señor, antes que el rey está la rey"—"My lord, the law is greater than the King."

It is said that this boldness and quickness of wit so charmed the King that Gálvez found himself well on his way to social distinction. By royal order Gálvez was made *alcalde de casa y corte,* or civil and criminal municipal justice, on November 25, 1764. He was quick to take advantage of this position as it brought him into close contact with the Council of Castile, which supervised the functions of the alcaldes. It was then that he made the acquaintance of the powerful Count Aranda and the two fiscals, Moñino and Campomanes, who spurred him on his way toward success in public service for which he gained much acclaim.

Gálvez entered into his new duties as alcalde with enthusiasm, but his career was soon to be interrupted. He was called to a more demanding and dangerous task.

Charles III faced a financial crisis. Recuperating from the war between England on the one hand and France on the other, Spain desperately needed to strengthen its sources of revenue. While it was true that the Treaty of Paris in 1763 brought hostilities to an end between the three countries, each considered the treaty binding only until it was ready to resume fighting. While France had been removed as a colonial power, Spain found that for the first time its North American territory adjoined England's. Spain watched with interest the English plan, set up in 1764, for taxing her American colonies to help defray the cost of the recent war and to help maintain the army of ten thousand soldiers remaining in America. Requiring additional revenues, England also was making plans to lay a stamp tax upon her colonials. Spain followed suit and in 1764 contrived a system of colonial taxation to gain assistance in paying off the costs of the war, to build a new navy, to reorganize the native militia, and to maintain the cost of the ten thousand troops to be sent from Spain as a counterbalance to those forces in the British colonies.

There was an overwhelming difficulty to overcome before all this could successfully come to pass. Spain's colonial finances were in a corrupt state. Disturbing reports coming from Mexico City accused the Viceroy and the courts in New Spain of complicity in graft. This was a situation calling for the most delicate handling since, from the time of Cortés, the Viceroy of New Spain had been the highest colonial official in all the territory.

The Viceroy was the King's alter ego and functioned in his place. He had all of the powers and the prerogatives belonging to the King, had the monarch been there in person. He was, however, subject to those checks and restrictions which the King saw fit to impose upon him.

The Viceroy exercised threefold duties and the ensuing power made him a real potentate. As *gobernador*, the Viceroy was responsible for the collection of all taxes both for local use and *derechos*, or those taxes for the satisfaction of the King's rights. He was also in control of levying duties upon commerce; administered numerous mines, which had their own code of laws; and was expected to increase revenues. He expended these funds, made appropriations to the military and public improvements. He directed the building and main-tenance of all public works—roads, bridges, fortifications, drainage canals, the creation of new towns, and the constructions of public markets, granaries, and foundling asylums.

The Viceroy, besides serving as president of the supreme court or audiencia as judge, appointed small army subordinates in the civil service. It was as captain general that the Viceroy possessed some of his most distinctive powers. The important functions of the supreme military command which he exercised over all of the military and naval forces, the militia of the provinces, and the capital police, far overshadowed the civil duties he performed.

Disturbing as the reports were of involvement of the existing Viceroy and the courts in graft, and the urgent need for a Visitador-General to be sent to correct matters, it was not an easy matter to find the proper person for this crucial task. The man selected would have need of utmost honesty, wisdom, courage, and unwavering loyalty to the King. He would also need delicacy and tact and have to be blessed with boundless strength and energy.

The Visitador was a typically Spanish concept of an administrative agency. If the visita was of major importance, the representative was called Visitador-General and his authority superseded that of all other powers within the jurisdiction of his visita.

Several men were given careful consideration for this arduous and important task. The man chosen would have to be capable of reforming the financial situation of New Spain, since the need for funds was critical; inaugurate a new system of taxation, including the tobacco monopoly; reorganize the native militia; and most impor-tantly he would have to investigate the conduct of the Viceroy and the judiciary.

It was finally decided to send Francisco Carrasco, later Marqués de la Corona, who had held various administrative positions. Carrasco, however, pleaded domestic difficulties and escaped the toilsome assignment. The choice then fell upon Francisco Anselmo de Armona, intendant of Murcia, who also endeavored to be excused from the King's command to go to the appointment as Visitador. Threatened with pain of imprisonment and confiscation of property for disobedience, Armona acquiesced and received his appointment in 1764, sailing for the New World that same year. Fate intervened and death aboard ship after fourteen days at sea released him from the unwelcome duty. Upon receipt of this news, the King appointed Joseph Gálvez, age forty-six, to be Visitador-General in 1765 at a salary of 12,000 pesos.

Gálvez quickly recognized that this was the opportunity he had been searching for and plunged wholeheartedly into the task.

Vain, arrogant, and egotistical as he was, Gálvez had a forceful and energetic personality. Rising from nothing to a position of respect and eminence partly by his own quickness of wit and partly by knowing the right people who fostered his career, and possessing an almost fierce sense of loyalty to the crown, Gálvez, ruthlessly at times, with sudden bursts of generosity and compassion at others, set about planning how he would put into effect the necessary reforms in the financial structure of New Spain.

He and his family landed at San Juan de Ulloa on July 18, 1765, and made the formidable old fortress his headquarters. This fortress San Juan de Ulloa was started about 1582 and was probably the strongest fortification in the New World. It was situated on Gallega island in the bay less than a mile off shore from Vera Cruz. When Gálvez landed it had 120 guns and 3 mortars. The main structure was in the shape of a parallelogram, with a bastion at each of its angles, each of these named for a saint. The one at the southwest corner, completed in 1633, was named for San Pedro and was surmounted by a high tower upon which was a revolving light. The lookout tower from which vessels were sighted was on the southeast bastion named San Crispin. A system of signals kept the mainland alerted. Facing seaward, the flanks of the bastions were covered with stakes of sharpened wood rising about two feet out of the water so vessels could not approach within musket shot at high tide. Seven large cisterns storing thousands of cubic feet of water were within the fort. Below it were moldy, damp dungeons where hardened criminals were imprisoned. A garrison of naval troops as well as infantrymen were quartered on the island.

From the fortress Gálvez looked over the brief span of harbor waters, less than a mile wide to the city which originally had been founded by Cortés in 1519 and named La Villa Rica de la Vera Cruz, or Rich Town of the True Cross. It was still, at this time, the only port of entry on the northern seaboard of New Spain.

Gálvez remained here until he had rested and fully recovered from the rigorous sea voyage before seeking an encounter with the Viceroy, Marqués de Cruíllas. Gálvez stepped upon the mainland as virtually the dictator of what was then the world's greatest colonial empire and was strengthened and fortified by the knowledge that he possessed the greatest authority ever granted to a colonial minister by the King of Spain.

CHAPTER V

VERA CRUZ TO MEXICO CITY,

1749-50

Everything appeared new and different. Even the sand underfoot looked sunburned by tropic rays as contrasted with the white beaches of Majorca. The water of the Gulf of Mexico was less blue than that of Palma. Parrots, with their strange stiff-winged flight and their plaintive cries, heralded the unknown. The smell of rotting seaweed was borne on the breeze. Ahead, the great sand dunes formed an immense barrier between the ocean and the jungle. The brooding towers of the San Juan de Ulloa fortress still were visible as the two solitary figures trudged northwestward toward their first goal, Antigua, still so fraught with the spirit of Cortés. The "new" Vera Cruz had been founded only forty-eight years before, in 1701, but already the original city of the conquistador captain was designed as the "old" Antigua.

History pressed in upon Junípero. Exactly here, he knew as any philosopher and student of history from the Llullian University would have known, the first sixteen horses ever to land on the American continent had stretched their weary bones and exercised their cramped muscles after being landed following the voyage from Cuba in 1519. Here the terrified Indians, who had never beheld such fearsome apparitions as horses and riders, were stricken with terror at these seeming centaurs. Stretching his own legs, feeling his own muscles respond after the wearisome ninety-nine days of the voyage, Junípero was confirmed anew in his conviction that he had done right in declining the King's offer of a mount to Mexico City, and depending on his own locomotion, a true "friale andariego," a walking friar.* Palóu,

* Concerning this episode, Father Maynard Geiger, the pre-eminent Serra scholar, has some interesting observations: "This decision of Serra's to walk on his initial American journey has given rise to the seemingly unconquerable legend that for the rest of his life he continued to walk, whether in the light of circumstances it made sense or not . . . On a number of Serra's journeys we know definitely from documentary evidence that he did not walk . . . In his decision to walk to Mexico City Serra simply declined to use the privileges his rule offered. He was in good health, felt he had the necessary strength to keep his rule in the hard way, and had the permission of his superior to do so."

having been critically ill, was forced to ride with the others and could not accompany his master on this walk.

Brooding on the western horizon, the towering snow-clad peak of Orizaba pierced the sky, accenting the difference between this wild upreared land and the comfortable small hills of Majorca. Off to the left, the jungle growth stretched inland toward fields of sugar cane. Lacy trees in a long stretch of forest ahead filtered the sunlight into dim cathedral-like recesses.

Junípero, just starting into his thirty-seventh year after having celebrated his birth date, November 24, on the pitching "Villasota" amid the islands of the Caribbean on the way from San Juan to Vera Cruz, was vigorous despite his small stature and frail appearance. The ordeal of the voyage, coupled with his natural abstemiousness, had honed him down so that he strode easily on the sand and through the matted growth alongside the trail. He was intent upon the journey, eager to reach Mexico City more than four hundred kilometers away—yet drinking in the sights and sounds around him so as to become familiar with the missionary task ahead. The thought of the heathen souls available for his ministration was constantly with him.

The December sun in this latitude only 19° from the Equator was hot by midmorning. The two friars, one from an "isle of the Hesperides" and the other from Andalusia so close to Africa, were unmindful of the warmth, having been accustomed since childhood to their own bright sun lands. The ever-faithful Palóu, when recalling what Junípero related to him about this trip, failed to mention the name of the friar who accompanied Serra. The two walked steadily, their eyes and ears alert for the unfolding vista, engrossed in their purposeful progression toward Antigua, with only their breviaries and faith to sustain them. Their coarse gray robes gave off the slight warm odor elicited from wool by the direct heat of the sun. Their sandals made slight slithering sounds in the sand.

As the hours passed, the steady pace was maintained. The forest on their left continued for many kilometers. From it came the songs of unseen birds.

The afternoon arrived and the sun began to descend toward Orizaba. Far ahead the giant trees along the banks of Río Antigua came in sight. Having been informed of this landmark, the friars increased their rate of travel, hoping to reach the river before dark.

It was then that the first of the three mystical experiences, which occurred to them on this journey, happened in the lonely area on the banks of the river.

Caught by the darkness of nightfall, the two friars could not find a place shallow enough to ford the river. A man seemed to loom up on the far side and Serra called out in a loud voice, "Hail, Holy Mary! Is there any Christian on the other side of the river?" A voice answered, "Yes, what do you want?" When the friars replied that they sought a place to cross the river and did not know which way to go, the voice instructed them to go upstream. They did this and crossed safely to find the benefactor waiting for them on the other side. He took them quite a distance from the river to his house and gave them supper and beds for the night. The next morning the friars thanked the man for his courtesy and in their bewilderment inquired what he was doing at that place the night before. They received the noncommittal response that he had been out on business. Leaving the warmth of his house, they saw that bitter cold had iced the ground during the night and they knew that they would surely have perished from the cold.

Palóu cautiously states that all this might have been purest coincidence, but that the two pilgrims attributed it to the singular protection of Most Holy Mary, and that they rendered humble, appropriate thanks.

The second episode occurred on the second day when the two, having traveled over rough paths through the intense heat of the sun, found themselves exhausted and stopped to rest along the way. A man on horseback proffered them two pomegranates to quench their painful thirst. The small fruit satisfied their thirst and seemed to give them strength to journey on without any signs of fatigue. As they walked they conjectured as to the identity of this second man, and both believed that from his aspect and mode of speech, he seemed to be the same man who had befriended them the previous night.

Another similar incident befell them on the third day. The two weary travelers had spent the night in an inn, and after offering Mass and saying farewell to the innkeeper, he gave them a loaf of bread to sustain them along their way. Soon they chanced upon a beggar who asked them for alms. They gave him the loaf of bread, which was the only thing they had except for their faith in the protection of Divine Providence. After traveling a long way they were exhausted and suffering from hunger which had brought on weakness, and sat down by the roadside to rest. Soon a man on horseback passed by and, after asking them their destination, broke a loaf of bread and gave each of them half of it. The man then went on his way leaving the bemused Fathers afraid to eat the coarsely prepared and unappetizing loaf for fear it would make them ill. Weariness and hunger pangs forced them to eat of the bread and they found it palatable and so nourishing they were able to continue on their way until they reached the next stopping place that night.

Palóu wrote that Serra frequently made reference to these experiences when exhorting the friars to put their trust in the Divine Providence, and used to say that this benefactor was either Patriarch St. Joseph or some other devout man whose heart the saint had touched.

During one night, Junípero suffered a bite on his left leg. In the morning he noticed a slight pain and itching around an inflamed spot. At first he paid little attention. Remembering the fierce buzzing of the *zancudos* the evening before, he attributed his discomfort to one of these mosquitoes.* As the day wore on, he began to feel feverish. Both feet swelled. The injured leg became double its natural size. He limped more and more but refused to halt.

His companion helped him over some of the rough rocky spots in the continual ascent onto the plateau.

By nightfall, Junípero could barely move. At sunset they came to a small jacal amid a clearing in the jungle. They were hospitably received. Junípero accepted a drink of water, lay down upon the rough cot assigned to him, and lapsed into a semidelirious state. In this half sleep he scratched instinctively at the burning spot. When dawn came his leg was lacerated and bleeding from his fingernails.

Obviously, he could not travel. His companion bathed the leg and persuaded Junípero to rest a day. All during the dragging hours of that day and the night, the leg continued violently painful. An abscess began to develop around the bite. Still, on the second morning Junípero insisted on proceeding.

* Controversy exists to this day over the cause of Serra's leg injury. However, after reading a report in *Today's Health* (July 1967) published by the American Medical Association, we wonder if the culprit has been found by Dr. Calvin J. Dillaha of the University of Arkansas. Dr. Dillaha reports on studies of the brown recluse, sometimes called the fiddler because of a violin-shaped mark on its back, which is a little-known spider with a potency far exceeding that of the notorious black widow. The brown recluse appears to have migrated into the United States from South America by way of Central America and Mexico. It has a severe and sometimes gangrenous bite and is dangerous because its appearance is insignificant to the point of innocence. The body hardly half an inch long, varies from faun to chocolate color and the spider bites only when it is disturbed and feels threatened. Because the bite is inconspicuous and the spider scurries away, the cause is often unsuspected. At first the venom causes only a stinging sensation, without much pain. Two to eight hours later, the pain may become intense, accompanied by nausea, joint pains, severe abdominal cramps, and fever. The wound blisters, is surrounded by hemorrhage; an ulcer may develop, followed by gangrene. The venom appears to contain a spreading factor, according to the toxologist, for the wound tends to enlarge in a downward direction. From what we can learn from Palóu, this appears to be a clinical description of Serra's injury.

He had suffered the injury which was to plague him the remainder of his life.

Despite the painfulness of this injury they continued on 'their way and in the afternoon of the last day of December 1749, reached the Sanctuary of Our Lady of Guadalupe where they remained for the night. The following morning, after saying Mass in gratitude, they went forth again.

Ahead, Serra saw the first of the Misterios. Word of these ornate stone monuments, each standing six meters high, had spread as far as Majorca. The prospective sight of them had stirred the imaginations of the missionaries while they were still in Palma discussing their trip. Now to view in actuality the ornately carved sculptures depicting the mysteries of the Rosary animated Junípero so that he moved his injured leg more rapidly to inspect the Misterio at close range. Along the *calzada* toward the city, the Misterios rose as if in frozen procession, fifteen of them at intervals and all dating back a century or more, and already showing the venerability of age.

Junípero knew, upon sighting them, that the city and the college were at last near at hand.

His emotion at being able in a single morning to visit both the Shrine of Guadalupe and the Misterios removed his thoughts from the constant pain in his leg. He hobbled, but his religious exaltation and his realization that he was approaching the college that represented the end of the long weary journey lessened his awareness of discomfort. As he passed each succeeding Misterio he studied the carvings for the message which the sculptor had been intending to convey. From each he drew new inspiration.

He and his companion moved steadily onward, and so came to the vast Cathedral at the zócalo, and then along the street that followed the route of an Aztec causeway straight toward the college.

The Church of San Fernando came in sight. At this moment Junípero, who had been almost unaware of the early morning bustle and clamor of the city around him, heard maddened screams. He awoke to his surroundings. The screams came from beneath the tower of San Hipólito, the hospital for the insane immediately adjacent to the College of San Fernando. For Junípero, it was as if the reason for his coming to America were personified. Souls in torment needed saving. He was ready for the task; this was his purpose.

At nine in the morning of January 1, 1750, he entered the doorway of San Fernando.

CHAPTER VI

THE COLEGIO DE SAN FERNANDO,

MEXICO CITY, JANUARY 1, 1750

When Fr. Junípero Serra stood before the Apostolic College of San Fernando of Mexico that morning on the first day of the year of 1750, the very size of the uncompleted edifice must have been overwhelming. The church, begun in 1735, and not as yet dedicated, was long and the largest in Mexico excepting the Cathedral. Its exterior of dark red *tezontle* stone and gray *cantería*, or hewn stone, common to many public buildings in Mexico, was formidable in appearance. The building with its single tower on the left and the adjoining two-storied monastery had none of the beauty nor grace of his beloved San Francisco de Palma. This would be his home for a while and then his headquarters for the remainder of his life.

Junípero and his companion went into the church to receive the blessing of the Lord in the Eucharist. The sound of the soft, rhythmic prayers of the friars chanting their office comforted his heart and turning to his companion he said, "Father, we can consider that our time has been well spent in coming so far and suffering so much, just to be allowed to have the joy of being members of a community which with so much ardor and devotion pays the debt of the Divine Office."

Dragging his painful leg a few steps farther, Junípero passed through the doorway into the college to be warmly welcomed by the guardian, Fray José Ortés de Velasco, and to kneel and kiss his hand. It was a joyous moment and the friars whose company had been broken up at Vera Cruz came together once again and Palóu and Serra were reunited. One of the older friars, who was among the founders of the college, recalled the words of St. Francis as he embraced Junípero and said, "Would that some one might bring us a whole grove of junipers such as this one." But Serra in gentle protest humbly replied, "It was not of this sort, Reverend Father, that our Seraphic Patriarch asked for, but of others quite different."

The indefatigable Serra, not allowing himself a single day to recuperate from the laborious journey from Vera Cruz, went immediately the following morning to request the Father Guardian to assign him a confessor. The venerable Father Fr. Bernardo Pumeda, a missionary of renown, and a great master of speculative and practical mystics, also serving as master of the novices at the college, was assigned confessor. Serra was overjoyed and presented himself to the master exclaiming, "The Prelate has been wise in his choice; this is what I need, to renew my novitiate."

Serra then implored the master to admit him as if he were the youngest of the novices and also to permit him to live in one of the novitiate cells. This was denied and he was assigned a cell with the other friars, but he was permitted to attend all of the special exercises of the novitiates. This plan was carried out and immediately upon completing his assigned duties in the community, Serra went every day to the novitiate and there recited with the director the Little Office, the Way of the Cross, and the Rosary as well as all of the other devout exercises performed by the novices. As Palóu says, "In these he was edifying to them, and himself received great benefit of spirit."

Serra's studying with the lowly novices has often been given as proof of the abiding humbleness of his nature, but there also was another deeper need that compelled him to take such action. He desired to return again to the wellspring of religious inspiration and to capture anew the freshness and fervor of his youth. He knew full well the demands the apostolic life he sought would place upon him. The Apostolic College of San Fernando of Mexico was but the training place for apostles dedicating their lives to the saving of aboriginal heathens. As he looked around him, he knew that some of his companions would not prove equal to the task just as those few had fallen by the way in Cádiz when they first saw the mighty ocean and weakness overcame them. He prayed that with the grace of the Almighty he would prove equal to the rigors of the life at San Fernando and be permitted to go forth as one of its apostles.

The Apostolic College of San Fernando was established by Royal decree on October 15, 1733, as an offspring of the mother apostolic college, the Convento de Santa Cruz in Querétaro. These apostolic colleges were an innovation of the Franciscans and were founded to prepare a carefully selected corps of priests of highest spiritual ideals, devoted to the strictest ascetic lives and austere living, to be missionaries bringing the Christian faith to the American aborigines. This concept, a totally new contribution to the mission field, was the work of another native Majorcan, Fray Antonio Llinás de Jesús María.

After serving for a period in the province of Michoacán, Llinás, returning to Spain in 1681, proposed his idea of sending carefully chosen religious to special convents for training in missionary work to Fray José Ximénez de Samaniego, minister general of the Order. The minister general countered with the idea of founding apostolic colleges. This concept received approval of the Council of the Indies, the all-powerful civil body passing on Indian affairs, and the apostolic colleges became colleges for the propagation of the Faith. Twenty-four missionaries recruited by Llinás were sent at government expense to start the colleges.

These institutions, independent one from the other, drew their recruits from all the Spanish provinces and were solely responsible to the Council of the Indies. A "guardian" governed each of the institutions. Elected for three years, he was assisted by his council or "discretory." The friars pledged themselves to serve ten years in the missions and to follow strict observances of the Franciscan rule. Members volunteered to serve in the Indian mission field and none could be forced against his will to do so.

Life at the colleges was strict and designed to prepare the missionaries for a life of hardship and austerity. Even the strongest of them would find the deprivations of frontier life beyond endurance were they not blessed with spirituality and obedience and hardened self-discipline. It was for this life that Serra prepared himself.

One day the friars were gathered in the cloistered garden for their recreation period. There had been great joy and happiness ever since the second contingent of volunteers gathered by Fr. Mezquía in Spain arrived on the first of April. Among the group were three Majorcans: Rafael Verger, Juan Crespí, and Guillermo Vicens, also a native of Petra. As they visited quietly, Father Ortés de Velasco joined them and expressed his pleasure at their coming. He told them of a difficulty which confronted him by the death of four of the missionaries serving in the Sierra Gorda Missions. Their college had assumed responsibility for manning these missions in 1744. The sister college, Santa Cruz of Querétaro, had volunteered to supply missionaries on an emergency basis for six months, but he felt that now that a new allotment of missionaries had arrived, Querétaro should not be expected to continue this service. He further explained to the friars that while the rule of the college required all newcomers to remain there a year before being sent out into the missions, circumstances dictated that the rule be changed. He said to them, "Now, who of you will volunteer for the Sierra Gorda?"

When Serra heard this he instantly responded in the words of the prophet, "Ecce ego, mitte me." "Here I am, send me." Seven others followed Serra's example with Palóu chosen as Serra's companion. These eight were advised to make their preparations so as to be ready to leave at the first notice. Palóu notes that, "As soon as our servant of God saw that he had been chosen for the Mission to the pagans he increased his spiritual exercises in order to be the better prepared to obey the voice of the Prelate."

The few remaining days of his stay at San Fernando were filled with prayer, study, and preparations for the assignment he had been given. But there was one more test which he was to face before departure for the Sierra Gorda. The annual feast of San Fernando and the religious festival accompanying it was one of the few occasions when the college was permitted to open to the people. Junípero was designated as preacher for this solemn occasion. Palóu once again sat in the audience and gave his reactions for, "when . . . they saw that he was so humble, silent, and retiring, they wanted to try out his learning."

Once again, as at Palma, Serra proved equal to the task. The listeners were so impressed by his eloquence and sincerity, many voiced doubt as to the wisdom of sending such a gifted and learned priest into the regions populated solely by ignorant heathen. They suggested to the guardian that Serra be retained at the college where his preaching ability and talents could have more effect upon the local citizens.

The guardian held firm and even went so far as to appoint Serra president of the Sierra Gorda, for it was his conviction the illiterate Indians had need of the compassion and talents of just such a literate man as this. Junípero humbly declined the honor of being president because of his inexperience, so the guardian acquiesced and withdrew the official patent.

"Here I am, send me." Serra had called out that day in the garden upon hearing of the need for missionaries in the wilderness of the Sierra Gorda. A lifetime of dreams and yearning for just such an opportunity was about to be realized. As a simple missionary—not as an appointed official—he was going forth to serve.

CHAPTER VII

THE CHALLENGE OF CACHUM,

1750–52

At last the day of departure for Junípero Serra and his companion Palóu to go to the Sierra Gorda arrived. They and the other friars named to this mission offered Mass, received the blessings of the guardian, and the good wishes of the priests who were to remain at San Fernando. Outside the college gates that morning of June 1, 1750, the Indians who had come down from Jalpan and a soldier escort with horses and pack animals awaited them. Despite the long, hard road that lay ahead of them, Serra, in his exultation, chose to make the journey on foot.

Which of the several possible trails to Jalpan they took is not known. However, no matter which way was selected, the road passed through swamps, over rugged mountains, and uninviting terrain. The shortest distance would have been close to two hundred miles from Mexico City. Palóu recorded that they made the journey in sixteen days, averaging fifteen miles a day, despite the worsening condition of Serra's leg. The extreme heat and dampness was hard upon all of them but especially upon Junípero, and his leg swelled painfully.

Rains, starting in May and usually continuing until October, made the roads nearly impassable. During the wet season cascades of water often ran off the water-soaked sides of the steep mountains plummeting hundreds of feet down into the canyon, frequently hurtling large boulders across the road and on down into the swiftly flowing Moctezuma River. This had to be crossed over a narrow suspension bridge, which perilously hung by cables and was sometimes washed away and destroyed by the onrushing floods.

As they trudged along the rutted, muddy road, Serra eagerly watched for glimpses of the wild life of the area. Tropical birds and raucous-shouting parrots flew deeper into the trees, resenting the intrusion. As the small band of pilgrims passed by, Serra tried to see the shy deer, coyotes, and small tigers who might possibly be stealthily watching from the dense growth.

Junípero knew the history of the Sierra Gorda country from the studies he made prior to leaving San Fernando. As they journeyed along he must have related all of this to his companions. The very thought of being entrusted with the responsibility for bringing the half-wild, unsubdued Pames, who lived in the mountainous regions of the Sierra Gorda, to the Faith exulted his soul, and he silently gave thanks to God for His generosity in granting to His unworthy servant this opportunity.

He spoke of this Sierra Gorda country as though from personal knowledge. It lay in the very center of the Sierra Madre Oriental range, which extends between the Atlantic seaboard and the central plateau of Mexico, running north and south. He told them about the proportions of this range, 250 miles long and 75 miles wide, the middle section of which was the responsibility of the Franciscans.

The Pames had lived in this mountainous region before recorded time and had carried on their barbarous ways—plundering, murdering travelers and merchants, and burning down the haciendas of the Spaniards. They had resisted all efforts, both military and religious, to subdue them. It was not until Colonel José de Escandón, accompanied by Father Mezquía, set out with a military expedition from Querétaro in 1743 that this tribe came under Spanish control. Escandón had previously battled with the Pames and defeated them at San Christóbal de Media Luna, but the purpose of the second encounter was to persuade them to quiet down and live peacefully. When he promised to send missionaries to teach and care for them, the Pames surprisingly agreed to his proposal and Escandón requested that the authorities at the College of San Fernando assume responsibility for the mission area.

Father Mezquía defined the territory to be under the supervision of the priests from San Fernando and drew up a set of regulations by which the Indians were to be governed. These regulations were to become the guidelines for all the missions sponsored by the apostolic colleges of San Fernando, Zacatecas, and Querétaro and their influence was to be evident as far away as California.

Five missions were founded: Jalpan, Landa, and Concá in the south; Tancoyol and Tilaco in the north. Escandón established a presidio or fortress at Jalpan and left thirty soldiers who were to be distributed between the five locales. The first friars from San Fernando faced the responsibility of feeding, converting, and reducing the Pames into the mission communities. Over seven thousand Indians were assembled by the self-sacrificing Fernandinos who often went without food to feed them. Five temporary churches were put up and farms started, but starvation and deprivations brought death to four of the friars, and four others, critically sick, were forced to return to the college. Disastrous epidemics killed off about two-thirds of the natives and the rest ran away and refused to return, claiming the vengeance of their abandoned ancient gods had caused the sickness to come. A plea of distress was sent to the colleges at Querétaro and Zacatecas and temporary relief came to man the five missions of the Sierra Gorda. This was the critical situation in the Sierra Gorda when Father Mezquía returned to Mexico City from Spain with his thirty-three recruits in January 1750. It was then, as we have seen, that a group of these men, with Serra as "acting prefect" and Palóu as his companion, volunteered to go into this wilderness and take over these missions, arriving on June 16.

With the first glimpse of the small village of Jalpan, situated on the sloping hillsides at the base of an eleven-thousand-foot mountain, Serra quickly realized that despite whatever work had been accomplished by the friars preceding him, he would have to start at the beginning. Visiting the four other missions, he found that all of the churches were but poorly constructed adobe buildings with primitive thatched roofs and in a state of crumbling neglect. Even worse was the condition of his so-called parishioners, who had reverted from their Christian teachings into lives of indolence, drunkenness, and moral disintegration, often indulging in bigamy and witchcraft.

Serra immediately put into practice the rules and regulations for the spiritual direction of the Indians which had been drawn up by Father Mezquía, whose experience in founding missions in Texas well qualified him for the task. At sunrise all of the Indians without exception were called to the church by the ringing of the mission bell. One of the Fathers then was to repeat the prayers and doctrines, with a Spanish explanation. Special classes for all children over five were held twice each day. Instructional classes for all those about to receive the Holy Sacrament were also held each day. All feast days were to be kept diligently and all persons were required to attend the principal Mass, which was to be explained by the priests with prudence and tact, according to the intelligence and simplicity of the Indians. Following the Mass, roll was called and the Indians came one by one to kiss the hand of the priest. In this manner absent members could be detected. The more intelligent and capable Indians were to be exhorted to frequent the Holy Sacraments, in addition to attending church even on the days when it was not obligatory to do so. The priests were to care for the sick with the greatest of diligence. The dying were to receive the sacraments if entitled to them, and all of the people were required to attend funerals. Finally, the priests were charged with the responsibility of helping the people to live in peace and Christian love and to do all in their power to do away with enmities. Above all, the priests were admonished that there be no scandal or evil example in the missions.

From the moment of his arrival, Junípero began to hear about the pagan idol. It was, in a way, the counterpart and rival of the Virgin Mary. The idol, sculptured in marble, was known as Cachum, the Mother of the Sun. It reposed in an Indian temple atop a hill amid the deep canyons, cliffs, peaks, and chasms of the Jalpan region. So sacred was the spot that the Pames had buried their mightiest chiefs alongside the long stone stairway leading to the abode of Cachum. The temple was a place of prayer. To it the Pames went with all kinds of petitions for celestial favors. They implored Cachum to bring them bountiful harvests, physical prowess, military victories, and suitable wives.

Junípero's first impulse was to emulate the patriarchs of the Old Testament and cast down the idol. This temptation was almost overpowering. His zeal for Christianizing the heathen led him inevitably toward a course of direct action. His youth and impetuosity cried out for obliteration of this idolatry, yet he held back. Some inner wisdom counseled patience.

Before long he began to realize the reason for this counterbalance, this restraint. Almost subconsciously he had been trying to be fair with the Pames because of the dreadful example being set for them by supposed Christians of Spanish blood living close to Jalpan. These apostates, Junípero learned, were indulging in many forms of witchcraft and appeasement of the devil. The perplexing question raised for Junípero was simple: How could he move against the Pames, immemorial heathen, as idolaters without seeming to discriminate against them when contrasted with the Spanish Christians who had lapsed into practices just as wicked, or possibly more so, because of their supposed enlightenment?

In this dilemma, he waited. To further his ultimate purpose, he called upon a childhood memory and began at once to make it a reality. In his mind's eye he could see, as plainly as if it were conjured up before him in reality, the gentle hill of Bon Any at Petra, crowned with its *Calvario* where he had visited so often as a boy. He determined upon a Calvario at Jalpan, a challenge to the temple of Cachum.

He lacked formal training as an architect and had studied the subject only from the standpoint of a philosopher, dwelling upon Greek, Roman, Persian, Spanish, and Anglo-Saxon buildings as manifestations of man's spirit transmuted into stone and mortar and soaring columns and lofty arches. Now he was confronted for the first time in his life with the practical problem of building a structure designed for a particular purpose. He knew it must be simple, both on account of his own deficiencies and also because of the lack of knowledge of the Indians who were to do the work. As a part of the plan he included fourteen spots leading up the hill to be used for the Stations of the Cross. This concept of erecting the Stations of the Cross was so relatively new, as granted by the Pope to the Franciscans, that to Junípero it always seemed fresh and challenging. He could remember in his own lifetime when he was eighteen the thrill of all Christendom when Clement XII permitted the use of the Stations in all churches under the condition that a Franciscan actually erect the Stations. This had grown out of the observance in the Holy Land where the Franciscans were in charge of all the places associated with the life of Christ.

In Jalpan the building of the Calvario and the Stations were undertaken with such enthusiasm that the lack of technical knowledge of building proved to be only a minor handicap.

Junípero knew he must dramatize the task for the Indians. He discovered as soon as he arrived in Jalpan that the native tribe, even in its idolatry, manifested a lively imagination. In their sorcery and witchcraft he saw an embryonic seed which could sprout into Christian faith if they were directed in the right path.

He tried to draw upon this resource of the aboriginal character. In a real sense the path up the hill back of the church to the eminence upon which the Calvario was to be built was a substitute for the "sacred stairway" leading up to the shrine of the Mother of the Sun. He knew that if he impressed the Indians properly, the fourteen Stations of the Cross would become as sacred as had been the graves of their chieftains lining the stairway of the idol. By signs and gestures as well as in the few words of the Indians' language which he had already learned, he began to impress upon the workers the exciting nature of the Calvario's construction. By now he was in the midst of one of the most practical aspects of the missionary task he had set for himself.

There in the awesome wilderness of Mexico, surrounded by potential Christian material, he called upon every resource of his background to attempt to cut short the process of learning how to interest parishioners. He received word that he had been appointed president without his knowledge and continued to serve for three years in this role.

So that the simple minds of the natives could fully comprehend the instructions in the Faith which he so earnestly gave to them, Junípero used every means his fertile mind could conjure and used all of the feast days of the Lord and the Virgin Mary, as well as those of the saints, to bring home this knowledge with dramatic impact. On Sunday nights there were torch light parades in Mary's honor.

During the Lenten season Serra especially strove to move the hearts of the neophytes. Beginning on Ash Wednesday and on every Sunday of this time of observance he instructed and preached constantly to them so that they would fully understand. On Friday before Easter he led the procession up the Way of the Cross to the Calvario upon the hill carrying a wooden cross, so heavy that Palóu states that he, so much younger and stronger, could not possibly have borne it, stopping at each Station and rendering appropriate prayers commemorating the sufferings of Christ. In this, Serra was not entirely play-acting for the benefit of his native parishioners, but was also devoutly performing as a penitent.

Holy Week was celebrated with drama and religious fervor which could not fail to reach the simplest mind. On Holy Thursday, Serra performed the "Washing of the Feet" ceremony on twelve of the oldest Indians, and that night made a procession with the image of the crucified Christ before all of the people. The Descent from the Cross on Good Friday was vividly portrayed by a lifelike figure Serra had made with hinged arms and legs. The manikin of the Lord was tenderly removed from the Cross of crucifixion and put into a special casket he had made for the purpose and then placed upon an altar. Easter Sunday was celebrated by a procession during which the image of the Risen Lord and another of the Holy Virgin were carried about the village. This was followed by High Mass after which Serra preached tenderly and lovingly about the significance of the mysteries of the Holy Week.

Word about the wonders of these holy dramatizations spread, and each year more converts came to be received into the flock and the nearby Spaniards also came to take part in the services and many remained near the mission until Holy Week had passed.

The message of Christmas was similarly portrayed with the day of the Nativity being celebrated by Masses. On the last night of the year, following the Midnight Mass, a simple play, telling of the birth of the Christ Child and acted by children trained by Fr. Serra, was presented—just as he recalled the Nativity plays of his childhood in Petra—and spoken both in Spanish and in native Pame.

During the eight and one half years Serra served in the Sierra Gorda mountains, there are records of his leaving and going to Mexico City only upon two occasions. The first of these visits was in 1752. Before leaving Jalpan he was presented with a most surprising gift by an old Indian whose purpose in life had been to guard and keep secret the Mother of the Sun idol, Cachum.

When the missionaries had started converting the people and erecting their churches, the old man had taken great care to hide the image deep in a cave among the rocks. He told about the time when the captain had sent soldiers out among the hills to burn the huts of the Indians to force them to move into the new town, and they came upon the hut that had once been the worshiping place housing the idol. Several times the soldiers attempted to start a fire but each time the hut would not burn. The sergeant cried out to his soldiers, "Put fire to it in the name of God and Our Most Holy Mother." The hut burst into flames and burned to the ground, giving off black smoke of a disgusting odor which filled the beholders with awe and fear. Possibly the old man grew weary of his secret task, or perhaps he had succumbed to Christianity. Whatever the reason, Cachum was given to Serra, who took it to the College of San Fernando in Mexico City and delivered it to the Father Guardian, "asking that it be put in the box of archives belonging to the documents and papers of these Missions as a memento of the Spiritual conquest."

CHAPTER VIII

NAILS, CARPENTERS,

AND A VIOLIN

Serra returned to the Sierra Gorda bringing with him some nails, several carpenters, a violin, and the official appointment of himself as Inquisitor for the entire area.

The violin was part of his youthful dream to follow in the footsteps of St. Francis Solano who played for the Peruvian Indians as he converted them. The nails and carpenters were also to be part of a dream—because fomenting in his eager mind were plans for building his first real church in the new land. His appointment as official Inquisitor was another matter—there was nothing joyous about that.

While in Mexico City Serra sent a petition to the headquarters of the Inquisition asking that an Inquisitor with jurisdictional powers be sent to the Sierra Gorda. He mentioned receiving reports of strange forms of depraved devil worship and witchcraft. What was most alarming was the fact that it was not the Indians who were indulging in these practices, but the *gente de razón*, or Spaniards. Serra gravely feared that these constituted a distinct danger to his impressionable Indian neophytes. He was immediately given this oath of office. There is no record of his ever having condemned any heretic to the stake during this period, but he safeguarded the spiritual welfare of his flock as well as their temporal needs.

He saw to it that as far as possible the Indians had enough to eat and sufficient clothing to wear so they would not leave the mission because of any lack. At first there was great scarcity of provisions and the priests shared and suffered the same frugal diet.

"Serra obtained a supply of oxen, cows, asses, sheep and goats, as well as seed corn and beans in order to make a planting for the current year," Palóu wrote, "and so it was that he soon was able to harvest a crop and each year the amount harvested increased so that every day he was able to distribute something to the people after the recital of prayers." Palóu neglected to make mention of the manner in which these unskilled men, highly schooled in the realms of theology and philosophy, but totally lacking in mechanical skill, became builders and tillers of the soil.

The harvest increased so abundantly that there was soon sufficient amount for the Indians to sell the surplus after their needs had been met, and Serra instructed them in the ways of doing this so they could buy more oxen and farm implements. Women and children were not neglected and each was taught some form of handicraft. So skilled did they become that they, too, were able to sell their products, all the while Fr. Serra guiding them so they could not be cheated. As the Indians became more knowledgeable about farming, those who were industrious were given their own parcel of ground. One of the Fathers went out each day personally to inspect the work and offered praise until the Indians no longer were indolent. The crops were abundant, the property of the religious community increased, and the Indians became more civilized and Christianized each day. It was then that Junípero Serra, seeing the interest his children took and the eagerness with which they performed their work, decided to build a church large enough to hold the entire congregation.

The Indians entered into the plan and greeted his idea with enthusiasm and agreed to bring in the stone and sand and to make the lime and mortar and to help in every way possible. Artisans he had brought from Mexico City quickly taught the Indians to be adequate masons, carpenters, blacksmiths, painters, and decorators. Working only in the dry season and when it was not necessary to labor in the fields, it took seven years for the church to be completed.

Serra worked as a common laborer in the building of his first church. He toiled in a torn habit bound around the waist with a piece of old altar cloth. Because of his small stature, it was necessary for him to pad his shoulder to increase his height while assisting a group of Pames in carrying a heavy beam. It was thus that Fray Bernardo Pumeda, his former spiritual father, chanced upon him and was greatly pleased at the humble manner in which his former pupil was making himself useful and commented upon it. Palóu, seeing nothing unusual in his master's behavior protested, "But he does this every day."

The beautiful Mission of Santiago at Jalpan still stands and functions today as the church of the Pame Indians. It was built in a combination of Baroque and Churrigueresque styles with an imposing tower over ninety feet high. The exterior walls are a mellow brownstone, but the lacy façade is a soft yellow. A graceful shell motif is above the wide wooden doors and atop this is the coat of arms of the Franciscan Order. Standing between two sets of graceful Churrigueresque columns are the statues of Our Lady of Guadalupe and Our Lady of the Pillar, patronesses of Mexico and Spain. A treasure of the church is the Cristo del Santo Entierro, or image of the dead Christ, kept in a glass case. The custom of removing this jointed figure and placing it upon a cross for Good Friday and then returning it in solemn procession to its burying place is practiced today just as it was during Serra's time. To the right of the church is the monastery whose sparsely furnished rooms open onto a large atrium with banyan trees and other shrubs. To Serra the quietude midst the lush green of the plants within this garden spot must have been reminiscent of his beloved San Francisco at Palma.

The missionaries, inspired by the beauty of this church, strove to copy Serra's efforts and built four other stone missions in the Sierra Gorda.

The pleasure and satisfaction Serra derived from seeing the untamed, barbarous Pames accept the teachings of the Church and become gentle, industrious, Christianized people was constantly marred by the irritants of a social and economic nature outside the religious sphere. Conflict and feuds between the missionaries, the military, and the Spanish ranchers had been in existence long before he came to Jalpan. Charges and countercharges were sent back and forth with the military claiming that the missionaries were usurping their farm lands for the benefit of the missions. The missionaries countered that the military was encouraging the Indians to revolt and run away and then refusing to return them when they were found. The Spanish settlers, who had originally been brought in to serve as examples for the Indians, were accused of using them as slaves. Finally the cable crossing over the Moctezuma River was captured and a toll charged, which the Indians could not pay.

Accusations became garbled and more acrimonious, until Serra standing steadfastly on the side of his Indians, circumvented the military and wrote directly to the authorities of the College of San Fernando, who in turn protested to the Viceroy. After considerable time an investigating board, appointed by the Viceroy with Serra as a member, came up with a solution which, while not pleasing to everyone, did seem to solve the vexing problem, and the interests of the Pames were protected against unscrupulous outsiders.

He left his beloved children in September 1758 when he and Palóu received a summons to return to the college and prepare themselves to take the place of two colleagues who had been killed at the Mission of San Sabá in Texas. Palóu wrote, "immediately this obedient servant, as soon as he received the letter, with his face radiant with a new joy and happiness, left the Mission in which he had labored for nearly nine years."

CHAPTER IX

THE SUMMONS TO SAN SABÁ

Junípero returned to Mexico City to find the city teeming with rumors and speculation about the great war in Europe and its effect upon Mexico. The capital was clamorous and almost frightening after the silence and primitive grandeur of the Sierra Gorda. It was necessary for him to become acquainted with the metropolis all over again. His stay in it had been so brief after his arrival from Spain— only during the six-month period from January 1 to June 1, 1750— that he was unprepared for the crowds, the traffic, the stores, the vast congregations in the churches, the almost nightly murders in the streets, the violence of the unemployed who roamed in bands.

He could look back upon his eight and one half years of missionary work among the Pames almost as a dream. Only the creation of the Calvario and the building of the solid stone church emerged as tangible facts in the midst of his labors for the salvation of souls.

Now his mind was totally occupied with the prospects of the four-hundred-league journey to San Sabá in the midst of the wild Apaches in Texas. Mexico City was to be only a way point on that dangerous journey. When he arrived September 26 one of his friends who had come with him from Spain, Fr. Miguel Molina, was still suffering at the College of San Fernando from the wounds he had received during the Indian raid in Texas which had taken the lives of Fr. Alonso Terreros and José Santiestevan.

Father Miguel Molina, the sole survivor of the San Sabá holocaust, related the dreadful events resulting in the massacre to Serra and the other priests who listened to the long sequence which started with two cousins who lived in Querétaro and of their resolve to further missionary work among the fierce aborigines of Texas. One, Fray Alonso Giraldo Terreros, a member of the Apostolic College of Santa Cruz in that city already had served as a missionary in Texas and greatly desired to extend his efforts into the land of the Apaches in the San Sabá area. He was aided by his cousin, Pedro Romero de Terreros, who had derived tremendous wealth from silver mines in Pachuca. Don Pedro agreed to finance these missionary projects providing certain conditions were met by the participating colleges of San Fernando and Santa Cruz: His cousin was to be appointed president of the new mission field; Don Pedro would finance each new mission for a period of three years, the government then to take over expenses; the military protection for the missions was to be borne by the government; and in case Fray Alonso died or left the mission field, he, Don Pedro was to have right of approval over any missionaries who might be assigned to replace his cousin. While the religious authorities were doubtful and hesitant to acquiesce to such a petition, they reluctantly agreed, lest the financing of such a generous benefactor be lost and the missionary work be prevented.

In April 1757 the small band of friars and soldiers made camp on the plains and established the Mission of San Sabá de la Santa Cruz and a military garrison San Luis de las Amarillas. At first there were no Indians in sight, but within a few days the Apaches began gathering around the mission. The friars were deceived into thinking they were going to be friendly and some of their apprehension was temporarily lulled. Then the Apaches began to jeer at the priests and started marauding in a threatening manner. The Apaches snatched gifts away from the Fathers readily enough, and then reviled them until the missionaries, recalling the treatment that befell their predecessors, began to comprehend that the Indians had accepted none of their teachings and were continuing in the same manner which led to inevitable tragedy. The Apaches would never become converted. Out of heartbreak and despair, letters telling of the Indians' great hostility were written by the missionaries and sent back to Mexico City. Despite the fact that discouraging messages expressing the hopelessness of their project had been sent to the Viceroy and to Don Pedro suggesting that the project be abandoned, they were told each time to remain and continue their efforts to convert the hostiles.

Finally the end came on March 16, 1758, when two thousand bloodthirsty Indians in war paint swooped down upon the helpless mission and slaughtered the priests who attempted to meet with them and assuage their wrath. Santiestevan was killed and beheaded as he prayed before the altar. The other priests were butchered and only Molina managed to escape with a bullet wound in his arm and to bring back the grim report.

The cousin, Don Pedro, upon hearing of the massacre, expressed his willingness and determination to defray the cost of reconquest of San Sabá. The Viceroy requested the Franciscan commissary general to appoint four new missionaries to the field. It was at this time the summons went forth to Junípero Serra and his friend Palóu at Jalpan in the Sierra Gorda to return to the college and prepare for the new assignment.

Serra listened to Molina's account of the massacre, but despite the dreadful events, he remained undaunted and fixed in his determination to go to San Sabá. "I realize my feebleness and nothingness for so glorious an enterpise," Junípero wrote his nephew, Fr. Miguel de Petra, who had just become a Capuchin priest in Majorca.

While expressing his unworthiness, as was a precept of the teachings of St. Francis, Serra knew deep within him that the practical training he had received and the lessons he had learned in the wilds of the Sierra Gorda were excellent preparation for coping with the Apaches at San Sabá. His religious fervor burned as ardently as ever, but he knew that he, along with being a saver of souls, was a builder of churches, a tiller of the soil, and a diplomat in dealing with vexing problems brought about by disgruntled people. He exulted in his heart and gave thanks to God for permitting him to have experienced the long hard years in the Sierra Gorda which gave him such strength.

While he waited for orders for his departure, he busied himself in the life of the college. He was not aware that the petulance of one man threatened the entire San Sabá mission. Don Pedro received word that Fray José García, guardian of the College of San Fernando and his counselors had chosen Serra and Palóu as worthy replacements for the martyred friars at San Sabá. Don Pedro Romero protested this action as a breach of friendship and faith and an usurpation of his rights and that according to the contract of 1756, he had the right to determine if the person selected to take the place of his slain cousin met with his approval. Letters of protest and letters of explanation went back and forth and time dragged on until the Viceroy died and the matter withered away. Palóu returned to the Sierra Gorda and became prefect of the missions, while Serra obediently immersed himself into the life at San Fernando. Thus capriciously was Serra kept from going to Texas where he might have spent the remainder of his days and of being claimed as a hero of that state.

The cloistered walls of San Fernando became a refuge. Serra rarely went out into the city, shunned social events, and took part in community life only through hearing the confessions of those who came to him. Still, the impact of world events penetrated even into his seclusion.

From the moment of his return, the seething ferment of distant events made itself felt not only in Mexico City but inside the cloister. The Franciscans, although less aggressive and worldly than the Jesuits, nevertheless kept themselves aware of happenings in Europe and the Americas as a necessity. They were dealing in many cases with individual parishioners who were highly educated and deeply informed on political and ecclesiastical events in Spain, France, England,

Prussia, Italy, Russia, and the American colonies of numerous nations. It was vital that the priests be aware of the trends of history; not only as a matter of information but also in their capacity as spiritual counselors so as to be able to champion those things they considered right and to oppose those they thought wrong.

Junípero necessarily was involved in all this in a city as large and cosmopolitan as the capital of Mexico.

CHAPTER X

THE *FRIALE ANDARIEGO*

(THE WALKING FRIAR), 1767

No further word was ever said by the guardian of the college concerning the fruitless plans for reactivating the Mission at San Sabá, nor was any mention made to Junípero about his returning to the Sierra Gorda. Palóu was ordered to return to Jalpan and to assume the duties of president.

Humbly and obediently Serra locked whatever disappointment he might have felt deep within his heart and dedicated the next seven years to furthering the missionary work of the college and the conversion of sinners as well as performing his other duties at San Fernando. He remained there until 1767 punctually and efficiently doing whatever was required of him, and often exceeding far beyond the demands requested. During this time he was not actively participating in the conversion of the heathen.

Once again the college was his refuge. He became completely detached from the world and from all secular life. He visited no one. Despite this withdrawal from the teeming world outside the college, Serra's charity and understanding nature caused his reputation to spread and those coming to him for Confession left his presence comforted and spiritually strengthened. Rigorously strict with himself, he was tenderly charitable toward those coming to him for religious comfort.

There is no record of the inner struggle which he must have undergone when he was thrust back into the cloistered world of the college after experiencing the rugged active life among the Pames. Serra was a man of action, a doer, a prime organizer as well as a scholar of great intellect and a man of religious asceticism. He kept his personal thoughts unto himself and not even his closest friend, Palóu, knew of his inner nature. Years later Palóu wrote of Serra's more notable virtues "which have been observed in him, and which his humility was not able to hide, and which, in order to fulfill the teachings of the Divine Master, ought indeed to be made public. . . ." These notable virtues were listed as being: humility, prudence, justice, fortitude, temperance, faith, hope, charity, and religion. Palóu found that he could not write about or discuss those other qualities of the inner man, which extreme reserve and shyness kept Serra from revealing, but about which all who knew him were keenly aware. Palóu flatly stated, "I will not take up a study of these inner virtues which he assiduously tried to hide even from his most intimate companions and from those who were nearest to him." Although the intimate friendship and high regard between the two dated from the year 1739 and Palóu was Serra's confessor for over thirty-four years, he found that he was able to speak only of Serra's outward life.

Whether the frustrations Serra felt, if any, at being placed in a quiescent role once again had any effect upon his religious asceticism remains a matter of conjecture. However, it was during this period about which so little is known, that Palóu, who is the main source of information, wrote of incident after incident concerning Serra's mystical experiences and of his constant self-mortification. While Palóu's veracity is not to be questioned, it must constantly be borne in mind that he was far away during much of this time and related years later, when an old man, what he recalled his venerated master told him of the events. It must also be kept in view that Junípero's spiritual exultation and his appreciation of the dramatic never left him, just as his religious fervor remained fresh and vital all the days of his life.

It was, therefore, with a sense of wonderment that Palóu wrote of Serra's self-discipline in denying himself sleep and the sufferings he bore because of his long and continuous vigils. Often Serra prayed until four in the morning and then retired, not to sleep, but to continue in prayer until the hour of Prime. He carried out this practice even while on distant missions and the sentinels, when they changed watch, were heard to say, "We don't know when Father Junípero sleeps."

Similarly, he exercised self-discipline in his eating habits. Meat seemed to be repulsive to him and he ate sparingly of fruit and vegetables and fish, often stopping in the middle of a meal to undertake the task of reading aloud to the other friars in the refectory.

Besides constant "mortification of his soul," as one observer wrote, Serra went far beyond the prescribed regulations of the Order in bringing his body into subjection to the Divine Will. As an act of Penitence he often stole away during the night, when he thought only God saw him, and silently slipped into the choir loft and flogged and lacerated his body with rough pieces of sackcloth made either of bristles or woven with broken pieces of wire. This bodily chastisement was stealthily observed by some friars who were, according to Palóu, edified by the sight. Serra was following the custom of chastising his body because of his own imperfections and sins, and also did it for the sins of others.

Once after exhorting the congregation to penitence, Serra, in imitation of his patron St. Francis Solano, dropped his habit to the waist and began lashing his own bare body so cruelly with a chain the whole audience broke into sobs. Finally a man rose up and hurried down to the pulpit, snatching the chain away from Serra. He stood upon the platform of the presbytery and then, imitating Serra, stripped himself to the waist and began making public penance. He lashed himself so unmercifully that he fell down before all the congregation after calling out, "I am the ungrateful sinner before God who should do penance and not the Father, who is a Saint." After receiving Extreme Unction and Holy Communion, the man died a little later.

Always aware of the importance of dramatic impact upon his audiences, Serra used various other methods of moving them into tears of repentence. Upon several occasions he hid a large stone in the pulpit and after delivering his sermon calling for repentance of sin, he would take up this stone in one hand, the crucifix in the other, and as an act of contrition beat his breast with such force that many in the audience were afraid he would injure himself permanently or kill himself before their eyes. In doing this he was acting as St. Jerome in the desert when he likewise bruised his breast with stones. Taking St. John of Capistrano as his model, Serra, when preaching on hell and damnation, would burn his flesh with lighted tapers. In performing such acts, Junípero Serra was acting in the accepted manner of his times. However, while the College of San Fernando did not disapprove such practices, the discretory did suggest that such measures be used only on rare occasions and then with great discretion.

Because of his impassioned and dramatic preaching, Serra was in great demand as a visiting preacher. It was the custom of the College of San Fernando to send the friars out on apostolic tours as itinerant preachers eight months out of each year, returning them to spend the remaining four months in the cloister. Interspersed with his other duties Serra traveled as an itinerant missionary, going through the dioceses of Mexico, Puebla, Valladolid, and Oaxaca. Always going on foot as a *friale andariego,* or walking friar, Palóu estimated that Serra walked more than two thousand leagues in seven years. Computing a league as 2.65 miles, the little friar with the crippled, ulcerated leg strode about fifty-five hundred miles in addition to carrying on other work at the college.

Heeding a request from the illustrious Bishop Buenaventure Blanco of the diocese of Oaxaca, Serra traveled a great distance from Mexico

City and conducted missions in those towns along the coast where a mission had never been held. It was on his way to Oaxaca in response to this invitation that Serra and his companions had to travel a week on the threatening Río Los Mijes, where they suffered many hardships because of the excessive heat and annoying flies and the constant dangers of the alligators abounding in the water. They were unable to disembark from the canoes because of the tigers and lions, snakes, and other poisonous creatures living in the region. After this hazardous trip, they still had to travel afoot for over a hundred leagues through equally dangerous terrain. Reaching Antequera, Serra preached a mission lasting from February through the Lenten season and performed the marriage ceremony for many persons living in sin.

One time while he was conducting a mission in the province of La Huasteca, there were many of the townspeople where he preached who did not come to hear the word of God, giving one excuse or another to explain their negligence. When the Fathers left this town, an epidemic broke out and many people died. It was then that the parish priest discovered that only those who had attended the missions were saved and those who remained away took sick and died. Once this fact was made known, a remarkable change in church attendance took place not only among the townspeople, but farmers and ranchers in the outlying districts came many miles to go to Mass. One man said he had not seen a church or a priest or heard a Mass in over eighteen years, and that it had been forty years since a mission had been conducted in that area. Palóu concluded this tale with the simple statement, "In all these towns a great deal of fruit was gathered for God who in this way abundantly rewarded the labors of his servant, Fr. Junípero and his companions."

One day at sunset when the missionaries, having finished their apostolic labors, were on the way back to the college, they found that night was coming upon them before they had found shelter and a bed. They decided they would have to spend the night out in the open and were looking for a place when they happened to see a house near the road. They were greeted warmly by a venerable old man and his wife and a child who fed them and gave them hospitality for the night. The next morning, after thanking their benefactors, the missionaries went upon their way and soon encountered some muleteers. In conversation with these humble men, the priests told of their night's experience at the nearby house. To their astonishment the muleteers told them, "In all the roads which you went over yesterday there is not a house nor a ranch, not even within leagues of the road."

This information astonished the Fathers, who in pondering the wonders of this considered, "That it was due to the Divine Providence that they had been favored with that night's lodging and that, without doubt, those who lived there must have been Jesus, Mary, and Joseph, a fact which was reflected not only in the cleanliness and neatness of the house in spite of its poverty and the affection with which they were lodged and entertained, but also in the inner extraordinary consolation which their hearts had felt. They therefore gave all due thanks to God," so records Palóu.

In one of these towns visited during the missions, Junípero was celebrating Mass, and immediately upon drinking from the chalice he felt a dreadful heaviness in his stomach. The pain was so severe he would have fallen had not his assistants carried him immediately to the vestry and, removing his vestments, put him to bed. All believed that someone had put poison in the wine cup in order to take Fr. Serra's life. When offered a well-known antidote, the venerable friar looked upon it and shook his head, refusing to drink. They then offered him oil to induce vomiting and he shook his head in agreement. He drank the oil and was then able to find his voice and speak the words of St. Mark, "If ye drink any deadly thing, it will do you no harm."

When the oil did not induce any nausea or vomiting, they marveled and then he told them, "It was not that I wanted to offend you or that I doubted the strength of the remedy or felt any repugnance about it, for in any other circumstance I should probably have taken it; but I had just eaten the Bread of Angels, which, because of the consecration, had ceased to be bread and had become the body of Christ. How then would you have me take so repulsive a drink after having taken into my mouth such divine food?"

Serra greatly enjoyed these apostolic tours during which he had the opportunity to serve people in distant places, but the six months of continuous preaching and hearing Confessions were taxing. Once a mission had been completed the friars spent sometimes as long as a month walking back to the college for a rest and the resumption of other duties. Serra served as vicar of the choir, as novice master for three years, and as commissioner of the holy Inquisition for New Spain and the adjacent islands. It was in this latter role that he sought out and condemned the books of the Encyclopedists.

These books were appearing in Mexico for the first time and Junípero became familiar with the name and the antireligious thinking of Voltaire. Sensing the inherent dangers of this type of thinking to the religious life, Serra could not possibly imagine that the influence of this movement and its subsequent consequences were soon to change the entire course of his life.

CHAPTER XI

JOSEPH DE GÁLVEZ COMES TO

MEXICO JUNE 6, 1765

Mexico City had its own printing press as early as 1535, a hundred and forty years before one appeared in the British colonies. By 1761 there were six presses to be found in the capital city and others in Puebla, Guadalajara, and Vera Cruz. Printers were permitted to work only under government licenses and so strict were the controls of the Inquisition on what might or might not be printed, books had to be smuggled from Europe. Especially true was this of books about philosophy and other topics considered heretical. Most of this smuggling was being done by the clergy.

Mexico City lacked a newspaper, in the usually accepted sense. Any current publications its citizens saw were mere listings of decrees and documents, devoid of interpretation, comment, or criticism. Even the *Gazette* from Madrid, when it arrived, after three or four months, in Mexico contained only this same kind of material. The actual news in which the people were truly interested came by word of mouth and was transmitted through the various layers of society. The doings of kings and emperors, the reports of battles, the naming of new ministers in the government, the gossip of the courts all filtered through the strata this way.

Junípero became necessarily more conscious all the time, as he gained in experience and perception, of the rigid social distinctions in the capital because they formed an integral part of the life with which he dealt every day. Confessions and deathbed rites, Baptisms and marriages, of which the priests were a part, were interlaced with the details of the caste system in which he found himself. As a peasant youth in Majorca, tending the flocks and working in the fields, he had become accustomed from infancy to these distinctions. He accepted them as a part of the world's structure but, over and above the practical limitations they imposed, he considered all souls equal in the sight of God and acted accordingly when he went into the priesthood.

In Majorca, there were essentially only the two groups, the peasantry and the nobility. Now, in Mexico, he had discovered that there were two more social classifications, rendering the complexities of dealing with them all the more difficult from the standpoint of the priests, who were bound by the conventions of the world even in attempting to deal with their spiritual duties. Junípero knew well the feeling of superiority animating the *gachupines,* the rulers and officials born on the home soil of Spain who were sent to this distant province with the aura of gentility emanating from the King himself. Ranked below them were the Creoles, the pureblood Spaniards born in Mexico, a circumstance of nativity which put them in an inferior position; even extending to a rule that they could not hold public office, although this often was forgotten in a practical sense. Junípero was deeply attached, in particular, to the other two classes—the mestizos, or mixed bloods, and the Indians. The Indians were the needy souls he had come to Mexico to help save, and in the Sierra Gorda and elsewhere on his missions he found his supreme challenge and delight in trying to bring them the Gospel so they could understand it and be saved. Lowly as they were in the estimation of the officials and soldiers, he saw them as material for the Lord's redemption, equal in spiritual potential to everyone else. The mestizos were so simple, friendly, and generous in sharing what little food or possessions they might have, that he found them more truly Christian than those in high places who merely professed religion.

To the Church of San Fernando came all classes, some imperious and aloof, others contrite and supplicating. Junípero ministered to them all, but in the meek and lowly, and the comfort he could bring them, he found his greatest joy.

As the years glided by, the outside world battered at the gates of the College of San Fernando and penetrated even to the sanctuary and the cloister. Junípero found himself hearing new names, learning of great events in the homeland, Spain, so that the movements of history enmeshed even the mendicant friends such as those of St. Francis whether they wished it or not.

Excitement prevailed whenever a courier arrived from Vera Cruz. All of Mexico City was intent upon every scrap of news which arrived from Spain. The sight of tired riders with their dispatch cases arriving at the palace of the Viceroy across from the Cathedral or at the Palacio del Ayuntamiento across from the southwest corner from the zócalo was a signal for speculation and surmise. The capital was so isolated from the Spanish, French, and English colonies to the north and from the Spanish colonies in South America that the thin trickle of information across the sea and then from Vera Cruz to Jalapa and then on to Mexico City became the one tenuous connection with the events going on in the world. The palace of the Viceroy was the listening post of all Mexico. Rumor and gossip spread out from it along with authentic news so that the capital was buzzing with every sort of report within a few hours after the arrival of a courier. In the social gatherings of leading citizens, the latest happenings in Madrid, Paris, London, Vienna, St. Petersburg, and Warsaw were discussed as avidly as in the salons of the Louis' or the royal chambers of the capital in Spain. Mexico City was justifiably proud of being the intellectual center of the New World. It could boast a population of almost one hundred thousand contrasted with the few thousand in the English cities of New York and Boston and the relatively small populations of Rio de Janeiro and Buenos Aires.

Life was carefree and gay for the most part in the capital and the theater was well attended. The performances began early, lasting until nearly midnight. The lavishly costumed audience took time out for visiting, *cigarrillos,* and light refreshments. Often the favorite performers were showered with gold and silver coins. Comedies, dances, popular music, and even operas were performed. These often were moralistic and quite dull, their titles indicating the themes such as "The Foolish Virgin and the Wise One," and "Prudence in Girlhood," while the *seguidillas,* or songs with dancing, were something humorous and naughty.

Social life among the colonial Spanish gentility moved along gracefully, governed by a code of elegant behavior. Affable relationships with the members of the French colony were a delightful source for witty conversation and grand balls. Following the afternoon siesta, beautifully dressed ladies and gentlemen drove along the tree-shaded avenues in their fine carriages imported from Europe and drawn by spirited horses. This complacency was scarcely interrupted when news reached the Spanish colonies in 1762 that Spain had entered into the long tedious Seven Years' War against England, the distance involved giving the war an air of unreality. It was not until the British seized Cuba that the Mexicans began to take the matter seriously. With the signing of the uneasy Treaty of Paris on February 10, 1763, Spain recovered Cuba but lost the island of Minorca and Florida. In return for the loss of Florida, France ceded Louisiana to Spain thus giving her a frontier abutting that of England which she feared. The members of the French colony in Mexico City were shocked to learn that France had lost most of her colonial empire.

The cost of this war and years of indifferent fiscal policies had depleted the coffers of the monarchy. Rumors of the King's dissatisfaction with the policies of the Viceroy and the courts were whispered about. All of New Spain awaited with dread the new taxes which they feared King Charles III would impose and pondered the controls which might be placed upon them. They did not have long to wait.

On June 6, 1765, Joseph Gálvez, Visitador-General, minister extraordinary of King Charles III, set foot upon the fortress island of San Juan de Ulloa off the shore at Vera Cruz. Within hours, the news had trickled into Mexico City and tongues began to wag excitedly. Diplomats uneasily tried to maintain their composure. No one knew exactly what was afoot, and all awaited the impact of the first confrontation between the new Visitador-General and Viceroy Marqués de Cruíllas. It was rumored that Gálvez had been the King's third choice before he could get anyone to come to Nueva España, so arduous was the task being assigned to his personal representative.

The confrontation between Gálvez and Cruíllas came almost immediately and resulted in a conflict over whose authority was to dominate. Gálvez, never one to permit rules and tedious protocol to stand in his way, dealt summarily with smugglers along the coast without consulting Cruíllas. An acrimonious argument ensued and Gálvez finally wrote an explanatory letter to the King demanding that Cruíllas be replaced because he was an obstructionist standing in the way of the best interests of the King. Just four and one half months after Gálvez arrived in Mexico, the King hastily summoned Marqués de Croix to his court in Madrid. On October 28, 1765, he offered De Croix the appointment of Viceroy of New Spain. De Croix accepted but did not leave Cádiz until May 3, arriving at Vera Cruz July 18, 1766, one year to a day after the arrival of Gálvez. De Croix was the first foreigner ever to receive the appointment of Viceroy and Charles III had to abrogate the law of the land since the new appointee was Flemish.

De Croix left Vera Cruz for the capital on August 11 and reached Otumba, some fifty miles outside Mexico City, to receive the command of the viceroyalty from Cruíllas as was the traditional custom. He took his oath of office before the audiencia the very next day, thus becoming the first Viceroy not to receive the festive welcome usually accorded. Since the time of Cortés, villages all along the way customarily vied with each other to do homage, decking the houses with colored paper and showering fragrant flowers in the path of the newly appointed official while Indians, dressed in full regalia, knelt and kissed his hand. This lack of courtesy for the new Viceroy and his own unseeming haste to assume his official position, was cause for bewilderment among the members of the official circles.

Once De Croix assumed office, the affairs of state seemed to progress smoothly. He and the Visitador-General worked together in harmony and the people relaxed under the agreeableness of their relationship, only to awaken one morning to dreadful silence. To their agonizing astonishment the affable Viceroy, in office merely nine months, had put into execution the dreadful secret commands for the expulsion and banishment of the Jesuits on the night of June 25, 1767—the night that changed the world.

Still reeling from the shock of this night's terror, the citizens were not permitted to regain their composure before another blow was dealt them later that same day. Viceroy de Croix issued a personal statement reinforcing the King's edict. De Croix stated that the King had "acted in order to fulfill the first obligation, with which God granted him the Crown, of preserving intact its sovereign prerogatives, and of keeping his loyal and beloved people in subordination, peace, justice, and for other grave reasons which he conceals in his royal heart."

The official notice which was posted throughout the city continued by pointing out that those who opposed the order would feel the wrath of the King, and De Croix decreed, "I shall see myself compelled to use the utmost rigor and military force against those that in public or in private for this purpose may have conferences, meetings, assemblies, talks, or discussions by word or in writing; for the subjects of the great monarch who occupies the throne of Spain, must henceforth know once and for all that they are born to keep silent and to obey, but not to discuss, nor to judge the lofty affairs of government." It was signed El Marqués de Croix, Mexico, June 25, 1767.

The imposed silence was observed rigorously. Palóu in his biography of Serra gives but passing mention to the expulsion of the Jesuits. These banished priests followed the edict themselves and made practically no statements either written or vocal concerning the cause of their expatriation and imprisonment. Only by whisper or by innuendo was the subject ever brought up for many years, so afraid were the people of the King's wrath.

Junípero Serra, busily carrying out his duties may have been totally unaware of Gálvez's arrival, the clash between the new Visitador-General and the Viceroy, and the subsequent appointment of De Croix to this position, or, possibly having heard of all this from one of his faithful parishioners, quite likely would have brushed aside the news as too petty for his concern. Thirty leagues from Mexico City, in the tranquil pueblo of Ixmiquilpan, a preconquest village with the Otomí name meaning "Where Edible Wild Greens Abound," he was unaware of the turmoil involving the Jesuits and he could not have dreamed of the role he was going to be playing as the result of their expulsion. His mind was on the holy message he hoped to give his people.

CHAPTER XII

THE CALL TO BAJA CALIFORNIA

Junípero hobbled into the capital by way of Guadalupe and the road beside the Misterios along the route that he had followed seventeen years before. Now he was struck with an enormous contrast. Then he had arrived early on New Year's morning and found a quiet and beautiful city. This time he encountered fear and anger, excitement and talk of rebellion. Along the way from Ixmiquilpan he had heard over and over again the reports of the expulsion of the Jesuits and of the riots and disorders during and after their departure for Vera Cruz. Junípero knew that his own summons must be in some way connected with the expulsion, but he had no idea what this might be. The message from the guardian of the college, Fr. José García, had contained no reason. It had simply bidden him to return at once to the college.

Rumors about the Jesuits were being whispered everywhere. Many were said to have died on the dreadful journey to Vera Cruz. Street battles were reported from Jalapa where the soldiers were reported to have had to fight their way through the crowds of sympathizers with the butt ends of their muskets. Sick and infirm priests were described as having fallen off their horses and to have been thrust back, bleeding and dying, to endure the horrors of more miles on steep mountain trails and through the jungle.

Visitador-General Gálvez was described alternately as a man in seeming-travail, torn between official duty and human sympathy; as permitting the Jesuits a final moment at the Shrine of Guadalupe, and then compelling them to endure the tortures of the damned along the route of their exile.

Serra found his fellow friars at the college silent, none voicing any criticism of the King's unreasonable action. From their sorrowful faces Serra knew that they were quietly mourning and praying for these outcast Jesuits now suffering the tortures of hell. They were remembering the martyrs of that Order who had gladly sacrificed their lives for the aborigines in the wild regions of Sonora. Fathers Kino and Salvatierra, among others, had explored vast regions and claimed them for Spain.

The priests at San Fernando, ever attuned to happenings outside the college, had heard of the Jesuit offer to relinquish one hundred or more missions in their charge and go elsewhere, wherever they could serve God and the King, when vicious calumny had been heaped upon them. Accused of avarice, of utilizing the missions for their own aggrandizement, and of fomenting revolt among the natives, this gesture of appeasement was made by the provincial of the order, Very Reverend Francisco Cevallos in 1766. The offer was refused by the Viceroy's council. The following year, the Jesuits had declined a legacy of 600,000 pesos willed to them by a devout Mexican lady, Doña Josefa de Arguelles y Miranda, for fear of rousing further enmity among the enemies of the Order. This gesture was misinterpreted by some and considered to be merely an astute political act. All conciliatory efforts failed and early on the morning of June 25, 1767, the stunning blow was struck, and from that hour the Jesuits were prisoners without ever having been informed of the charges against them.

Immediately after the announcement of the expulsion of the Jesuits, the Viceroy requested that the now-abandoned missions of Lower California be taken over by the apostolic Fathers of the College of San Fernando. The Reverend Father Guardian was most reluctant to comply since the college was already taxed beyond its capabilities and lacked sufficient friars to carry on this new assignment. However, the college felt compelled to oblige and asked for twelve volunteers among its members.

The Reverend Father Guardian welcomed Serra when he arrived at the college on July 12, and after giving him his blessing, told him of the new assignment. Junípero rejoiced that the burden of acting as president of this company had been assigned to him without his having been consulted. To him it was an act of devotion and obedience and his acquiescence was immediate.

All was ready, the Viceroy having supplied the equipment necessary for the long journey of over two hundred leagues to the port of San Blas. Every comfort had been provided so that the Fathers would be protected against illness on the lengthy journey through the hot country during the rainy season. Since the roads would be of poor condition, the priests were permitted to ride.

They left their school of San Fernando on the morning of July 14, 1767, after bidding a tearful farewell to the community and to their prelate. Scarcely able to hold back his tears, Father García, realizing as they all did, that this would be the last farewell for some of them, spoke to them tenderly. "You go," he said, "Fathers and beloved Brethren, with the blessing of God and with that of Our Holy Father, St. Francis, to work in that mystic vineyard of California which our Catholic Monarch has confided to us. Go, and go comforted with the thought that you have as your superior the good Father Fr. Junípero, whom by this patent I name as the president over your reverences and of all those Missions, and I have nothing more to say to you than that you should give to him the same faithful allegiance you would give to me, and I also ask that you continue to commend me to God." His voice choking, with tears streaming from his eyes, he silently gave Serra the patent. He received it wordlessly and in all humility, without being able to express his emotions.

Kissing the hand of their Reverend Father Guardian whom they thought they were leaving until eternity, they went outside the gates and found the entire square filled with grieving parishioners. The friars mounted their horses and began the long journey into the unknown, which would take some of them into the almost mythical land of Alta California and would cost others their very lives.

It had been decided to send eight Fathers from San Fernando who would proceed to Querétaro or Guadalajara where they would be joined by five coming from the Sierra Gorda. Palóu lists the eight Fernandinos as being: The reverend father preacher, Fray Junípero Serra, doctor and professor de prima of sacred theology, commissary of the Holy Office, and president of the mission, of the holy province of Majorca; Father Fray Francisco Palóu, son of the same province and missionary of the college named; Father Fray Juan Morán, missionary, from the province of La Concepción; Father Fray Antonio Martínez, of the province of Burgos; Father Fray Fernando Parrón, son of the province of Extremadura; Father Fray Juan Sancho de la Torre, of the province of Majorca; Father Fray Francisco Gómez, of the province of La Concepción; Father Fray Andrés Villaumbrales, of the same province.

Those coming from the Sierra Gorda were Fathers Juan Crespí, José Antonio Murguía, Juan Ramos de Lora, Miguel de la Campa, and Fermín Francisco de Lasuén. Father Rafael Verger went to Spain to gather more recruits for the missions.

Traveling at the rate of fifteen to twenty miles a day the missionaries passed through villages with such names as Tlalneplantla, Cualtitlán, Coyotepec, Tula, and Huichapan to San Juan del Río where they crossed a stone bridge dated 1710, and then dropped down into the expansive plains or *bajío*, dotted with small pueblos and farms. On the outskirts of Querétaro they passed by the aqueduct which carried water to the city. They marveled at its seventy-four arches, standing ninety-six feet high in some places. Entering Querétaro, then a town of eighteen thousand inhabitants, the weary travelers walked over the cobblestone streets, lined with single-storied adobe homes, and their hearts quickened with anticipation of seeing the mother apostolic church of the Americas. Santa Cruz was Serra's home whenever he was in Querétaro, but some of the priests were visiting the church for the first time. Here they rested briefly. Their friends from the Sierra Gorda had not yet arrived and so the caravan pressed on, hoping to encounter them at Guadalajara.

The Camino Real continued through the bajío and the fathers went on through Pueblito, Apaseo, Celaya, on through Salamanca, Irapuato, Silao, and León until they came to a slight rise leading to San Juan de los Lagos, where stood the beautiful shrine to Our Lady, second in the hearts of the people only to that of Guadalupe, and dating back to the sixteenth century. The road went through gentle hills and then dropped down to Guadalajara, a city then of about nineteen thousand persons, all living in an area of about ten blocks, going out in all directions from the Cathedral which dated back to 1561. Five blocks south of the Cathedral they came to the Colegio de San Francisco.

San Francisco, with its large monastery, housed about seventy Franciscans during Serra's time and was the provincial headquarters and the home of Indian missionaries. The traveling friars, once again not finding their members from the Sierra Gorda, pressed on leaving San Francisco with its beautiful atrium and gardens.

The roadway became more spectacular, as the plains gradually rose and approached the high mountains ahead. Passing through Amatitlán and Tequila, the way rose rapidly along the mountainside from which they had a wide view of the great barrancas. Descending rapidly through a long narrow valley, the road dropped into more tropical vegetation and passed through small villages until the descent of over two thousand feet from Guadalajara to Tepic was reached. The San Fernando contingent of friars arrived in Tepic after thirty-nine days while the members from the Sierra Gorda did not arrive until August 25.

Tepic, founded in 1524 by Gonzalo de Guzmán, was the site of the modest church and hospice built by the province of Jalisco in 1744, and this became a temporary home for many missionaries. Serra was to stay there four times. The Convento de Santa Cruz de Zacate, built upon the side of a hill, was so named because of a cross of grass. This grass, parched and brown during the dry season and verdantly green during the wet, was protected by a high wall and left open to the sky. The grass cross was deemed to have miraculous healing powers, and crudely lettered and primitively painted pictures, expressing the gratitude of those receiving cures, were tacked on the walls of the church.

Tepic was teeming with missionaries and soldiers and the Fernandinos were welcomed by the superior, Fray Antonio Zamudo, who extended an invitation for them to stay at the hospice of Santa Cruz de Zacate. The treasurer of the troops came and told Serra that he had an order from the Viceroy to provide everything the missionaries required. Serra, expressing his appreciation, told him the friars preferred to remain in the hospice with the other religious, and the money was then paid to the syndic of the convent.

Among the missionaries they found at Tepic were fourteen being sent out from the mother college of Querétaro and these were destined for the far regions of the Pimería in the north; and eighteen friars from the province of Jalisco, also being sent to the Pimería and parts of Nayarit. The soldiers were going to Cerro Prieto, in the province of Sonora, by way of Guaymas, and were being detained because the two boats Gálvez had ordered to be constructed at San Blas were not finished. A small sloop was to carry Don Gaspar de Portolá, the newly named governor of Sonora, a troop of soldiers and dragoons and their color sergeant and a chaplain, Bachelor Don Pedro Fernández.

Serra went personally to call upon Colonel Don Domingo Elizondo, who was in charge of the whole force to request permission for some friars to accompany them on the voyage. Because the boat was so small, only two friars were to be permitted to go and Serra chose Fray Juan Ignacio Gastón and Palóu. They embarked and the sloop set sail from Matanchel August 24. A launch carrying saddles and equipage of the military accompanied it.

The small vessel, overloaded and top-heavy, immediately encountered tempestuous seas. It was the season for tropical storms and tornadoes and on the afternoon of August 28 while off Cape Corrientes a storm of such fierceness and duration came up that the crew prepared to die, so badly were they being buffeted about. Governor Portolá, after making his Confession, suggested to Palóu that they make a promise to a saint, in order to escape with their lives. Fr. Gastón reminded Palóu of the sprig of grass he was carrying as a relic from the holy cross in Tepic. Promising to make a Mass for the holy cross, and that everyone aboard would attend it, Palóu tossed the stems of grass into the turbulent ocean. He later recorded, "And I can sincerely say that as soon as the grass fell into the sea, it was pacified and became calm, but I cannot assert that it was a miracle, but I can say that everybody regarded it as a prodigy and a great mercy of God."

Portolá ordered them to return to Matanchel, since it was not the proper time of year for the voyage, and they reached the hospice in Tepic on September 6 and found that the five members of their college had arrived from the Sierra Gorda.

Serra, never able to tolerate idleness, suggested to the president of the Querétarans, Fray Mariano Antonio de Buena y Alcalde, that a useful occupation for the friars awaiting embarkation would be to hold a mission in Tepic. However, because of the general confusion and the apparent unreceptive mood of the people, it was deemed advisable to postpone the mission.

Colonel Elizondo notified Serra that he and his missionaries should make preparations to sail about the middle of October. Portolá, having decided to sail in the sloop, had assigned a launch for the Franciscans. Serra wanted to see for himself if this launch was large enough for the purpose. He felt free to leave, for brotherly harmony appeared to be well established despite the crowded conditions at Santa Cruz. The fourteen Franciscans from Querétaro, assigned to the Pimería in the north, and the eighteen blue-robed Jaliscans, who were destined to replace the Jesuits in the Pimería and in Nayarit, amiably associated with the Fernandinos. Father Zamudo presided over the entire group.

Serra departed for San Blas, forty-five miles distant, leaving Palóu in charge of the delegation from San Fernando. Junípero had been away from the hospice but a few days when Father Zamudo received a letter from Viceroy de Croix. The letter shattered the seeming tranquillity of the convent. Informed of the contents of the letter Palóu was aghast.

Something had gone wrong. The orders to the missionaries had been changed. He sent an urgent note to Serra advising him to return to Tepic immediately.

CHAPTER XIII

THE CONVENT OF SANTA

CRUZ DE ZACATECA, TEPIC

All was new. The road itself was freshly slashed through the dense jungle growing on the steep slopes leading down from Tepic toward the harbor of Matanchel and the recently established port of San Blas was just now beginning to be settled. Along the way, Junípero saw Indians and Mexicans with machetes flailing at the lush growth brought out by the summer rains and threatening to clog the trail with creepers and tendrils. The October sun in this latitude shone with such brilliance that autumnal growth proceeded with incredible speed although the equinox was already come and gone.

Junípero was awaiting his first sight of the Pacific Ocean. His missions in Mexico had taken him to many parts of the country, including visits to the regions where he could see the Atlantic again following his initial landing at Vera Cruz, but this was his first opportunity to view a portion of the vast body of water to the west.

The country itself, as he descended from the pleasant three-thousand-foot elevation of Tepic into the steaming jungle land below, closely resembled the region surrounding Vera Cruz except that the stench was greater. The land was stinking in its own offal. So rampant was the growth that it flourished, blossomed, bore fruit, crumbled, died, and turned into putrefying masses of vegetation within a period of a few weeks, and then started the process all over again. Even the cultivated banana plantations along the route joined in this riot of fecundity and decay. The long lower leaves yellowed, dropped off, and joined the mat below while the continual process of the ripening of the fruit went on. Only the coconut trees, imported to the region by the earlier settlers, appeared to stand cleanly aloof, as if holding their high clusters of fronds distant from the wormy masses surrounding their bases.

A slight limp, as always, marked Junípero's walk. His ulcerated leg never seemed to get any better. At the rare intervals when he had time to contemplate the sores, he speculated on the reason for the continuing infection but there was hardly ever any opportunity to seek treatment. His life was too busy. It had been nearly eighteen

years now since he had suffered the insect bite on the road from
Vera Cruz to Mexico City and he had, in a way, come to regard
it as a mortification of the flesh imposed for his sins. He accepted
it as such, and permitted himself to think about it only when the
pain became so severe that it threatened to interfere with his missionary
activities.

Today, trudging at his steady pace lower and lower into the
jungle where increasingly large numbers of parrots screamed and
the heat grew more and more intense, he was preoccupied with all
the manifold details of trying to arrange the passage of his party
of friars across the intervening waters to their new assignments in
California. Loreto, he knew, lay out there somewhere to the northwest
across the roiled and tempestuous ocean but as yet it was only a
vague and indistinct goal, mysteriously distant amid the heathen.
More real at the moment were the problems of transportation. He was
determined that, regardless of the wishes of the temporal authority,
he must be satisfied of the safety of his brother priests on the voyage.
The news that they were expected to embark in a mere launch,
intended primarily for coastal use in the Matanchel vicinity rather than
for crossings to California, had impelled him to make the trip to the
harbor. He must be sure that he was not endangering the lives of his
companions.

Necessarily, his thoughts dwelt, too, upon the plight of the Jesuits
summarily removed from their posts after so many years of service,
and even now awaiting the voyage across from California to the
mainland and an unknown fate ahead. Like his Franciscan brethren
and the Viceroy and the Visitador-General, Junípero from ingrained
habits of obedience accepted the King's authority and the decree of
expulsion for the Jesuits without outward question, yet, as a human
being, he shared in the pity for them as other human beings. He
knew from his own experience in the Sierra Gorda and elsewhere
how slow was the process of communication, and that there would
be weeks or months of travail and suffering for the disgraced Jesuits
after they were contacted in their remote outposts in California
before they could congregate at Loreto, and be brought over for
their long enforced march to Vera Cruz.

Loreto . . .

The lyrical name of the community for which he himself was
bound kept recurring to him. At one moment it seemed remote and
impossible of attainment, situated as it was on the coast of Baja
California some three hundred leagues from Tepic across the treach-
erous waters of the Gulf of California, as if it were enmeshed in a
dream; at others, it beckoned close and confiding as though it were

his natural destination, easily attainable. Its association with "Our Lady of Loreto" was familiar to him. The community was observing its seventieth anniversary in this year of 1767, having been founded by the Jesuits in 1697 and named for the shrine in Italy, which housed the reputed home of Mary, Joseph, and Jesus after its miraculous transportation across the Mediterranean in 1291 during the Crusades. Junípero knew the story well from his boyhood reading. Now that he was indeed destined for the "new" Loreto, namesake of the holy spot so far away, he was fascinated by every word he heard about the California port. From it came fantastic stories of riches from enormous pearls, of the giant and fearsome man-eating manta rays waiting to snare unwary divers, of brilliantly colored fish flashing through its blue waters, of the treasures reputedly gathered there by the Jesuits, and now hidden following the order for their removal.

One practical aspect of Loreto concerned him in particular. The launch he was going to inspect in regard to its safety belonged to a celebrated resident of the fabled port, Don Manuel de Osío, who had started as a soldier at Loreto, had become rich in the pearl fisheries, and then had developed a silver mine at Santa Ana, several leagues inland. Osío conveyed trained miners and supplies from the mainland at Matanchel and elsewhere across the tempestuous stretch of ocean to Loreto, and sometimes rented his boats to the government. Junípero knew that Osío's launch in which his companions were scheduled to make the passage had succeeded in the crossing before, but he still was determined to make a personal inspection before giving his approval to the embarking.

This determination, this fixity of purpose, once he had decided on an objective, had become more and more apparent to his brethren at the College of San Fernando, to his companions in the Sierra Gorda, and to the missionaries who accompanied him throughout Mexico to preach the gospel. It was a growing characteristic which had transformed Junípero since his landing at Vera Cruz. Then he had still been primarily the scholar, the academic professor of philosophy from the Llullian University at Palma, the more or less impractical teacher whose knowledge came from books, whose horizon was a cloister, whose meditations were upon saints and heroes of the Church rather than upon pagans and active sinners in a foreign land. That had all been changed. The professor suddenly had lost his cloister and come in contact with naked savages and idolatry and open wickedness and the most venal aspects of primitive and unthinking mankind.

An adjustment was thrust upon him. A revolution in thinking was required. A daily necessity of dealing with ugly facts arose.

In this situation, Junípero retained an almost naïve spirit of obedience to his religious superiors and to what he considered the manifest will of God. Yet, at times, he as a man, he as a priest, he as a servant of the Almighty was compelled by reality to make hard decisions of his own, to wrestle unaided with evil, to determine courses of action, to maintain a goal.

Out of this came his growth, his maturing, his development of an inflexible determination in the cause of right as he saw it.

Now as he limped ahead on the flatlands through the towering, lace-topped trees and the heavy undergrowth after having descended from the hills, the sound of chattering voices came to him suddenly amid the parrot cries. Ahead, on the banks of a rushing stream he saw women washing their clothes. Children played in the shallow water amid the rocks on the banks. Men lolled in the shade. The water was high and dark with silt at this season but the women washed as if it were emerging crystal clear from some deep spring. Clothing and bedding, already washed and surprisingly clean, was spread to dry on the rocks.

As Junípero approached, he was greeted with respect, and the people crowded around him. In their pleasantries and laughter he felt a sense of excitement.

One of the little boys pointed upstream and cried:

"Boats! Boats!"

Junípero realized the boy must be speaking of the new vessels, ordered by Visitador-General Gálvez on a visit to the area many months before, and since then under construction on the Santiago River ten leagues to the north. During this period of high water they were undoubtedly being sent down a tributary to the new fitting-out yard at the inner harbor of San Blas close to the older part of Matanchel, for use on voyages to California.

Junípero forded the stream at the place indicated by the natives and hurried on toward Matanchel. He was aware that it would require much time for the preparation of the vessels before they could go to sea, yet he caught some of the excitement of the people in the forest at the idea of having new large ships to link the settlement with other ports.

He knew soon that he must be approaching his destination. The delightful aroma of sawn cedar came to his nostrils, which effaced the smell of rotting vegetation. The cedar of San Blas was famous for its strength and durability in shipbuilding, and an immense supply of timbers was being cut at San Blas for fitting out the present vessels, the *San Carlos* and the *Principe,* and for the building of others. Its clean tangy smell was becoming an emblem of the new community under construction close to the harbor.

Serra had been in San Blas but a few days and scarcely had time to inspect the ships in the harbor at Matanchel when a special courier brought him a message from Palóu telling of the distressing events at the hospice. By the latest edict of the Viceroy, the orders for the Fernandinos had been changed. They were to go to the Pimería with the Querétarans, and the Jaliscans were to take over the original assignment of the Franciscans and go to Lower California. A letter written by the Jaliscans to the Commissary General of New Spain, Fray Manuel Nájera, inferring that a feeling of disharmony toward the Jaliscans on the part of the Fernandinos had developed while at the hospice in Tepic. The message suggested that since the Fernandinos and the Querétarans were members of sister colleges, they would undoubtedly be more congenial working together and hence were assigned to the Pimería; the Jaliscans were to be assigned a separate location in Baja California.

The jubilation of the Jaliscans was like salt in the wounds of the saddened Fernandinos. They had volunteered for missionary work in Baja California and preferred to return to their headquarters in Mexico City if there was to be a change. Palóu checked with Colonel Elizondo and found that the new instructions were true. Since no lack of harmony had been observed by anyone at the hospice, Palóu could only believe that the move had been a fabrication of the Jaliscans, who preferred going to Baja California instead of among the warlike Apache Indians. He considered the change in orders and the insinuations of the Jaliscans as insults against the entire College of San Fernando.

Similarly, the Querétaran friars were embarrassed at this affront to the good name of their college, and their president, Buena y Alcalde, prepared a legal paper disclaiming the truthfulness of all alleged accusations of disharmony. He signed this himself and requested that the president of the Jaliscans also sign; then all of the members of the various Orders signed under oath.

Serra rushed back to Tepic to find his friars in a state of dejection. He wrote a letter to Father García pointing out the injustice of the accusations and the impracticalities of the new orders and recommended that his friars be returned to their original college. Serra, acting with the independent directness he had learned while in the Sierra Gorda, decided to bypass regular channels of protocol and sent Palóu and De la Campa to Guadalajara to mail the letter or to press on to Mexico City should they deem it advisable.

The two left Tepic on October 19, the same day the Jaliscans sailed from Matanchel to take over the Jesuit missions in Lower California, and traveled the seventy leagues to Guadalajara without rest. Once there Palóu decided to go directly to Guanajuato for a personal confrontation with Visitador-General Gálvez to inform him of the "insidious and false" charges so skillfully presented by the Jaliscans.

They reached Guanajuato on November 1 and on that same afternoon had an interview with Joseph Gálvez, who told them he had just been informed of these changes and that he disagreed entirely. He gave them a letter expressing his views and suggested that since they had come so far, they might as well go on to Mexico City and report to the guardian and the council of the college. Palóu delivered the letters eight days later to the authorities of the Order who decided to have him report in person to the Viceroy.

On November 11, De Croix, impressed with Palóu's arguments and obvious sincerity and after reading the letters, signed an order countermanding the decree he had issued under the false representation of the Jaliscans. The Viceroy suggested that the two weary friars remain for a brief rest at San Fernando and sent the message back to Tepic by special courier. After the welcome respite, Palóu requested and was joined by two additional friars who were to complete their contingent. Fathers Dionisio Basterra and Juan de Medina Veitía were selected to go and the four departed from Mexico City arriving at Tepic the last day in December, where they were greeted with "demonstrations of the utmost joy."

With the Jaliscans departed for Lower California, the troops and the Querétarans off to Sonora, the Fernandinos alone were left behind. Serra decided that the time had come for the proposed mission to take place. All fifteen were in agreement. Serra and a few others gave a mission in Tepic while Palóu, De la Campa, and Medina Veitía went to the nearby pueblo of Campostela to conduct another. This village, a brief twenty-four miles from Tepic, was famed as the place where Coronado, in February 1540, assembled his army and marched northward seeking the fabled Seven Cities of Cíbola. The friars had not finished their mission before they received an urgent letter from Serra recalling them to Tepic. He had received official word that they were soon to sail on the *Concepción*. Word had come to him that the ship also brought news of the wily Jaliscans who had reached Baja California but had not as yet been assigned their missions.

The *Concepción* also brought the subjugated and expatriated band of Jesuits from this region to San Blas—the first stopping place on the journey to Vera Cruz and exile.

*   *   *

The dreadful responsibility of carrying out the royal orders expelling the missionaries from Baja California was given to Don Gaspar de Portolá by Joseph Gálvez. Portolá, a pleasant, genial man, enjoyed wide popularity, but withal was brave and honest. He was ordered by Gálvez to embark from San Blas taking fifty well-armed men and, by force if necessary, drive the Jesuits from the missions. Two years before the Jesuits had voluntarily offered to relinquish these missions but their offer had been refused. Portolá sailed with his soldiers divided among three ships and accompanied by fourteen Franciscans who were to replace the Jesuits. Violent tropical storms buffeted the ships so mercilessly, the two ships carrying the soldiers and the Franciscans were driven back, but the third, carrying Portolá and the dragoons, came to the Port of San Bernabé close to the Mission of Loreto on November 30, 1767.

Records show that Portolá acted with compassion and understanding. He summoned Father Benito Ducrue, the superior of all the California missions, to come to Loreto for a conference. Traveling the fifty miles from the Mission Santa María de Guadalupe, Father Ducrue with three others arrived at Loreto during the time of the Christmas vigil. Portolá immediately told him of the awful royal decree and ordered the superior immediately to summon all of the members of the Jesuit Order under his command to hasten to Loreto for embarkation to San Blas and thence on to Vera Cruz. They were to take an inventory of all the goods belonging to each mission before departing, and to take with them only articles necessary for the journey. They were to be permitted to carry away three books apiece.

Portolá also requested Father Ducrue to direct the missionaries to preach to their Indian converts and to tell them to obey and continue to be quiet and obedient to the new priests who were coming to be with them as they had obeyed their present Fathers. From the gentle, humble manner in which Ducrue accepted his demands, Portolá realized that a simple letter would have served and that armed force never had been necessary.

The childlike Indians received the heavy blow that they were to be parted forever from the tender ministrations of their beloved priests with bewilderment and sorrow. When the Indians at Mission San Borja heard their Father Wenceslaus Link was to be taken from them, they broke out in rioting. Because of a foot injury, making walking impossible, the Indians carried Father George Retz the hundred miles from Mission San Ignacio to Loreto. Father James Baegert wrote years later in his diary: "I wept not only then, but throughout the journey; and even now as I write tears fill my eyes." Not only were the priests leaving the orchards, vineyards, and fields they had cultivated in this sterile inhospitable land, but they were being forced to abandon two thousand spiritual charges they had converted while at Mission San Ignacio.

When the Jesuits had completed their sorrowful task of taking the inventories of their missions, they made their farewells to their charges, who weeping disconsolately, followed the long distance to Loreto which they reached by the first of February. Here they received word that the replacement of Franciscans, after a harrowing voyage of eighty-three days, had landed farther to the south. On the morning of February 3, Fathers Ducrue and Retz officiated at the farewell Mass aboard the tiny vessel. There was not space enough for sleeping accommodations so they had to sleep on deck. The craft was becalmed until the next morning when a wind came up and the vessel slowly departed as the Fathers stood together chanting aloud the litany of Our Lady of Loreto. The Indians and soldiers remained watching upon the shores as Portolá wept.

Distressing as all of this had been to Portolá, within a few months chance was to decree an even more agonizing experience for him when a boatload of sick and dying outcast priests was blown into the shelter of Puerto Escondido by strong winds.

As he was enforcing the decree of expulsion in Baja California a similar fate was being dealt to Jesuit missionaries in the north and west. Knowledge of the decree did not reach the black-robed priests of the missions of Sinaloa and Sonora until July 25, 1767. These missions were among the most famous in the history of the missionary effort of Spain for these intrepid, Jesuit priests had pushed forward the frontiers of New Spain by their explorations and, during their labors, had baptized hundreds of thousands of Indians and established close to two hundred missions.

Father Juan Nentvig, rector of the north, called all of the priests of the two provinces to meet with him at Mátape near the upper Río Yaqui. Manuel Aguirre, vice-provincial and general superior of the western section, in the meanwhile, deeded over all of the church properties to the King. The fifty-one Jesuits who gathered at Mátape were ordered to go to Guaymas on the coast to await a ship which would take them to San Blas. They were kept at Guaymas for months and housed in rat-infested, crumbling barracks made of mud and straw. The stench was unbearable because of the lack of windows. They were not provided with chairs or tables and were fed tainted food and not given sufficient potable water to drink. One of their members, José Palomino, died and all of them were desperately ill, some barely able to stagger, and others had to be carried on litters when the ship arrived.

Despite the fact that it was the time of year when no experienced seaman would have embarked upon the stormy and turbulent seas, they sailed in May. Tossed and buffeted upon the tempestuous sea, all sick with scurvy and suffering from lack of water, they finally, after a dreadful voyage of twenty-four days, were blown upon the coast of Lower California and took shelter, to escape the battering winds, in the Puerto Escondido. Once out of the winds, the heat became stifling in that sheltered pocket where they anchored. Forbidden to land, they rotted with sweat and scurvy in the scorching heat. They were near the embarkation spot from whence the Jesuits from Lower California had sailed four months previously. Soon word spread out over the countryside that other black-robed missionaries were off the coast and the Indians paddled out to bring food and to kiss their hands as acts of devotion. The superiors of the Franciscans came out to visit them and to bring spiritual comfort to the beleaguered Jesuits in their desperate situation. Portolá feared the wrath of his superior, Joseph Gálvez, and was too timid to allow the priests to be brought ashore despite the pleadings of the Franciscans.

Finally, Portolá actually boarded the ship, and saw at firsthand their acute suffering and permitted them to leave the terrible inferno of the ship. Many of them were nearly dead, but revived when they drank the juice of the fresh mescal plant which the Indians brought to them daily. Portolá received word of the arrival of Visitador-General Joseph Gálvez in Baja California and gave orders for the immediate departure of the Jesuits for San Blas. He commanded the captain of the vessel, under pain of death, not to land in any other port. Portolá gave a dinner for the superiors the night before but was on hand the next morning and did not leave the shore until the vessel disappeared from view.

After a voyage of unspeakable horror, the Jesuits landed twenty-six days later at San Blas. The villa of San Blas, but recently founded, consisted of crudely constructed pole huts. The climate was damp and enervating and the inhabitants sickly and weakened by the constant humidity. The Fathers were rain-soaked and sick with fever by the time they were permitted to go on their way to Tepic. The rainy season made the roads virtually impassable and even those priests on horseback were in danger. The water often came above the horses' bellies and they stumbled and fell, nearly causing the wayfarers to drown. Despite the kindliness they received at Tepic, many of the Jesuits were broken in body and spirit, and by the time they reached

Ixtlán a strange malady struck them. Twenty of the fifty died and were buried with respect and honor by the local people. Doctors were brought from Guadalajara, but they were helpless. It was later written that the bodies turned black as death approached, and even as the priests lay in their caskets a deadly sweat oozed from their corpses. Those who managed to survive went on and came to Guadalajara where they were treated with great veneration. Finally, despite all of the hardships and sufferings, some did manage to reach Vera Cruz and depart for Cádiz where they arrived after two years of painful travel.

The day of the "Old Society," as modern day Jesuits refer to these early representatives of their Order, was over. The long history of their missionary work, begun in 1591 by Gonzalo de Tapia, and then carried on by Kino to Arizona, and by Salvatierra, who carried it across to Lower California, making possible the extension of Spanish claims into Alta California, came to an end. During the 176 years of Jesuit missionary work in New Spain, it is estimated that approximately two million neophytes were baptized. The work of twenty-four colleges and six Jesuit residences came to an end; eleven seminaries were discontinued and many Indian schools collapsed. The approximately two hundred thousand Indians under the ministrations of the Jesuit missionary Fathers were virtually abandoned and either wandered back into their former homes and pagan ways or remained beside the missions and suffered great want.

The missions in many instances declined or disappeared for lack of enough trained missionaries to replace the expelled Jesuits. Portolá and his soldiers ransacked several missions, hoping to find the hoarded Jesuit treasure-trove. Finding none, Portolá left one of his soldiers at each mission to assume charge and to keep the Indians from looting. Conditions at the missions deteriorated rapidly.

The Fernandinos under Serra's supervision would arrive to find crumbling buildings and demoralized Indians who, for the most part, had scattered and fled into the wild, bleak country to escape from the severe treatment of the military.

CHAPTER XIV

GÁLVEZ FORMULATES A PLAN

Not even the warmth of the sun shining down upon his shoulders brought him comfort as he rode along the El Camino Real from Guadalajara toward Tepic. Once he would have looked forward with great anticipation to making this journey again to the small port of San Blas for which he had such great plans. It was to be the key that would unlock the barricades of indifference and procrastination impeding his path toward the dream and goal of his life—California.

He knew well the fables and facts of that distant place and their lure beckoned to him constantly. Eager as he was to move ahead, his pace was slowed by the burden of bone-weary fatigue which now accompanied him every inch of the way. His eyes burned from lack of sleep and his eyelids were half closed. His head ached as though encircled by a metal band.

Joseph de Gálvez, Visitador-General of the King of Spain, slumped in his saddle and his usually spirited horse plodded slowly as though sensing his master's mood. The road Gálvez and his retinue traveled this day early in May 1768 passed the shrine of Our Lady of Zapopan several miles northwest of Guadalajara and then entered broad, fertile plains. It was a pleasant countryside and one which customarily brought him great pleasure. He gave it scarcely a glance as he continued his silent way. His mind churned restlessly and spasmodically as the events of the comparatively brief time since his arrival in Mexico crowded into his tired head in a mad, giddy, kaleidoscopic whirlwind. He raised a gloved hand as though to brush away the tormenting, jumbling thoughts and his staff members drew back, troubled by his unfamiliar lassitude.

Scenes from that fateful night of June 25, 1767, flashed vividly before him as though they had just happened. Bad as that night had been, the following morning of the actual expulsion of the Jesuits and the ensuing days and months following the event, had been worse. Gálvez inwardly smiled grimly as he recalled Viceroy de Croix' naïveté when he gratefully commented upon the docility of the people in peacefully accepting the expulsion without protest. Just as Gálvez anticipated, this quietude was short-lived. De Croix' complacency was quickly shattered when couriers began arriving bearing urgent messages from the outlying provinces telling of violence and rioting raging in San Luis de la Paz, Valladolid, Pátzcuaro, San Luis Potosí, and Guanajuato, where trouble with the peasant classes had always been chronic.

The Viceroy, believing the trouble entirely due to the expulsion, planned to send one of his ministers to cope with the situation. Without dissuading the Viceroy from this belief, Gálvez offered to go himself to quiet the troubled areas. He suspected that many of the disorders were due to the peasants rebelling against the renewal of restrictions against carrying firearms, to the collections of tributes, and to the duties recently put upon local liquors, and he further believed that he would have to resort to force before the recalcitrants would be subdued. Accompanied by five hundred hand-picked troops, Gálvez went into these areas where pillaging, rioting, and civil disruption were more violent and placed the Indians under martial law. Arrest followed arrest with Gálvez acting as judge in each instance when the malcontents were brought to trial.

He was absent from the capital four and one half months and during that time three thousand Indians were brought before him to be tried. All were found to be guilty of having hearts full of malice and a desire to do the Spanish mischief. Gálvez sentenced 117 to banishment, 640 were condemned to life imprisonment, 75 received the lash, and 85 were put to death and the worst offenders decapitated and their heads stuck upon spikes and put on public display. Private lands were confiscated and the lower classes were taxed to pay for the housing and upkeep for the unrequested and unwelcomed soldiers Gálvez left to keep them in submission and to quell any further uprisings.

All classes of society throughout Mexico, even the judiciary, were repelled and terrorized at the actions of Gálvez. The tumult of shocked criticism, coming from all sides, probably reached him and may have prompted him to write De Croix a letter stating his views:

> If I have been able to work with any success, and to take any measures which merit the approval of yourself and the satisfaction of his majesty in the zeal and fidelity with which we strive to serve him, this is the only reward I seek as the final recompense for my wakefulness and fatigue, that I may carry to my grave the inner satisfaction and consolation that I have not been a servant entirely useless to my master and to my nation.

He then added piously, "But I assure you before God, and with all sincerity that I have not upon my conscience the slightest scruple of having exceeded the limits of justice, for I mitigated my sentences always with clemency and mercy."

He sensed that behind his back vile stories ridiculing him were being whispered. One such tale, which spread from one end of Mexico City to another, was that Gálvez, troubled by the burden of decision, prayed long hours asking the Virgin Mary for advice on what to do with the rebels. At length he would then lift his hand for a pen to write down the judgment the Virgin had given to him —and the sentence was always death!

Despite the fatigue which continued and the persistent sleeplessness, for often he could not snatch more than three hours of rest a night, Gálvez turned an anxious eye toward the conditions in the remote northern frontier. This was the frontier which held his interest from the moment he had stepped ashore at Vera Cruz to assume his duties as Visitador-General. He had thoroughly familiarized himself with the various reports being sent back by missionaries and explorers. Doubtlessly he had carefully read Burriel's *Noticia* setting forth the advantages of conquest. He also was firmly convinced that there would be a tremendous personal advantage to himself. Just how, he could only conjecture, but he believed that vast resources and benefits could be derived from this wild, untamed frontier both for himself and for Spain.

During the last days of 1766 and the early part of 1767, Gálvez made his first visita and took careful note of what he saw. Everywhere he went as Visitador he saw signs of decadence in the colonial government. Soldiers were poorly equipped and indifferently performed the most routine duties. He chafed to see the inefficient working of the mines and he noted that commercial agriculture and manufacture were at low ebbs. Everywhere the provinces of New Spain had settled into stagnation and needed new regulations and controls which would restore vitality and life.

Gálvez raged within himself to think that he had evolved just such a plan immediately upon reaching Mexico, but had been thwarted on every side by the jealous and ineffectual Viceroy Cruíllas. It was just such blind fools as this, he thought, who kept Spain from pressing onward in its exploration into the west and north. Procrastination, a characteristic which was an anathema to him, was the greatest evil infecting the Spanish government. For over a century and a half no exploring vessel had sailed up the Pacific coast. Petty wars and political turmoil drained the royal treasury, and despite the fact that the Crown was in full possession of complete information of the most detailed sort about the coast line, the land, and the people and had exact descriptions of the ports of San Diego, Monterey, and Port Reyes or San Francisco, nothing was done to seize them firmly for Spain.

Once he had succeeded in the removal of Cruíllas and De Croix had come as the replacement Viceroy, he was able to make some progress in his plans. He and De Croix worked together in perfect amity, and it was to him that Gálvez reported the unstable conditions he found in the provinces. He recommended that the Royal Edict of October 1764, which had been delayed by quarrels between himself and Cruíllas, calling for prompt pacification of the northern Indians be immediately enforced. De Croix, in complete agreement, called the junta of September 1765.

Plans were formulated for the reconquest of the frontier with an expedition to be sent the first of the new year. Two companies were to be dispatched immediately. Gálvez volunteered to obtain money for the financing of such a project, there being none in the royal treasury for the purpose. It was further decided to organize flying companies of presidial soldiers and settlers, the latter to be paid only while on active duty. Two brigantines were to be built on the Pacific coast for more direct transportation of troops and supplies to Sonora in a formal expedition. The Council of the Indies had previously urged construction of such vessels for the commercial need on the west coast.

The following June 17, 1766, Gálvez reported progress to the King in the collections of funds for the enterprise. He claimed that over 200,000 pesos had been promised to him by the consulates of Cádiz and Mexico, by ecclesiastical bodies and individuals, and that he believed the expedition could be made "without cost to the royal treasury." The shipbuilding project was started and an experienced naval shipbuilder from Vera Cruz, Lieutenant Alonso Francisco Pacheco, appointed supervisor. Pacheco immediately established a new shipyard twenty-six miles from San Blas on the banks of the Río Santiago and started construction on two boats.

It was not until the following November 19, 1766, that the King gave his reluctant approval, expressing grave doubts as to the efficacy of a formal expedition. He also questioned the wisdom of gathering up settlers from the restless, undesirable class of poor residents in the large cities and transporting them to the frontier to serve as a defensive wall against the savages.

In all of his tremendous plans Gálvez was greatly aided by De Croix who called two juntas, one on December 6, 1766, and another on January 8, 1767, to get their agreement to move troops northward immediately. The total number of forces to be used in the Sonoran campaign numbered eleven hundred. Among these were to be veteran dragoons, fusiliers, half of these to be from Havana, militiamen, and three hundred Indian auxiliaries. When the fusiliers were not forthcoming from Havana, a company of Catalonian volunteers sent from Spain took their places. These would later march on to Monterey in Alta California under Lieutenant Pedro Fages.

In April of 1767 the military expedition proper under command of Colonel Domingo Elizondo, a contingent of 350 men, set out for Tepic on the west coast to remain until the completion of the brigantines which were to carry them on to Sonora. Gálvez faced great opposition against his plan not only from his opponents and critics, but the King lacked enthusiasm for it as well. A man with less drive and ambition would have abandoned the entire effort rather than face such overwhelming obstacles.

De Croix called a junta for the purpose of selecting a leader for the expedition in January of 1768 and to no one's surprise, Gálvez was the choice. The time for departure was set for the middle of April and he was to go with the full powers of the Viceroy to reorganize the affairs of the government and to establish colonies along the frontier the moment the military forces had restored peace.

Gálvez presented a fourteen-point program which was enthusiastically accepted. While suppression of the Indians along the northern borders and the establishment of new colonies were of primary importance in the vast scheme, Gálvez also proposed setting up a new form of government independent of the viceroyalty of New Spain. In this he was adapting ideas which had previously been proposed as early as 1751 when it had been set forth in the Sanchez proposal that the government in Mexico City was too far away to handle the affairs of these wilderness regions properly. This was to be called a commandancy-general. He further suggested the establishment of a system of intendancies to increase the profits of the Crown. Three of these were to be located at Durango, Sonora, and the Californias to collect internal revenues. Gálvez placed great importance upon the threats from other European powers and emphasized the safety precautions against attacks which would result from his plan.

Gálvez sometimes thought that he was the only man fully aware of the need for extending the Mexican boundaries farther north. For years the Manila galleons sailing back from the Philippines by the northern route, their crews wracked with scurvy and lack of fresh water, their hulls badly in need of repair, frequently careened laboriously down the California coast line badly in need of supplies and a sheltering relief harbor. Countless requests for such relief stations coming from seamen throughout the years went unheeded by Spain. Ports and presidios along the California coast were imperative if commerce was to be maintained with the Orient and the encroaching threats of other countries were to be stopped.

Now, he, Joseph Gálvez, with the aid of De Croix and the reluctant consent of a doubting King, was about to rectify this situation.

He had left Mexico City on April 9, 1768, with a group of settlers for Sonora ostensibly to make a visita or tour of inspection to Guadalajara and Tepic and to make a hurried visit to Baja California on his way to the northern frontier of Sonora, but his prime objective was to found the royal naval department at San Blas. The previous January, Viceroy de Croix, at Gálvez's insistence, had issued instructions for the establishment of such a base, deeming it indispensable to found a port which would be the base of supplies for New Spain once the frontier of Sonora had been subdued and for the advancement of the Californias. Gálvez, according to a report of one of his secretaries, had been hard at work drawing up plans for such a naval department in December of 1767, a month before the Viceroy issued his instructions.

Gálvez arrived in Guadalajara on April 22, 1768, and remained in that city until May 4. He appeared before the audiencia and laid before them his plans for the establishment of a system of intendancies in New Spain. He adroitly explained that the present system of government was too unwieldy, placing too great a burden upon the Viceroy. Under this plan the collection of revenues would be made by eleven intendants. He explained that this plan had received official approval at the junta of February 25. The audiencia of Guadalajara likewise endorsed the plan and sanctioned Gálvez's appointment as executor.

So far, all was going according to his plan and now, two days after the Guadalajara meeting, Gálvez was riding on toward Tepic. He took little interest in the dramatic change in the scenery when the road passed through the narrow valleys of the rugged barrancas. His very bones ached and his head throbbed continuously. His eyes, customarily so keen and penetrating in their glance, smarted from lack of sleep which would not come at night despite his great physical exhaustion. Gálvez did not notice the sounds of commotion at the rear of his retinue and was unaware that a messenger had arrived until an aide handed him a letter from De Croix telling of Russian explorations in the Americas.

Marqués de Grimaldi, the Spanish minister of state, had written to the Viceroy telling him about the rumors of Russian activities, relating that news had come from the Spanish minister to Russia that the Russians had actually made a landing in North America and had a battle with the Indians in which three hundred Russians had been killed. The exact place of this invasion was not known. The message continued by describing the threat from Russian merchants who were moving across the Bering Strait and pushing southward along the mainland of Alaska.

Gálvez hastily scanned the letter and his pulse throbbed with excitement when he read:

> The King has ordered me to inform Your Excellency of all that has just been set forth, so that you may make it known to the man appointed governor of California, giving him instructions about the vigilance and care that he ought to exercise in order to observe such attempts as the Russians may make there, frustrating them if possible, and giving notice of everything promptly to Your Excellency, so that you may report it to His Majesty.

While this letter did not give instructions for an expedition to Monterey, it gave Gálvez an opening wedge. It was all that he needed. Whatever authority was lacking, he would assume. The plans for this expedition to Alta California had long been fomenting in his active brain. With a sudden surge of energy coursing through his veins, all fatigue vanished. He spurred his horse, and with an imperious wave of his arm, ordered his retinue to do likewise. They hurried on, stopping for a brief rest at Tepic and then pushed on, reaching San Blas on May 13. He delayed in answering the Viceroy's letter and telling him of his plans until May 20. While the letter from the Viceroy did not specifically order an invasion and occupation of Alta California, Gálvez quickly formulated his plans and wrote to De Croix,

> . . . recalling to mind the many conversations and reflections which we have previously had concerning the supreme importance and utility of taking possession of the port of Monterey and establishing a presidio there, I am obeying your orders to take such measures as I deem fitting for reaching that place by land or sea. As you leave to my discretion fulfillment of this order, it has seemed to me both fitting and necessary that I should inform you from here of the resolutions which it was thought proper to take in this weighty matter.

His first act was to make a thorough inspection of the former shipping center at Matanchel, three miles east of San Blas which had been built by the Jesuits in 1750. Supplies from Mexico City were transported by way of Guadalajara and Tepic and finally brought to Matanchel from whence they were ferried across the gulf to the

Jesuit missions of Lower California. Despite all this, Gálvez selected San Blas for the new government supply center and maritime base.

The seeming haste in which this decision was made would seem to indicate that the choice of the permanent naval depot had been predetermined in conversations between De Croix and Gálvez in Mexico City before the start of the visita. The disadvantages of San Blas as an important port were many: the inclement weather, the smallness and shallowness of the harbor, and the vast distance from the capital.

The weather, hot and humid in the summer and with torrential rains during the winter months, made the area exceedingly unhealthy. Noxious odors from the rotting vegetation and swarms of mosquitoes coupled with poor sanitation made it necessary for those who could to escape into the higher and healthier regions of Tepic. The harbor was small and shallow with many sand bars forming dangerous obstacles. Although the inner port was sheltered there was room for only four vessels at one time. The outer harbor had a five-mile beach and provided ample anchorage for large vessels.

In Gálvez's mind the advantages far outweighed the disadvantages. San Blas was strategically located and would provide the most direct route for troops and supplies both to the Sonora frontier and to the regions of Upper California. There also was an abundant supply of natural resources—rich timberlands, mineral deposits from which revenues would be obtained, easy access to agricultural crops and livestock, and nearby salt deposits which were an additional source of revenue.

Probably the plentiful supply of the light, durable cedarwood for shipbuilding was the determining factor in his selecting San Blas. Soon vast amounts of cut timber were stored up and the expansion of the lumber industry provided jobs for scores of workers. The timber was used not only for shipbuilding but also in the construction of small homes for the one hundred new settlers De Croix induced to venture into the new port.

Gálvez remained at San Blas two weeks. During this brief time he officially designated San Blas as the new maritime base and held a council of war or junta. His plans were approved and it was decided that a voyage should be undertaken, using the newly constructed brigantines *San Carlos* and the *Principe*, the largest and strongest vessels on the coast. The voyage was to start in June or July and at the same time a land expedition was to be sent from the northern missions of Baja California to take possession of Monterey and to build a presidio. Immediate preparations were started in collecting materials to be sent by the ships as soon as they returned from carrying troops to Guaymas for the Sonoran war. These vessels were to be outfitted and hastened to Cape San Lucas.

In addition, he issued a decree directing that the yearly salt revenues be placed on deposit with the treasury of San Blas and he organized a minor revenue division of the tobacco monopoly and directed that this money also be used to support the naval operations.

On May 20, 1768, he wrote a formal report to Viceroy de Croix summarizing the progress made. Boarding the bilander *Cinaloa*, Gálvez departed from San Blas on May 24. His party of settlers embarked in the packet *Concepción* and the bark *Pison*. A severe storm forced the *Cinaloa* to anchor at Isabella Island on the seventh day. On the eleventh day at sea they put in at Tres Marías, the other vessels sailing on.

Gálvez took six days to explore the islands and took formal possession of them in the name of the King. He is supposed to have left an inscription carved on the tallest tree which read, "Gálvez took possession for Spain, June, 1768." Sailing from the Tres Marías they encountered rough seas and violent winds which drove the vessel to Mazatlán. After a journey of forty days they reached Cerralvo in Lower California but it took the other two vessels nearly three months to reach La Paz. During this interval Gálvez worked diligently on the organizing of the affairs of the peninsula.

He was finally in the land of his dreams.

Gálvez came to Baja California three months after the arrival of Fr. Junípero Serra. Although well known to each other by means of correspondence, they had not met. The extraordinary partnership between these two men of vision, courage, energy, and singleness of purpose, which was to influence the course of history, was yet to be formed.

CHAPTER XV

SERRA ARRIVES AT LORETO,

FEBRUARY 1768

Junípero Serra and his fifteen missionaries boarded the packet boat *La Purísima Concepción de María Santísima,* commonly called *Concepción,* about eight o'clock on the night of March 14, 1768. They set sail with a lively faith that they were to have a fortunate voyage despite the realization that this same ship, which had been at anchor in the port of San Blas since that fateful day in February when it brought the expatriated Jesuits from the peninsula, was now carrying the Fernandinos as replacements for these unfortunate missionaries. Their hopes for a good voyage were not in vain for after eighteen days sailing, despite a contrary north wind, they anchored in the roadstead of Loreto late on Good Friday, April 1.

Governor Don Gaspar de Portolá boarded the packet immediately to welcome Serra and to see what his plans were for landing. Because of the lateness of the hour, Serra decided that just he and Palóu would go ashore with Portolá, the others to land in the morning. Going immediately to Loreto Mission, Serra encountered Father Manuel Zazuárregui, the president of the Jaliscans, who had administered the missions for eighteen days, and had already issued orders recalling his friars so they could be returned to San Blas and go to Sonora as originally planned.

Serra and Palóu spent the night in two rooms of the mission living quarters. From these rooms Serra could look out upon the village of Nuestra Señora de Loreto. The capital town and the mission lay quite close to the California Gulf. Despite his excitement at being in the place he had so long dreamed about, he experienced a slight pang of dismay. The bleakness of the pueblo, with not a single bush, tree, or blade of grass, must have caused him nostalgically to recall the lush beauties of his homeland of Majorca. Coming so recently from the rampant verdure of tropical San Blas, Loreto must have appeared harsh and uninviting.

Close by the mission was a shedlike structure serving as guardhouse and barracks for the unmarried soldiers. The married soldiers and a few sailors, with their wives and children, lived in small mud huts, resembling cow stables rather than houses. In addition there were two rows of mud huts in which Indians, men and women and children, were all crowded together. There was no running water and the only supply, which had a strong, brackish taste, came from holes dug in the sand.

The mission dwelling consisted of a small one-storied quadrangle of adobe brick with a flat roof. Three of the wings had six rooms each about twenty feet square and with a door facing out to sea. These were the kitchen and storerooms from which the military men and their families could buy trinkets such as straps, ribbons, tobacco, sugar, linen, shoes, hats, and similar goods. Near this quadrangle were four other walls or lean-tos where beef, tallow, lard, sugar, chocolate, cloth, leather, wheat, and corn, all infested with bugs, were stored. One wing of the main structure was partly built of limestone, as was the church.

This church, originally built by the Jesuits, was a plain flat-roofed building with a beamed ceiling of cedarwood. Simple as this un-adorned mission appeared, Serra was to learn that with its many fine paintings and richly wrought vestments, it was the finest in all Baja California.

Sounds of voices singing the "Salve Regina" reached him as the remaining fourteen friars left the ship and walked in procession toward the church. Serra was joined by Portolá and his soldiers and sailors who gave the friars a hearty welcome as they entered the sacristy to give thanks for their safe arrival. Following the brief service, Portolá turned over the church to Serra, but reserved the residential portion of the mission for his own supervision and allotted two rooms to Serra and his assistant. Each was given a table, a chair, leather bed, a candleholder, and a bookstand. They were to remain as the guests of the governor, eating at his table, the cost of their food to be charged against the mission.

Easter Sunday, April 3, Serra celebrated the Solemn High Mass with the other friars forming the choir. He then preached with great warmth and feeling on the mysteries of the day.

Following the Mass, Serra and Palóu met with Portolá and listened in bewilderment as he read to them the letter from the Viceroy. The Jesuit missions with churches, furniture, and sacristies were formally turned over to the Franciscan, but they were to be in charge of spiritual administration only. Temporal matters were to continue in the hands of the soldier-commissioners the governor had appointed for the purpose when the Jesuits were removed.

The Franciscans had assumed they would be permitted to carry on in the same manner as had the Jesuits with full authority over the Indians in all matters. Despite his immediate realization that his missionaries would be powerless to advance the spiritual affairs of the missions with this divided control, Serra quietly acquiesced to the plan and stated that they would not interfere with temporal matters. Portolá, evidently sensing his dismay, went on to explain that he had placed the soldiers in charge of the abandoned missions to keep the Indians from despoiling the property and that the Viceroy had approved this action and had suggested that it be continued. He added that perhaps the mission properties and full authority over the Indians would be restored when the Visitador-General Don Joseph de Gálvez arrived.

Serra, wise from his Sierra Gorda experience, knew the value of waiting until he had thoroughly investigated the situation before taking the matter directly to Gálvez. In the meanwhile, there was much to learn and to do. He called his missionary brothers together and gave them a solemn talk. He reminded them again of the purpose they all had in coming to this far-off region, and urged them to work zealously among the Indians and to do all they possibly could to reclaim the natives into the ways of the Church, and to uphold the good name of their College of San Fernando. He asked them to offer twenty Masses for the repose of the soul of any of their brotherhood who might die at the missions. Serra also told them of the spiritual compact he had entered into with the Querétaran friars who were stationed in Sonora. The missionaries of each group were to offer nine Masses for the departed soul of a friar.

In his gentle manner he spoke affectionately to each friar, offering encouragement and counsel, promising to visit whenever possible. "This very special gift of counsel," Palóu recalled years later, "which was a fruit of his prudence, was not only noticeable to us, his subordinates, who were in close contact with this Servant of God, but it also was helpful to as many as consulted him. All were edified and convinced of the value of his advice when he made them see the right and freed them from their doubts."

Serra had informed himself about the various missions now entrusted to the Franciscans, and having learned the needs of each and its distance from the others, proceeded to assign his friars to the various locations. Palóu listed the assignments as follows:

Beginning with Cape San Lucas, for the Mission of San José, at that cape, he appointed the father preacher Fray Juan Morán;

For Santiago de las Coras, the father preacher Fray José Murguía, son of our College;

For Nuestra Señora del Pilar, commonly called Todos Santos, the father preacher Fray Juan Ramos de Lora, son of the holy province of Los Angeles;

For Nuestra Señora de los Dolores, commonly called La Pasión, the father preacher Fray Francisco Gómez;

For San Luis Gonzaga, the father preacher Fray Andrés Villaumbrales;

For San Francisco Xavier, he named me;

For San José Cumundú, the father preacher Fray Antonio Martínez;

For Purísima Concepción de Cadegomó, the father preacher Fray Juan Crespí, of the province of Majorca;

For Nuestra Señora de Guadalupe, the father preacher Fray Juan Sancho;

For Santa Rosalía de Mulegé, the father preacher Fray Juan Gastón;

For San Ignacio, the father preacher Fray Miguel de la Campa; For Santa Gertrudis, the father preacher Fray Dionisio Basterra;

For San Francisco de Borja, the father preacher Fray Fermín Lasuén;

For Santa María de los Angeles, the father preacher Fray Juan Medina Veitía.

And for the mission and royal presidio of Nuestra Señora de Loreto he designated the father preacher Fray Fernando Parrón, the reverend father president remaining in it as minister, with Fray Fernando as companion.

The friars were all pleased with their assignments and gave thanks for the posts. They were eager to learn more about the country and their mission duties. They busied themselves by preparing the articles to be taken with them and consulted with Serra on a uniform plan for administering the missions. It was part of his administrative genius that Serra managed to see to it that his subordinates were happy and content under his orders. "He always brought it about," wrote Palóu, "that his subordinates were well satisfied with the Mission to which he assigned them, and he was accustomed to visit them once a year when this was possible. With this visit they were always consoled, made happy and zealous in their Apostolic ministry, resting under this leafy shade so happily that we may say of them what the holy text says of the Prophet Elijah, namely that 'he lay down and slept beneath the shade of a Juniper tree.' For although it was a tree of no great height and we were all stretched out over this region of more than two hundred leagues, in spite of the fact that the shade is supposedly small in comparison with the size of the tree, it covered us all with its continuous and efficacious counsels which were ever being sent out by his well-cut pen. And these counsels not only served to direct us but also to comfort and inspire us, and others with us, in the work of the Conversion of the Gentiles and in the spiritual and temporal development of the Missions."

The Fathers departed for their assignments the morning of April 6. They left their president at Loreto and the farewells of those who had lived and journeyed so long and closely together were sorrowful. The first group of six including Fathers Palóu, Murguía, Ramos de Lora, Gómez, Morán, and Villaumbrales set out and in about an hour the later or second contingent departed. These remaining eight missionaries, Fathers Martínez, Crespí, Gastón, Sancho, De la Campa, Basterra, Lasuén, and Medina Veitía, followed along the same road. They were to rendezvous the first night out at Mission San Xavier and the following morning would then divide and head north or south, whichever was their destination.

They reached Mission San Xavier at eight in the evening after traveling about twenty-two miles southwest of Loreto over a dusty, rutted road. The next morning, after a Solemn High Mass, they divided and five turned south for their assigned missions, and the eight others turned northwest. Palóu remained at the Mission San Xavier.

The missionaries continued celebrating Solemn High Mass along the way until only three were left. Finally each reached his destination. Father Medina Veitía at the extreme northern portion of Baja California found no church standing at all, as did Lasuén at San Francisco de Borja. Father Morán, at the most southern tip at Mission San José del Cabo, likewise found that he had no church or living quarters.

Undaunted, each missionary, now entirely upon his own, entered into the hard physical labor immediately demanded of him, as well as the difficult task of learning the native dialect. They took advantage of the Easter time to begin their pastoral work by trying to get the Indians to come and make their annual Confessions. All the while their work was impeded by the restrictions placed upon them by the divided authority under which they had to toil. At each mission the soldier-commissioner turned over to each missionary the church and sacristy, as well as all religious and household goods, and presented an inventory made in duplicate. The soldier signed as did the missionary and one copy was kept at the mission while the other was delivered to Serra and he in turn sent it on to the College of San Fernando in Mexico City. The priests received their meals from the soldier-commissioner who reimbursed himself out of the mission's property over which he had complete control.

It was a most humiliating position for the priests who no longer had any means by which to attract the childlike Indians, either by firmness or by gifts of food and clothing. The Indians quickly became aware of the new Padres' weak position and took advantage of them. The Indians refused to attend Mass and to do any work. The missionaries struggled against the declining influence of the missions. They could only hope that their president could effect a change with Don Gálvez when he presented the facts to him. In the meanwhile, they tried to learn about their elusive charges and sought ways to administer to their spiritual needs.

CHAPTER XVI

BAJA CALIFORNIA

THE LAND AND THE NATIVES

Once the Fernandinos had reached their assigned missions, they found they were strung along the barren peninsula for a distance of five hundred miles or more. Dreadful roads made traveling the long distances between the missions almost an impossibility and the priests had to face relentless and unrelieved loneliness in an inhospitable land. The former practice of the Order, which required two priests to be stationed in lonely outposts at the same time, was impractical because of the shortage of friars.

They were in a land where there was a perpetual shortage of water and very little rainfall. The Baja California peninsula is a desert country with tremendous extremes in temperature, with occasional heavy rains and some snow in the northernmost portion. The central desert is the driest portion and has vast forests of strange desert plants. Rugged mountains run the entire length of the peninsula, which is about 800 miles long and varies from 30 to 145 miles in width. The highest mountains, some reaching more than 10,000 feet above sea level, are in the north, while the southernmost tip from La Paz down, being partly in the tropic zone, with summer rains and hurricanes, has a more equable climate and more luxuriant vegetation.

Mission settlements were established only where there was enough water for irrigation and the watering of livestock. The first missionaries found that often the Indians had a tolerance for alkalinity in the water which the Fathers and the newly introduced plants could not endure. Many springs that had served native rancherias had to be abandoned and a sweeter supply of water located. A study of the mission locations of Lower California would provide virtually a list of the water resources of the peninsula.

The natives inhabiting this land were among the most primitive people on the North American continent. They were divided into many tribes, each with a different language, and were of a nomadic nature. The Indians engaged in practically no agriculture and lived by hunting and fishing with crudely constructed weapons. Some of the coastal tribes had clumsy rafts and used fishing spears and nets but they preferred to catch fish by the simple means of trapping them in tidal pools. They lived, for the most part, in poorly built shelters made of stones and branches piled haphazardly together or, in many instances, out in the open, wandering from water hole to water hole. Always on the verge of starvation because of long dry spells, they ate everything—insects, mice, owls, dogs, cats, mules, grubs, and reptiles, but principally they fed upon wild plants, seeds, roots, and fruits.

When a deer was killed, and this was very infrequent, it was the custom among some of the tribes to tie a string to a piece of the meat and for the first Indian to chew, swallow, and then pull the morsel up and hand it to the next man until there was nothing left of it. During the summer and fall seasons when the fruit of the pitahaya cactus ripened, they stuffed themselves upon the delicious pulp which was filled with tiny seeds. The various tribes mixed together and often family ties were forgotten as the Indians gorged themselves and indulged in a common orgy. When the fruit was eliminated by the Indians, they dried the excrement and then sifted and sorted out the undigested seed of the pitahaya fruit. This "second harvest," as the Spanish referred to this practice, was then roasted and ground into a powder for use during the winter months.

The natives were well formed and physically attractive. The men went entirely naked and the women wore small aprons, or as Serra commented, "were very honestly covered." He was charmed by their pleasant natures and the physical beauty of both the men and women.

Completely isolated from the rest of the world and living their simple nomadic existence, these Indians had no native physical immunity or resistance to withstand their first European contacts and were susceptible to every communicable disease. Late in 1533, or early in 1534, Hernán Cortés, the conqueror of Mexico, sent out an expedition from Tehuantepec to explore the northern coast. The crew mutinied and the commander, Diego de Bacerra, was killed by the pilot, Fortún Ximénez. Sailing across the Gulf of Mexico, the mutineers arrived at La Paz, where most of them were killed by the Indians. Cortés arrived at the same bay in 1535, named it Santa Cruz and established a colony which lasted barely a year.

The pearls Cortés found at La Paz excited the interest of Spanish pearling expeditions for centuries afterward. Serious efforts at colonization of the peninsula were made several times and each failed because of the lack of suitable sites for farming and the difficulty of obtaining supplies from the mainland across the turbulent Gulf of Mexico. The Viceroys made poorly prepared efforts at colonization during the times of Sebastian Vizcaíno (1596), Francisco de Ortega (1632–36), and by Porter Casanate (1648–49). The famous Jesuit missionary explorer Padre Eusebio Francisco Kino accompanied another colonization attempt which was made by Atondo y Antillón during the two years between 1683–85.

It was not until Father Juan María Salvatierra, as leader of the Jesuits, arrived at Loreto in 1697 that the first permanent settlement was established. The dreadful poverty and primitive living conditions of the Indians shocked the Jesuit missionaries, who during the next seventy years founded twenty missions. They reduced the Indians into living quarters around the missions, sometimes by force if other forms of enticement failed, and tried to bring them the teachings of Christianity. The Indians were supplied clothing, which the men wore mostly to church on Sundays, and were instructed how to build houses and churches and to till the soil as well as to recite the catechism.

As this reduction of the Indians into small confined areas continued, sickness began to take its toll. Perhaps the enforced change in living habits and alterations in diet reduced the resistance of these nomadic tribes and as the mission influence became stronger, the native death rate increased. New diseases were introduced by the first European contacts.

It has been said that the Spaniards brought salvation, smallpox, and syphilis to the Indians. It is ironical that the dread social disease, which was supposed to have been brought from the New World to the Old by the crew members with Columbus on his first voyage, was returned to infect the Indians on the opposite side of the North American continent. The role of epidemics in the destruction of the Indian population can clearly be determined by a study of the baptismal records in the various missions. Often as many as a thousand deaths a year occurred at separate missions. The Jesuits' strict control over the lives of the Gentiles somewhat impeded the spread of the disease, but with the coming of the Franciscans and the greatly increased civil and military activity, syphilis virtually became pandemic. It was generally recognized by the missionaries in the late eighteenth century as the dominant force which was hastening the extinction of the missions and the extermination of the race.

Whether the crews of the Manila galleon first infected the Cape region in 1735 or not, by the time the Franciscans arrived the Indians of that area were thoroughly infected, while little or no mention was made of its being prevalent on the central desert. With the shifting of the Indian population and the passing of so many soldiers and muleteers through the region, the entire population became infected, despite the preoccupation of the missionaries with the sexual morality of their converts. They built women's houses and at sundown locked in all of the unmarried women, and those whose husbands could not be with them at night, until morning. These houses were unventilated and possessed no sanitary facilities or simple comforts. Many of the women sickened and died.

The missionaries, from the time of their first arrival on the peninsula, had made a vigorous attempt, for moral reasons, to keep all of the Indians above the age of puberty in a constant state of matrimony. The legal age for girls to marry was twelve and most of them were pressed into immediate marriage. If a husband died, the wife was urged to remarry as soon as possible. While the mission records showed a high marriage rate and an equally high birth rate, deaths among infants were frequent and only a small portion of the children lived to reach puberty. Finally, there seemed to have been a rise to almost total infant mortality. While the cause for this tragic situation was undoubtedly pandemic syphilis, the polluted water supply in some of the villages brought about onslaughts of diseases such as diarrhea and typhoid.

During the Franciscan period an epidemic of an unknown disease spread from north to south killing off about 15 per cent of the central desert population. This may have been smallpox followed by a devastating attack of measles. Consumption was prevalent and catarrh was general throughout the missions.

One of the several recorded epidemics in 1772 killed a third of the Indians at missions San Borja and Santa Gertrudis. This was a combination of typhus and malaria brought about by contaminated drinking water. The pattern of recurring epidemics involving four or five different diseases—particularly serious diseases—struck only about once in a generation, but the cycles of the various diseases varied so much that specific epidemics struck about every five years.

When the Jesuits first came to the peninsula, the native population was estimated as being about forty thousand. The first census taken by the Franciscans at Gálvez's orders revealed that this number had dropped to a mere seven thousand in 1768.

Learning the dialects of the various tribes proved to be extremely difficult and communication by means of sign language at first was nearly impossible. The Franciscans found some of the Indians mentally alert and quick to learn. However, most of them were dull-witted and all of them resented having to labor on behalf of the missions. Possibly generations of disease had so depleted their energies the natives existed in a state of inertia. The Franciscans despairingly continued their efforts toward drawing these nomads back into the protection of the Church.

CHAPTER XVII

GÁLVEZ IN BAJA CALIFORNIA

The forty wearisome days aboard the *Cinaloa* were put to good use by Gálvez. During the days of enforced idleness he had his first opportunity to devote all of his time and thinking into planning for the northern expedition to California. He had taken every precaution for the success of the venture, even to ordering the construction of a smaller, faster supply vessel, the *San José*, before he left San Blas. As he reviewed his plans, he believed that all would go well.

Joseph de Gálvez landed at Cerralvo, Baja California, on July 5 and immediately wrote to notify Father Junípero Serra of his arrival and confidentially informed him of his intention to occupy Monterey.

As soon as Serra received the letter, he publicly announced the arrival of the Visitador-General by ringing the mission bells and by holding a thanksgiving Mass. He sent word to all the missionaries instructing them to pay the same homage at each of their missions. Junípero then wrote a congratulatory letter to Gálvez and eagerly offered to go in person as the first volunteer "to erect the holy standard of the Cross in Monterey." Later that month Gálvez responded to this letter and expressed his appreciation for the president's enthusiasm over the projected northern expedition by stating that he had depended upon support from his "beloved brethren of the College of San Fernando of Mexico." A steady flow of correspondence between the two continued, Gálvez writing from the mining camp of Santa Ana, where he had set up headquarters in the home of the wealthy mine-owner, Manuel Osío. It was from here that the Visitador-General planned to direct the reorganization of the government and the missions before organizing the northern expedition.

Gálvez requested a detailed report from all of the missionaries asking them to set forth the exact conditions existing at their missions. He sent a similar demand to the soldier-commissioners in charge of temporal life and stated that, after receiving and reviewing these reports, he planned to make a personal investigation of the missions before deciding upon any course of action.

Serra completed his report and sent it to Gálvez before starting upon a tour of several missions in the north. Junípero wished to obtain the facts for himself and to take this opportunity to talk over the proposed California expedition with his friars.

The first mission was that of San Xavier with its large stone church of Moorish architecture, which was begun in 1744 and completed in 1758. A small spring about a half mile from the town supplied the water for the orchards of many kinds of fruit and the mission gardens. San Xavier was, and still is, the finest example of the churches built in Baja by the Jesuits. Two bells in the tower bear the dates 1761, and the third bell, of a later period, is dated 1803. The statue of St. Francis and the gilded *altar mayor* was brought from Mexico City in thirty-two large boxes. Extensive gardens are still to be found behind the church with two stone reservoirs, dating back to the Jesuits, supplying water. Serra was delighted to see a reminder of Majorca in the gnarled old olive trees which were grown from seeds by the Jesuits. At San Xavier Serra conferred with Palóu and then went on northward over a crude road cut through sharp lava rock to Mission San José de Cumundú.

Nestling at the bottom of a steep canyon, Cumundú was an oasis with several springs supplying sufficient water to irrigate hundreds of acres of fertile soil. The mission, built in 1750, stood beside the small plaza. There were date palms planted and small whitewashed houses built at the base of the precipitous walls of the canyon. Father Martínez welcomed Serra for the brief visit.

Again traveling northward, Serra traveled along the road that crossed many stream beds until it reached the Mission La Purísima de Cadegomó, built on the left bank of an arroyo, where his longtime friend, Father Crespí, was in charge. Serra moved on to reach Father Sancho at the Mission of Nuestra Señora de Guadalupe which was founded in 1720. He completed this inspection trip of two hundred miles in three or four weeks, going over extremely difficult terrain.

Gálvez, in the meanwhile, was also visiting missions but toward the south in the region of Cape San Lucas. Arriving at Mission San José del Cabo and discovering there was no church, he immediately ordered the royal commissary to assign 800 pesos for the purpose of building one. He then had to postpone construction until a master mechanic and suitable laborers could be located.

His wrath and disappointment increased as he continued his inspection tour. Everywhere he saw mismanagement and destruction of church property caused by the wastefulness, indifference, and dishonesty of the soldier-commissioners. He was dismayed to see that only by threats or bribery could the Indians be persuaded to attend prayers and divine instruction. Gálvez came to the realization that spiritual and physical affairs of the missions were deteriorating at an alarming rate and that only by restoring full control of all mission property to the Franciscans could they be expected to promote the spiritual life of their charges. On August 12 he decreed that all the military commissioners were to turn over the temporalities of their missions to the missionaries. He also instructed them to make a full written report of their period of management. This order was to be put into effect at all the missions except Loreto, and the Franciscans, like their Jesuit predecessors, were to assume full control of the missions.

From his personal observations and from reading the reports sent to him, Gálvez readily saw that flagrant abuses had been committed by certain of the commissioners and thought that they should be severely punished. The priests, however, tried to intercede with him on behalf of the soldiers, and asked him to temper his punishment. Some of the offenders he merely discharged, but others he ordered to be sent on the proposed expedition to Monterey, evidently thinking the rigors of this trip would be punishment enough.

He was further irritated by the information which his couriers, going to and from the various missions, brought back to him. The same day that he issued the decrees restoring mission property, he indignantly wrote to Palóu:

I have returned in good health from my pilgrimage to Cape San Lucas, and I have discovered important things. Today I am sending out nine decrees for the missions of that part of the Peninsula, so that the temporalities may be transferred to the direction of your Reverence and be delivered from the harsh rule of the soldiers of the presidio. Come out, then your Reverence, in regard to that rascal whom you have in that mission, and do not cover up anything that he may have hidden. I promise him my justice, if this should be necessary to induce him to confess what he may have concealed, for by this means only may severity be abated; and although blood may not flow, I shall know how to give him his deserts.

As Gálvez continued studying the reports sent to him, he grew increasingly irate. He angrily read of the wanton destruction of crops and cattle by the wastrels during the six-month period they had been in charge. One soldier reported that six hundred head of cattle had been killed, another four hundred, and yet another three hundred. The devastation among the crops and wines was so bad that if it had been allowed to continue another year, the missions would have been left destitute and entirely ruined.

The missionaries, fully realizing that their missions were being destroyed by the mismanagement of the soldiers, and that spiritual progress among the Indians was being impeded by this division of authority, nevertheless now were reluctant to assume the management of the temporalities. Perhaps all their interest at this time was focused upon the expedition to Alta California and the work they expected to accomplish there. Whatever the reason, some of the Franciscans did not seek or welcome this responsibility. Gálvez prevailed upon the missionaries to assume full control by explaining how necessary it was to have both temporal and spiritual matters under one head so that the welfare of the souls would advance. He also pointed out, and this may have been the deciding factor, that since a friar was a vassal of the King, he owed this service to his Majesty.

"The friars had to admit," wrote Palóu, "that in this way they might further the missions in the spiritualities, which is the principal aim of our institute. In a short time this began to be apparent, for they observed in the Indians more obedience, submission, and punctuality in attendance at catechism, prayers, and other services of the church."

During the remainder of the time he was to spend upon the peninsula, Gálvez continued his interest in the management of the missions and issued constant instructions to the missionaries. Some of his orders met with their approval, with others they disagreed but had to carry out his work for economic betterment because they were his only agents. Gálvez would sometimes heed their remonstrances and yield to their point of view, but upon important matters he made up his own mind.

His most drastic action was the redistribution of the Indian population. Some missions lacked sufficient water and arable land to maintain the Indians living there while others, with an abundance of water, lacked enough Indians to farm the land. Gálvez observed that at some of these more populous missions where land was scarce, the Indians were obliged to live in outlying areas or were forced to resume their primitive methods of wandering from place to place like deer, gathering food from whatever was at hand. He believed that this was injurious both spiritually and physically to the Indians and he issued orders for a more equitable distribution of the native population. He did so with disregard for the feelings of the Indians and looked upon the matter from the practical point of view entirely.

He considered it necessary to abolish several of the missions which would never be able to support themselves or the Indians. Consequently, he moved the eight hundred natives from missions Dolores and San Luis Gonzaga to Todos Santos, where good land and water were plentiful and which he considered to be the best site of all the mission lands. The few natives of Todos Santos, whom he thought to be afflicted with syphilis, were taken to Santiago where there were others with the same sickness, so that they all could receive treatment from the noted physician, Dr. Pedro Prat, when he returned from the northern expedition. Mission San José del Cabo received some Indians from San Xavier, and in the north the Indians from Guadalupe were distributed to missions San José Cumundú and La Purísima de Cadegomó. The only missionary who objected to the inhumanity and impracticability of this move was Father Fermín Lasuén at Mission San Borja. He adroitly circumvented every decree Gálvez issued for the displacement of the Indians at San Borja despite the fact many were hungry and going naked. Lasuén wrote that since most of the Indians were but tender recent Christians, a forced move might make them renounce Christianity forever. An interesting correspondence between the lonely missionary and the powerful Visitador-General ensued with Lasuén out-parrying Gálvez at every turn.

With the abandonment of the missions, two additional priests became available for the northern expedition, which was always uppermost in Gálvez's thoughts. He could not, however, devote his entire attention to this expedition until he had put into effect his plans for the betterment of the entire peninsula. He sternly prohibited card playing and gambling at the missions; instituted a government monoply on tobacco; and regulated the purchase and distribution of salt. He established an industrial school at Santa Ana under the direction of Reverend Ibarzábal for the training of four Indian youths who were to be selected from each mission in the industrial and mechanical arts. These boys in turn were to teach their people on their return to the missions. Orphan boys were to be brought to Loreto for instruction in ship handling.

Gálvez paid special attention to the colonization of Baja California with Spaniards. He issued a decree on August 12, 1768, setting forth the privileges to be offered to Spaniards of good character whereby they were to be permitted to buy government lands that had been separated from the lands of the missions. For this privilege, the colonists were to make improvements and pay a small tax to the King. Discharged sailors and soldiers from Loreto were the first to avail themselves of this offer.

Three other colonies were established by Gálvez. The first was the organizing of the mining settlements of San Antonio del Oro and Santa Ana, with a few small ranchos, into a district to be called Real de Minas. Reverend Isídro Ibarzábal, who had orginally come over with the Jaliscans, but had remained after they departed, was placed in charge, along with his duties of running the new industrial school. Gálvez ordered the sum of one thousand pesos to be paid to the new curate from the royal store for the building of a church. The priest was granted one dollar a day for personal living costs. Gálvez appointed a lieutenant-governor with jurisdiction in civil and criminal affairs and organized three companies of militia for the protection of the colonists. One of the local mines was to be worked solely for the payment of these expenses, which would formerly have been charged to the royal treasury.

Two other colonies were established by Gálvez. One was begun at the Bay of San Bernabé and placed in the control of a lieutenant and three soldiers. It was to serve as a protection and relief station for the Manila galleon. Another colony was founded at La Paz with Manuel Morales, the captain of a militia company, appointed commissary to superintend construction of buildings and with authority to act as judge in the name of the King. A sergeant and two soldiers were also stationed there to protect supply ships arriving at the port.

Thus the Visitador-General made every effort to put the affairs of the peninsula in order. Many of his ideas were too precipitant and some of them could not be carried out and caused difficulties and dissatisfaction at the missions. However that might have been, Gálvez was ready to turn his thoughts and indefatigable energies toward the preparation for the northern expedition, which had been delayed too long by vexatious civic problems.

*   *   *

He knew well the challenges that confronted him in successfully accomplishing the northern expedition when he first arrived at Cerralvo that July 5. His task was to advance into, take, and hold possession of a distant country. While considerable information had been reported back from Cabrillo, Viscaíno, and other explorers, much was still to be learned about this almost mythical land of California. His additional charge, therefore, was to discover more about the place, to build presidios or forts, to defend it against foreign invaders, to colonize, and to Christianize the heathen.

This religious part of the undertaking had not played a very large part in his original plans. In his report to the King six months earlier, in which he outlined his carefully thought-out plans for conquest and expansion of the boundaries in the northwest, Gálvez had suggested the establishment of a new see and the appointment of a bishop whose "ardent zeal and Apostolic ministry would immensely advance the conversion of the Heathen, hastening their reduction by influence near at hand, and conquering many souls for the Creator, at the same place with which new domains are acquired for the Sovereign, who is His Immediate Vicar in the world." In other words, with the bishop taking care of all spiritual matters, Gálvez could be spared worrying about them.

His thoughts were to follow the time-tested plan by which the Spanish mission system had functioned so well for many years. Originally, missionaries went into the land of the hostiles alone to convert them to Christianity. At first these solitary men of God met with success, but when the Indians began to turn against them in some instances in bloody massacres, the Crown started sending soldiers to guard the missionaries. As time went on, the mission became the principal instrument for advancing the frontiers for Spain. While the missionaries never lost sight that their prime function was to convert the Indian and save his soul, the government, on the contrary, looked upon the missions as a means of civilizing the natives and training them into self-supporting, tax-paying Spanish subjects. The Indians also were expected to serve as buffers against invasions from other savage tribes and were taught how to protect the colonial settlements.

Gálvez also had written in this memorial to the King that by taking the resources from neighboring mines to finance the project, he could send settlers overland with a protective guard escort, and others by sea from the provinces farther to the south. He also could send ammunition and soldiers in sufficient quantity to protect the harbors and stores until the country could develop to the point that such supplies would not be required. All this could easily be accomplished with five hundred soldiers and sufficient funds. Until the King found time to read his memorial and supplement his plans, Gálvez had to do what he could without royal support.

In La Paz he found conditions in such a deplorable state that the hopes of most men would have been completely dashed. He immediately went to the presidio at Loreto to confer with Governor Don Gaspar de Portolá, and his seasoned commander Don Fernando de Rivera y Moncada, who had been on the peninsula for over twelve years. They informed Gálvez that not more than forty soldiers, at most, could be spared from the garrison and withdrawn from the mission posts. Gálvez would have to recall some of the troops recently sent to Sonora, and this would take considerable time.

A further disappointment came in the realization that there were barely four hundred *gente de razón*, people of reason or civilized people, on the peninsula, and these were mostly employees and the families at the mines. Gálvez readily perceived that no great number of colonists could be drawn from these, and colonists were a vital part of his over-all plan.

The more he studied, the more Gálvez came to the realization that he would have to depend upon the missionaries for a greater role than had ever been required of them. With a mere forty soldiers he could not defend the entire length of Alta California and thus he must look to the priests to convert, train, and change the Indians from savages into peaceful, law-abiding, loyal, and obedient subjects of the King.

It was plain that the missions of Alta California would necessarily have to assume a larger political purpose than missions had ever had before in Spanish foreign policy. There was but one man to whom he could turn for assistance in this almost hopeless task. This was a man Gálvez had never met, but whose successful record among the Sierra Gorda Indians he knew well, and with whose character he had become familiar through considerable correspondence.

He immediately wrote to Father Junípero Serra and asked him to come directly to his headquarters at Santa Ana for a conference.

CHAPTER XVIII

THE HOLY EXPEDITION BEGINS—1769

The old, troublesome infection in his leg flared up again as soon as Serra arrived on the peninsula and began his duties. His foot was swollen, doubtlessly greatly traumatized by the long inspection tour of the missions and the jagged volcanic ground over which he traveled to reach them. "Great and incessant were the pains which the Servant of God, Fr. Junípero, suffered on account of the sore in his foot and the swelling in his leg with which he was afflicted from the year 1749 until his death, as we have already seen; yet he never complained," wrote Palóu, and then added ". . . in spite of the severe pains which he suffered, it seems that he found consolation in them to such a degree that he forgot to ask for medical treatment."

It was probably his being incapacitated by this painful foot and leg which delayed Serra's going to meet Gálvez. He must have responded in such a manner to one of the many letters Gálvez wrote him during this period because on August 13 Gálvez wrote of deep concern about Serra's welfare:

> I would feel bad if your Reverence would not be well and strong enough when the day comes to begin the overland march and you resolved to make the journey to Monterey, for it will be one fraught with hardship owing to the distance. However, I shall see to it that some provision shall be anticipated which will facilitate the journey in so far as it is possible. But I repeat that I will never consent to Your Reverence going by sea.

They continued writing until the time when Serra would have recovered enough to make the journey for a personal conference. Late in September Gálvez wrote to tell Serra that the two packet boats, the *San Carlos* and the *San Antonio* (formerly *Príncipe*), possibly would arrive later that month at La Paz and suggested that he select the priest who was to sail with the first ocean contingent of the expedition. He gave his approval to the suggestion Serra had sent him proposing that the new missions should not be farther apart than one day's travel and with one missionary stationed at each. He further agreed that if San Diego, Monterey, and San Buenaventura were to be the only missions established, two missionaries should be located at each. Gálvez planned to station soldiers somewhere between the missions for their protection.

In another letter to Serra, Gálvez listed the names he had assigned to the new missions to be constructed in Alta California. Since the explorer Viscaíno had already given the name San Diego on November 12, 1602, to the first port the expedition would occupy, the mission would likewise be called San Diego de Alcala. San Carlos Borromeo was the name he selected for the mission at Monterey, thus named in honor of King Charles III of Spain, the Viceroy Carlos de Croix, and the famous Cardinal Archbishop of Milan, Carlos de Borromeo. San Buenaventura was to be named in remembrance of an exclamation made to St. Francis by one of his friars.

Serra and his missionaries were not entirely pleased with Gálvez's choice of names and were disappointed that the name of the founder of their Order was not included. When Junípero in gentle protest wrote Gálvez, "Is there to be no mission in honor of our Holy Father St. Francis?" Gálvez is supposed to have answered, "Let him find the port bearing his name and he will have his mission there."

Gálvez, in an attempt to hasten the time for their conference, wrote to Serra offering to send a launch to aid him in traveling. A severe storm caused the launch to bypass Loreto. Then Gálvez wrote again and outlined the instructions he had drawn up defining the rules for the economic and domestic life of the missions and asked Serra to send him his frank opinions about them. At this time, he also offered to send mules and an escort to bring Serra to his headquarters. It was not until October 22 that Serra felt he could make the trip to Santa Ana and this time because of the direct request from Gálvez that he do so.

There is no record of what transpired at this first encounter between the two former shepherd boys from Spain, grown to manhood and following the same dream but along divergent paths, to converge, at last, in this out-of-the-way spot at a most propitious moment in history. Whether the tiny, crippled priest, clad in his drab woolen robe adorned only by his crucifix, his bare feet shod in frayed hemp sandals, dominated the meeting no one knows for sure. However, history does note that immediately following the conference, a marked change was noted in the attitude of the arrogant, domineering, ambitious, hard-working Visitador-General clad in satin knee britches, lace at his throat, bewigged, and with glistening buckles upon his finely made shoes.

From that moment the missionary part of the undertaking took on a new aspect of importance. Gálvez, both in his manner of speech and in his correspondence, began to express a spirit of deep piety, as though he fully realized that the success of the expedition depended mainly on the role the missionaries were to take.

They discussed many matters pertaining to the present missions and those to be organized, and Serra entered enthusiastically into the plans Gálvez set forth. A financial schedule was determined and the annual allowance for the missions in Lower California was set at 400 pesos. The last and most distant mission founded by the Jesuits, that of Santa María de los Angeles, was granted 700 pesos and 1000 pesos was the amount set for the government for every new mission to cover the cost of construction of buildings, for household goods, and farm equipment. This was not to include the sum required for vestments, sacred vessels, and other needs for church and sacristy. That money was to be taken from the Pius Fund which had been created by religious benefactors and given to the Jesuits for the propagation of the Faith among the savages.

Gálvez explained in detail his plans for both sea and land expeditions and once again Serra volunteered to go. They discussed which of the missionaries were to accompany the various parties. Three priests were to go north by sea and three by land. Serra suggested the secularization of several of the missions, thus enabling his priests to become available for the journey. At his suggestion, Gálvez wrote the Viceroy who in turn requested the College of San Fernando to send additional priests. This the college was loath to do because of the shortage of their members and a general belief that the entire project was too impractical for any possible success. They felt compelled, however, to send Fathers Juan de Escudero, Juan Vizcaíno, and Benito Sierra all of whom reached Cape San Lucas in February 1769. Father Vizcaíno was chosen to go with one of the expeditions while the other two were to replace Fathers from the missions.

Gálvez further explained that from his study of the reports and inventories sent him from each mission, he had decided to call upon each of the old establishments for small donations of vestments, sacred vessels, and other church furnishings that could be spared. He authorized Serra to collect whatever he thought necessary from each of the missions he visited while Gálvez himself would collect what he could. Cattle and farm implements were to be considered as loans and were to be repaid by replacements rather than by money. The missions were to make gifts of surplus food and grain.

The first land party to be sent out was to gather up the cattle and drive the herd to Santa María, the northernmost outpost west of the Gulf, and there permit the livestock to rest and graze until the provisions, which were being shipped up the coast to the Bay of San Luis Gonzaga, arrived and were transferred to Velicatá, thirty miles farther north. This was to be the place of rendezvous and point of departure for the long awaited expedition to Alta California. Captain Rivera was to be in charge of this division.

The supplies for the new missions were gathered at Loreto and Gálvez impatiently awaited the arrival of the vessels which, in the age-old custom of the sea, had been given nicknames by their crews. Hence the *San Carlos* was familiarly called *El Toison* or the *Golden Fleece*; the *San Antonio* or *Principe* or *Prince* was the flagship; and the supply ship *San José* was called *El Descubridor* or *Discoveror*. The *San Carlos* and the *San Antonio* were large, two-masted sailing vessels similar to brigantines, displacing up to two hundred tons.

After a tempestuous journey against heavy winds and angry seas, the *San Carlos* finally hauled into port early in December. It had taken her almost three months to complete a voyage which usually required fifteen or twenty days. The pride of the naval department, the newest and largest of Spain's maritime units, limped into La Paz with her tackle and rigging in shreds, two broken anchors, and so weakened by the battering seas some of the oakum was cast off its seams, through which water rushed at the rate of six inches or more per hour. Her cargo was damaged and the *San Carlos* was without any fresh provisions whatsoever.

A lesser man would have given up in despair, but once again Gálvez, by personal encouragement and determination, supervised the difficult task of careening such a large vessel on the beach and its complete overhauling. Having anticipated the possibility of such trouble, he had standing by in readiness a complete crew of skilled workmen, including a master builder, six naval carpenters, three blacksmiths, two calkers, and two ropemakers, plus tools and equipment. Gálvez personally assisted in the refurbishing of his prize ship during the whirlwind fifteen days it took to perform the miracle of restoring the *San Carlos*.

In order that ample provisions be stored aboard for the long voyage to California, he had constructed six new storerooms and living compartments for the troops and seamen. He then ordered a great *matanza*, or slaughter of livestock, to supply fresh and salted meat as well as lard and tallow. A supply of beans, corn, lentils, and other produce was shipped from the mainland, and, as a final effort, he ordered that an ample supply of fish be caught.

Don Vicente Vila, a lieutenant of the royal navy, was captain of the *San Carlos* and had as his mate, Don Jorge Estorace. The crew consisted of twenty-three sailors, two boys, two blacksmiths, and four cooks. The passengers were Lieutenant Don Pedro Fages and the twenty-five soldiers of the Catalán company, Gálvez had ordered returned from Sonora; Ensign Don Miguel Costansó, as engineer of the expedition; Don Pedro Prat as surgeon; and as chaplain, Father Fernando Parrón.

The official manifest signed by Vila reveals that the *San Carlos* carried the following as cargo:

4,676 lbs. meat, 1,783 lbs. fish, 230 bushels maize, 500 lbs. lard, 7 jars vinegar, 5 tons wood, 1,275 lbs. brown sugar, 5 jars brandy, 6 tanates figs, 3 tanates raisins, 2 tanates dates, 300 lbs. red pepper, 125 lbs. garlic, 6,678 lbs. common bread, 690 lbs. white bread, 945 lbs. rice, 945 lbs. chickpeas, 17 bushels salt, 3,800 gallons water, 450 lbs. cheese, 6 jars wine, 125 lbs. sugar, 275 lbs. chocolate, 10 hams, 11 bottles oil, 2 lbs. spice, 25 smoked beef tongues, 6 live cattle, 575 lbs. lentils, 112 lbs. candles, 1,300 lbs. flour, 15 sacks bran, 495 lbs. beans, 16 sacks coal, hens for the sick and for breeding.

"The total of pounds here is 45,051. Estimating the water at 10 pounds per gallon (the weight of an imperial gallon), the cattle at 1000 pounds each, the coal at 200 pounds per sack, the sixty-two members of the crew and passengers at 200 pounds each, and the church furniture plus all of the foodstuffs and supplies, the total did not exceed 108,000 pounds or 54 tons. To carry all this, neither of the ships would need to be above the 60 or 70 tons capacity. The *Mayflower*, which brought 102 persons, men, women and children, with supplies and all their furniture for their houses, was a ship of only 180 tons."*

Once the provisions had been stowed on ship it was time for the loading of the church goods which had been collected from the missions. Father Serra and Father Parrón, who had been chosen to make the voyage, began carrying the religious articles aboard. They were soon joined by the exuberant Gálvez, who later in a letter to Palóu, prankishly boasted that he was a better sacristan than Father Presidente since he had packed the vestments and other objects for his personal mission of San Buenaventura more quickly than did Father Serra for his mission of *San Carlos,* and that he even had to help Father Junípero.

"The zeal of the illustrious Visitador," wrote Palóu, "was such that he wished to adorn the new missions as if they were cathedrals, for, as he said to the Reverend Father President, they must be beautified as much as possible, and the vestments must be the very finest, so that the heathen might see how God our Lord was worshipped, and with what care and purity the Holy Sacrifice of the Mass was said,

* Clinton A. Snowden. *History of California.* Ed. by Zoeth Skinner Eldredge. New York, 1915. V. 1, p. 193.

and how the house of God our Lord was adorned, so that by this means they might be induced to embrace our Holy Faith."

In obedience to these instructions Serra took from the government warehouse in Loreto "five yards of scarlet damask, five of China silk, three of blue taffeta, five yards of green cloth with gold flowers for a chasuble, and the necessary lining of scarlet taffeta, gold lace and fringe of the same for a muceta, a sash and its lining which he ordered made, some more of the same for another muceta with another sash which he made new, and a print of the Immaculate Conception with a tortoise-shell frame." From these were to be made "some little necessities which were lacking" and which were to be taken by Serra on the land expedition according to Palóu, who then inventoried the entire list of religious articles taken from the various missions. Among these were:

7 church bells; 11 smaller altar bells; 23 altar cloths; 5 choir copes; 2 surplices; 4 carpets; 2 coverlets; 3 roquetes; 3 veils; 19 sets sacred vestments, different colors; 6 old single vestments; 17 albas, or white tunics; 10 palios, or short cloaks; 10 amitas, or pieces of linen; 10 chasubles; 12 girdles; 6 hopas or cassocks; 18 altar linens, or corporales; 21 purificados, or chalice cloths; 1 pall cloth; 11 pictures of the Virgin; 12 silver or gilded chalices; 1 cibary, or silver goblet; 7 crismeras, or silver philas for chrism, or sacred oil; 1 custodia or silver casket for holy wafers; 5 conchas for baptism; 7 insensarios, or silver censers with incense dish and spoon; 12 pairs of vinegras, silver and glass cruets for wine and water; 1 silver cross with pedestal; 1 box containing statues of Jesus, Mary and Joseph; 1 copper platter for baptismal font; 2 copper baptismal fonts; 29 brass, copper, and silver candlesticks; 1 copper dipper for holy water; 1 silver jar; 1 tin wafer box; 3 statues; 2 silver suns or dazzlers; 4 irons for making wafers; coins and rings for arras at marriages; 5 arras, or consecrated stones; 4 missals and a missal stand; 1 Betancurt's Manual.

By noon on January 9, 1769, all was in readiness for the *San Carlos* to start on the expedition from La Paz. All of the crew were on hand and received the sacraments of Penance and the Holy Eucharist and attended the High Mass sung by Father Serra in honor of the patron saint of the voyage. Two months before, Gálvez had named St. Joseph patron of the expedition because the image of this saint and his divine intercession were said to have saved the crops of Cape San Lucas from clouds of locusts that threatened them. The litany of Our

Lady of Loreto was then chanted following which Gálvez addressed the crew.

He spoke to them with sincerity and reminded them that theirs was a glorious mission, that they were going to plant the Sacred Cross among the heathen, and charged them in the name of God, the King, and the Viceroy, to respect their priests and maintain peace and union among themselves. Father Serra then quietly pronounced a formal blessing on the pilgrims, their vessel, the flag, the crew, and on Father Parrón, who was in charge of the spiritual welfare of the entire company.

The San Carlos, floating wth the rising tide, took up her anchors and slowly left the harbor of La Paz, her sails barely fluttering in the faint breeze. Gálvez and Serra followed in the smaller Concepción for a final leave-taking at Cape San Lucas. At vespers on the evening of the fourth day, the two vessels anchored in the Bay of San Bernabé and Captain Vila made his final official call upon Gálvez. Sunday morning dawned fair and calm and everything was made ready on board deck for the final farewell ceremonies. The Visitador-General came aboard, Mass was said, and after giving the captain explicit orders to follow his instructions carefully and to proceed, Gálvez took his leave. The rest of the day was taken up with the chore of filling the water casks and at seven o'clock that Sunday, the sixteenth, the ship slowly headed out to sea.

Gálvez watched from atop a hill for the next five days as the San Carlos lay becalmed. At the end of the first day she was not more than three miles off the coast, but on the evening of the twenty-first she spread all her sail to catch the rising wind and slowly disappeared over the horizon. With a sigh of relief and a prayer that God would prosper her journey, Gálvez turned and walked down the hill.

Shortly before the departure of the San Carlos, word was received that the San Antonio (Principe) had made the crossing of the Gulf without having to endure all the structural damage which befell her sister ship. Captain Juan Peréz notified Gálvez of his arrival after making a landfall in Bahía de Pulmo south of La Paz. He was then forced to sail southward because of unfavorable winds, finally anchoring on January 25 in San Bernabé. Although she had received her cargo at San Blas and was not in bad shape, Gálvez decided for the safety of the crew to unload her and give the San Antonio the same overhauling and provisioning given to the San Carlos.

He used two launches and the old Concepción to transport his workers to the southernmost tip of the peninsula. The work was accomplished with the same efficiency, and in eighteen days the ship was ready to sail northward on the fifteenth of February.

Besides Captain Juan Peréz, a veteran of the Philippine run, and his mate, Miguel del Pino, there was aboard the *San Antonio* a crew of twenty-eight men, and Fathers Juan Viscaíno and Francisco Gómez. After the High Mass in honor of St. Joseph was celebrated and those who were making the voyage received Holy Communion, Gálvez spoke to the members, exhorting them in a similar fashion to the message he had delivered on the *San Carlos*.

He then directed Captain Peréz to sail directly for San Diego and to wait only twenty days for the *San Carlos* before proceeding to Monterey. If by any chance neither the *San Carlos* nor one of the land expeditions arrived, he was to leave some sign and go on, not tarrying.

On the same day the *San Antonio* had departed, the smaller ship *San José*, which Gálvez had ordered built just as he was leaving San Blas, arrived with a broken mast and was ordered to La Paz for repairs. Gálvez continued his inspections of the southernmost missions and then having arranged everything for the missions to his satisfaction, boarded the *Concepción* for Loreto from where he departed on May 1, 1769, for the coast of Sonora. His vessel was accompanied by the *San José* which made the return voyage carrying a cargo of beans, a quantity of fish, fifty arrobas (25 pounds) of figs, four hundred arrobas of dried meat, raisins, eight casks of wine, two casks of brandy, and a quantity of plain clothing for the naked Indians of the north. Palóu put aboard the three tower bells and all the vestments that Serra had taken from the northern mission and sent to Loreto.

Three months later, after having been driven about the Gulf, the *San José* arrived at the Bay of Escondido again badly damaged. When Gálvez heard of her plight he ordered the *San José* back to San Blas for repairs. Palóu cautiously removed the church goods he had ordered and sent them on to Velicatá. Once the ship was put in order she returned to Cape San Lucas carrying a load of foodstuffs, and took aboard the religious articles Gálvez had ordered from Guadalajara. Fr. José de Murguía, who was to have gone with the *San José*, had fallen sick near unto death and had gone to Loreto. It was the most fortunate act of his life; for the *San José* did not arrive at her destination nor was she ever seen again.

CHAPTER XIX

THE PAINFUL JOURNEY

When the maritime section of the Alta California expedition finally sailed northward along the coast, Gálvez was able to turn his undivided attention to hastening the departure of the land division which was to go from Loreto to San Diego. Years of dreaming and planning were about to become a reality. Because the journey, through rugged unknown country peopled by pagan savages, presented serious hazards, Gálvez decided to divide the company into two groups. Thus, if accident happened to one, the other might pass through unscathed.

The roads they were to traverse were merely rough, natural tracks, which wound through the desert and along the steep sides of the barren mountains. It would have been easier going had they been able to follow the sandy beds of the dry streams, but this was not possible. On rare occasions when rains occurred, flash floods sometimes came rushing down from the surrounding mountains, turning these arroyos into raging waters, and coming with such rapidity that unsuspecting travelers were caught and engulfed. Because of this great danger, travelers in Baja California usually tried to avoid riding in the bottom of these arroyos and never camped in them at night.

Gálvez appointed as first commander, Don Gaspar de Portolá, captain of dragoons and governor of California, and as second in command, Don Fernando Rivera y Moncada, captain of the armored company of the garrison at Loreto. Rivera was to leave with the first section and explore all the region which as yet was unknown. Besides exploring the land, he was to open roads, build bridges, locate camping places with enough fresh water and grass for all the animals, and erect temporary shelters when necessary. Portolá was placed in command of the second division, which Father Serra was to join when he had completed his tour of gathering donations of religious articles from the various southern missions.

Gálvez gave Rivera instructions for the trip and told him to select as many soldiers as he thought wise and proper from the company of armored troops, and if necessary to recruit others. Rivera was also instructed to procure muleteers for the handling of cargo and baggage, and was further ordered to travel by way of all the missions and to requisition from them as many horses and mules as needed, as well as any other provisions he could obtain. He was to sign a receipt for what was taken in order that the missions could be repaid. He then was to proceed until the frontier of Santa María de Los Angeles was reached, taking from this mission two hundred head of cattle. He was also ordered to keep an accurate record of all which might happen on the journey as well as the length of time required to complete the trip.

Serra and Gálvez had counted upon an early departure for the land party, but unforeseen difficulties delayed them until September 28, 1768. On that afternoon, Father Lasuén gave a final blessing and the first of the land divisions set forth on the long trek to Alta California. Besides Rivera, as commander, the party consisted of twenty-five soldiers from the presidio at Loreto, José Cañizares, master's mate of the vessel *San Carlos,* who had been detached for land duty, three muleteers, a band of neophyte Indians who were to act as pioneers, and Indian servants armed with bows and arrows.

Serra watched the picturesque procession as it slowly departed from Loreto and began to wend its way over the hills. The spirited horses ridden by the officers had to be reinchecked to keep them down to the slow pace of the ladened mule train. Hoarse shouts of the muleteers prodding their animals into line wafted back to him until the cavalcade had nearly disappeared from sight.

The soldiers wore a *cuera,* or sleeveless jacket, which was made of six or seven thicknesses of tanned deerskin and served as armor against arrows. As a protection against thorns and brambles while riding through thickets, the soldiers also wore a divided leather apron fastened to the saddlebow and this gave some protection to the horses as well. The soldiers carried shields on their left arms. These shields were made of two thicknesses of tough bull hide and striking arrows glanced off their surfaces making a drumlike sound. As weapons, the soldiers carried a lance, a sword, and a small carbine or musket. The colorful uniforms of the officers were in brilliant contrast to the drab woolen cowled robes of the friars. The nearly naked Indians straggled at the end of the column.

Rivera arrived on the "frontier of paganism" as Palóu referred to it. Not finding a suitable spot for making camp, he reconnoitered the area and after traveling farther for eighteen leagues toward San Diego, came upon a desirable place with good forage and plenty of water. He immediately sent word to Gálvez and to Serra that he had arrived at this destination with all of the pack animals and that the freight, which had been sent ahead by boat was waiting for him, and that he would remain there until the end of March before moving on.

Upon hearing from Rivera, Serra notified Father Juan Crespí, whom he had previously named spiritual adviser for this division, to hurry and join the group at the place of encampment which the Indians called Velicatá. Crespí, Serra's former philosophy student and Palóu's classmate, who also served as the diarist for the Portolá expedition to Monterey and who was to go on to achieve great fame as an explorer, traveled the 180 leagues and arrived at the camp on March 22, 1769, which was Wednesday of Holy Week. The party was joined by Father Lasuén who had come from Mission San Francisco de Borja on Thursday to care for the Easter religious obligations of the party. After receiving Holy Communion, the command was given two days later to march, and Rivera and his retinue, after traveling fifty-two days, arrived at San Diego on May 14 to find the ships *San Carlos* and *San Antonio* at anchor in the bay whence they had arrived on April 11 and 29, consecutively.

In Loreto all was in readiness for the last of the expeditions to set forth. Junípero Serra, who was to serve as chaplain and diarist of the second section, went to Governor Portolá and suggested that they proceed without him since he had further duties to perform. He asked Portolá to leave behind two soldiers and a servant and told him they would start a little later and catch up with the expedition before it reached the frontier.

Portolá quickly observed the suffering Serra was undergoing from the foot and leg infection which had become increasingly worse since his trips to the south. Fearing that the condition had become cancerous and that Serra was physically incapable of making such a long and difficult journey, Portolá tried to persuade him to abandon the idea of going and to appoint Palóu, who enjoyed youth and vigorous health, in his place. Portolá, an experienced soldier, realized that such an ailing member could delay the progress of the expedition and keep it from reaching its destination. He pointed all of this out to Serra who quietly responded that he trusted in God and that He would provide strength for the journey not only to San Diego, but to Monterey as well. Junípero urged Portolá to start and appointed Father Miguel de la Campa from Mission San Ignacio to go with him.

Portolá and his company of soldiers left Loreto on March 9 and made Mission San Xavier their first stop. Immediately upon arrival, the governor told Palóu of the venerable Father's painful condition and expressed his deep concern saying, "In spite of what I have told him, and the delay which he may cause to the expedition if he should become unable to proceed farther, he insists upon going and I have not been able to persuade him to remain behind and to let Your Reverence go in his stead. . . . It looks to me quite impossible for him to carry out this plan and so I have written to the Visitador."

Portolá urged Palóu also to write Gálvez and make a similar report in the hope that Serra could be dissuaded from making the taxing journey. Portolá then left with his contingent of 15 soldiers, under Sergeant José Francisco de Ortega, a servant, 14 muleteers and Indians, making up a company of 44 persons in all. Thus the two land parties were comprised of 178 persons, 200 head of cattle, 38 horses, and 144 pack mules to carry provisions and all of the church furniture and religious articles. Their destination was the outpost of Santa María where they would await the arrival of the provisions being delivered by vessel to the Bay of San Luis Gonzaga, make arrangements for the herd, and where Serra planned to join them.

Great as his longings were to accompany Portolá, Serra remained behind because of one final obligation to his parish. Easter week was approaching, and since this would be the anniversary of his first sermon to his people, he felt in his heart he could not leave until he spoke to them again at this holy time.

Serra waited until after the Holy Week celebrations of the Church had been observed with solemnity and devotion and preached his farewell sermon. Then, as he wrote in his diary, "On the day which punctually fulfilled an Ecclesiastic year of my having preached to them since the first time when I took possession of spiritual matters . . . I set forth after Mass of the said third feast." On March 28, 1769, he left the mission after beseeching the protection of Our Lady of Loreto and arrived at Mission San Xavier to be welcomed by his disciple, Francisco Palóu.

Palóu embraced his teacher and wept as he saw the swollen and ulcerated leg of the tired and hungry Padre. The mule Serra rode was a broken-down dispirited creature which had been supplied by the military commissioner of Loreto. Junípero was without extra clothing and had almost nothing to eat, for as he wrote, "From my Mission of Loreto I did not take more provision for so long an excursion than one loaf of bread and a piece of cheese. For I was there all the year, so far as temporal matters go, as the mere guest for the crumbs of the Royal Commissary, whose liberality at my departure did not extend further than the aforesaid."

Palóu gave him clothing and comforts for the trip and supplied him with warm food and tender care until Serra noted in his diary, "Not even I myself could have managed to contrive them, tho' for my sins I do not cease to be fond of my convenience. May God repay so much charity."

Serra remained with Palóu for three days that they might rejoice in each other's company and recall the early, happy days when they were on the island of Majorca as pupil and teacher. There was also much business to discuss concerning the presidency since Palóu had been named vice-president in the original patent from the College of San Fernando and was to serve as president in the absence or death of Serra.

"But before the treating of these matters I called attention to the deplorable condition of his foot and leg," Palóu recorded, "and told him that naturally it would be impossible for him to take such a long journey and that he might be the cause of bringing disaster upon the expedition, and if not he might greatly retard it." He continued by begging Serra to remain behind and volunteered to go in his place.

"Let us not talk about it," responded Serra as soon as he heard Palóu's proposition. "I have put all my trust in God, from Whose goodness I expect that it will be granted me not only to arrive at San Diego and to set up and dedicate in that port the standard of the Holy Cross, but also to go on to Monterey."

There was nothing for Palóu to do but to yield to the fervent determination and faith of his friend who, so obviously, was ready to sacrifice his life in the pursuance of his apostolic labors. So they spoke of other matters until the time came for Serra to depart.

"The pain of our good-bye was very greatly increased when I saw that in order to mount or dismount from the mule which carried him, he needed the services of two men who lifted him up bodily and adjusted him in the saddle," again wrote Palóu, whose compassionate heart pained when he thought of "how much he still had to suffer in the rough and difficult trails which he must traverse before reaching the frontier and the other unknown trails which he would have to traverse farther on, without other doctor or surgeon than the Divine aid, and without further protection for his lame foot than a sandal, as he never would use anything else in all the journeys which he took both in New Spain as well as in California, saying that he could not use shoes or stockings or boots because it was better for him to have his foot and leg bare."

Once mounted on his sorry mule, Serra called out to Palóu, "Good-bye till I see you in Monterey, where I hope that we shall come together again to work in that vineyard of the Lord."

Palóu gloried in the little priest's courage and faith, but could only softly respond, "Until eternity." For this he received a gentle, affectionate scolding from Serra for having so little faith.

Junípero had been gone but a brief time when an answer to Palóu's letter arrived from the Visitador-General. Palóu had written to him of Serra's poor health, and had expressed doubts as to his being able to keep up with the expedition. Gálvez responded by saying, that he, too, was concerned and had brought up this matter with Serra both at the camp in Santa Ana and at La Paz, and that knowing of his great spirit was sure Serra could go on. "I am very glad," he wrote, "that our Reverend Father is going with the expedition and I praise him for his great faith and confidence that he will get better, which, may God grant, and that he may arrive at San Diego. I fully believe that he will do so. . . ."

Palóu could only continue his prayers that the health of the venerable Father would be restored and asked for the good success of his expedition.

Junípero Serra plodded on traveling from mission to mission visiting the priests and comforting and counseling them. Having left San Xavier at dawn on April 1, he was able to reach San Jose Cumundú about eleven in the morning where he found that his old time friend of the Sierra Gorda days, Father Antonio Martínez, had gone to Mission Purísima, where, since Crespí's departure with Rivera, he had alternated between the two missions. However, in anticipation of Serra's arrival he had made every provision for his friend and superior's comfort. The next day being Sunday, Serra heard confessions, offered a High Mass, preached a sermon, and generally busied himself while the *arrieros,* or muleteers, repaired the harnesses, which were in bad shape from neglect. Martínez arrived at midmorning and proffered Serra the resources of his mission and urged him to take whatever was needed.

The following day both rode to Purísima, a mere ten leagues distant, and arrived before noon. Father Juan Crespí had left ample provisions for his friends and had instructed the soldier, Don Francisco María de Castro, major-domo and escort of that mission, to deliver these to Father Serra. The Indians welcomed him with a dance performed with all the solemnity possible. Part of that day and the next was spent in loading the provisions, supplied through Crespí's thoughtfulness, onto the mules.

At daybreak the next morning, Serra bade farewell to his friend and took off for Mission Guadalupe, a journey of thirty-seven leagues through rough terrain. Serra walked all day, stopping briefly for a bite of food and a rest, but found himself in the open country when night fell and he prepared to sleep upon the ground. He encountered ten Indian families from Mission Guadalupe who, because of lack of provisions, had been told by Father Sancho to go into the wilds and forage for themselves. They had not found anything to eat and the babies and children were crying with hunger. Serra could only give them two bowls of *atole,* or corn meal mush, from his own meager supplies because his pack mules were far behind and were not expected to arrive that night. He prayed with the Indians and comforted them by telling of the food supply which was on its way by ship and urged the Indians to return to their mission. While Serra rested, the Indians, who were noted for their sweet voices, sang a "tender song of the love of God," and he received great consolation in hearing them.

"On the 8th I set forth from said place, and over those so painful hills, arrived at the Pueblo of San Miguel, which is a visita [branch] of that mission, about midday," wrote Serra. Here he found more Indians and fed them from his meager supply of food. Some of these Indians followed him for a while as he went through the dusk to reach Guadalupe after nightfall and "well tired." He had now come to the end of the previously traveled part of California which he knew well. From this point, all would be unknown land of the pagan Indians.

As official diarist for the Portolá section of the expedition to Alta California, Serra kept a careful record of his experiences while traveling from Loreto to San Diego during the time of March 28 to June 30, 1769. The diary of his first *entrada,* or entrance, into California fills thirty-four folio pages of finely written manuscript and is a very human document of hardships endured, physical suffering, courage, indomitable faith, and an occasional flash of wry humor.

Interestingly, Serra started the diary by relating barest details and told nothing of the plant or animal life of that great central desert region which had to be crossed. He made no mention of the fantastically wonderful vegetation and the strange plants so characteristic of Baja California. Possibly the realization that the first part of the journey had been traversed and recorded by Father Juan Salvatierra, the Jesuit explorer priest, gave Serra reason not to put forth the effort. One can but assume that the physical pain he was enduring at the start of the journey kept him from having the energy or enthusiasm to make mention of these unique botanical specimens which, as a genuine lover of nature, would surely have attracted his attention.

For this region abounds in such plants as the bisnaga or barrel cactus which grows to a height of over five feet and is said to be a source of water for the parched desert traveler. There are the cardons, giant in size, one species having the comblike spines which is known as the "comb of the aborigines." There is the chirinola or "creeping devil," a thick-stemmed cactus which grows recumbent; and the "jumping cactus" or cholla; as well as the strange spectral toretes or "elephant tree" with its thick, tortuous trunk and pinnate leaves, to mention but a few. The cirio or idria, a slender tree with a columnar trunk and short horizontal branches perhaps is the weirdest plant of all. After a rain, leaves spring forth and the yellow flowers appearing in a tuft at the tip of the trunk make this strange plant appear to be a giant upside-down carrot.

In the rugged mountains wild game abounds and deer, or *venado*, is to be found everywhere on the brush-covered mountainsides as well as in the more isolated ranges. There are lurking mountain lions, *leones* or *pumas*, sometimes reaching six feet and weighing nearly two hundred pounds. An occasional bighorn sheep, *borrego*, shyly lives in the extremely dry desert mountains while the pronghorn antelope, *antílope*, gracefully roams the open desert areas. The bark of coyotes can be heard at night, and wild pig *jabalí*, can also be seen. At dusk the small jack rabbits, *liebre*, come out. Overhead the buzzards soar silently and gracefully with widespread wings in the cerulean blue skies. It is a strange land of angry, untamed, and haunting beauty. The rising or setting sun hurls colors into the skies which have such brilliance that they come with an almost physical impact upon the beholder while changing shadows and light play upon the jagged mountainsides. All the while, there is a pervading, haunting sensation of intense serenity.

Serra mentioned none of this. It is not until his physical well-being improved on the journey that he began to indicate his customary joy in the beauties of nature and made note of all that he saw and enjoyed.

At Guadalupe Serra took a badly needed rest. He had correspondence and reports to write. Then, too, the pack mules, weary and sore, were three days late in arriving. Junípero's friend, Father Juan Sancho, graciously extended the hospitality of the mission to him and out of solicitude gave him a fresh mule to ride, and several for pack replacements, to relieve somewhat the burden of the tired pack animals. "For of all the beasts saddled for the expedition, none were so forlorn as those they assigned to me," said Serra. Despite all this, several of the original mules were so old and exhausted they soon died along the road.

Father Sancho gave Serra a little page who had served at the Mission Guadalupe and who spoke Spanish and could read. He was about fifteen years old and named Juan Evangelista Benno. The good padre gave him a complete change of clothes and fitted him out with all of the trappings to make the trip. Dressed in his leather jacket and boots and astride his own saddle mule, the boy was content to go and his parents looked upon this as a stroke of good fortune for their boy.

Serra remained at Guadalupe five days and was delighted when his friend from Spain and his coworker in the Sierra Gorda, Father Juan Gaston, traveled from Mission Santa Rosalia de Mulegé to bid him farewell. This mission, being so far off the main road on the coast of the Gulf of California, was the one mission of the entire chain that Serra did not intend to visit because of the worsening condition of his bad leg. The parting of the two old friends was particularly poignant and they consoled each other with the thought that "all was arranged for the greater honor and glory of God." Serra then gathered up the religious articles that could be spared from the mission and Father Sancho agreed to send everything to Mulegé on the coast for shipment to Loreto where all of the goods for California were being assembled. To expedite matters, Serra ordered the ladened mule train to depart a day previous to his own leaving. He and his young page and their soldier guard left the next morning to go to Mission San Ignacio.

They passed a place called Santa Cruz and by nightfall had reached a ranchería, called San Borja and made camp. Father Juan Medina Veitía, minister at San Ignacio, thoughtfully sent Indians to the camp with a warm supper for the weary wayfarers who were to sleep that night on the ground. The next evening Medina Veitía came out to give Serra a personal welcome. They traveled along the trail for a short distance and then the priest rushed back to the mission so that, dressed in surplice, stole, and pluvial, he could extend formal welcome at the entrance to the church. The former priest of this mission had been Father Miguel de la Campa, who had departed with the first land division with Rivera.

The following was Sunday the sixteenth and the day of the Profession of the Order of St. Francis on which they celebrate the feast of the Holy Archangel St. Raphael, who is the patron of travelers. Serra quietly and reverently united with his brothers around the world in renewing his vows as a Franciscan. Earlier Palóu had written in the biography at the time Serra took his first vows in Palma, "So very great was the joy and the happiness which his profession caused him that in all his life he never forgot it; but rather he renewed his vows and profession every year not only on the day of Our Holy Father St. Francis, but also whenever he assisted in the receiving of any novice."

Two days later, Serra failed to awaken early and could not cover much distance because of the warm day. At noon the sun's intense heat forced him to seek shelter and he rested in a cave until the coolness of evening, when he went on to a place called San Juan. That night and the following night, not being able to reach the desired destination, he slept on the ground. He arrived at Santa Gertrudis very early in the morning and was greeted by Indians dancing in front of the church where stood Father Dionisio Basterra formally clad in religious vestments and accompanied by acolytes with a Cross, candlesticks, incensory, and holy water. Serra venerated the Cross and blessed the people with holy water. Then he entered the church to pray. Once Basterra had removed his vestments, the two embraced warmly and tears welled into their eyes. They had not seen each other for years, since parting at Loreto. They recalled the experiences shared while companions on the preaching missions in Oaxaca and Puebla while they both were stationed at San Fernando in Mexico City.

Serra tarried at this mission for five days to bring companionship to the young priest who had become melancholy over enforced loneliness with none but the Indians around him. Rivera had confiscated his servant and soldier guard for the expedition and the priest had no one with whom to converse. Basterra in his loneliness wrote letters to Serra at Loreto beseeching him to send some relief, but all the president could do was respond with letters of consolation. Appeals to Gálvez proved fruitless, and so the disconsolate priest wept in loneliness.

Official business also claimed Serra's attention since he had been requested by Gálvez to try to persuade the Indians at this mission to move to Purísima where field workers were needed. Using all of his persuasive powers, Serra thought he had convinced the Indians of the benefits they would derive from such a transfer when some of them agreed. However, they quickly had a change of heart and decided to remain in the area where they had always lived and do without the proffered food and clothing. They threatened to revert to pagan ways rather than move.

Mission San Borja was two days' travel away and Serra reached there on the morning of April 28 to be welcomed by Father Fermín Francisco Lasuén, whom he held in the highest regard. The mission and houses were crudely constructed of adobe. Lasuén had found neither church nor hut there upon his arrival and had done what he could with the unskilled Indians. Despite the barren land and scarcity of water, Lasuén refused to heed Gálvez's demand to move the Indians since they were such recent Christians.

Despite his eagerness to hasten on and join up with the expedition which was at the next mission, "Out of especial affection for this minister," Serra stated in the diary, "I tarried the two days following, which for me were of much enjoyment, owing to his lovable converse." After considerable talk about the expedition, Lasuén urgently requested that he be permitted to join. Serra preached to the Indians and then started the final portion of the journey to the frontier mission of Santa María, some forty leagues away.

The next four days he spent in traveling toward his goal, stopping only to rest out in the open at night and to offer Mass on the Day of

Ascension at the ruins of the old Mission Calamajué which was merely a jacal, or hut, made of branches. Rising very early the next morning on May 5 and traveling over a "most grievous road," Serra arrived at Mission Santa María de los Angeles. Here he found Portolá and Father de la Campa; the remainder of the retinue having gone on to Velicatá to find forage for the animals. "We were mutually glad to see ourselves already joined," wrote Serra, "to begin anew our peregrination through a desert land populated only with Infidelity, with innumerable Gentiles."

Having to wait a day until the provisions and cargo of grain were brought from the beach of San Luis Gonzaga, and for the muleteers to repair the harnesses and ropes of the beasts of burden, Serra, Father de la Campa, and Portolá explored the surrounding terrain to check upon water supplies and the amount of arable lands. Gálvez had instructed them to do so and to move the Mission Santa María to Velicatá should they deem it advisable. They did not find the land to be as poor as it had been presented to them and wrote to Gálvez recommending that the site be retained, a decision that Palóu later claimed to have been unwise. They had not seen the region during the season when the streams dried up, and the land being alkaline, was useless.

Serra remained at Mission Santa María de los Angeles from May 5 to May 10. He occupied himself by preaching a sermon to the Indians who were among "the poorest" he had yet seen. Serra took very little from the poverty-stricken Mission Santa María, and he signed a receipt so that all would be replaced by Gálvez.

On the eleventh and twelfth of May Serra noted in the diary that they set forth and traveled along an arroyo which seemed to have water sufficient for irrigation of fruit trees in the future and could sustain a mission. There were native palms and grass at this place. Continuing on their way, he noted that they came to a place called *ponza de agua dulce*, or sweet water well, and saw recent tracks leading up to little rancherías, but, he stated, "Not one, big or little, let himself be seen; their retreat mortifying my desires to talk to them and to caress them."

The morning of May 13 Serra requested permission from Portolá that they go ahead in light order to reach Velicatá in one day, rather than to continue at the slow pace set by the pack animals, and so arrive there on the day of Pentecost. It was agreed and so Serra, Portolá, and Father de la Campa, accompanied by two pages and the soldier escort, moved ahead, reaching the camp of the advance guard the next evening after passing more of the little huts set in the barren countryside, which was virtually without vegetation except for an occasional cactus, but not seeing a single Indian as they went.

"The number of soldiers that were there received us with much content," wrote Serra in the diary, and it was with much content and prayerful thankfulness that the weary little Padre lay down to rest. At last he had reached the place of departure into the wilderness where, he hoped, countless pagan Indians or Gentiles were waiting to receive the blessings of the Church.

His injured leg and foot throbbed with pain, his body was sore and stiff from the long journey, but his heart rejoiced, for on the morrow he was to found his first mission.

CHAPTER XX

ENTRADA TO ALTA CALIFORNIA,

JULY 1, 1769

Serra arose early that morning of May 14, the day of Pentecost. Already the little jacal was being cleaned and adorned with the religious furnishings he had brought with him. This crude shelter, made of palisades, had been built by the members of Rivera's division as they passed through, and had been used by Father Lasuén to preach the first Mass in Velicatá. He had administered Communion to the captain and the soldiers in preparation for the expedition.

The pack train had not as yet reached the camp with the required supplies for a proper religious observance, but Serra determined to proceed without the use of candles or incense, disappointing as this would be. He later wrote at length in the diary describing the events of this great day:

> In that jacal, then, the altar was arranged, the soldiers were drawn up under arms, with their leathern jackets and shields, and with all the neatness of Holy Poverty I celebrated Mass on that so great day, with the consolation that this was the first of those Masses which must continue with the permanency of that new Mission of San Fernando which dated from that very day. The Mass while it lasted was solemnized by the very repeated discharges of the muskets of the soldiers; the fumes of the powder supplying in this instance, the place of incense, which we could not offer because we had it not. And as there was no more wax that would burn, except for a short end of a candle that I found, the Father's only taper for that day was the Mass, and the Father heard the Mass with the rest in fulfillment of the precept.

After they had sung the "Veni Creator," Serra planted the standard of the Holy Cross and made Father Miguel de la Campa the first minister of the new mission. According to instructions from Gálvez, the new mission was given a fifth of the herd that had been assembled there, and Serra shared his store of supplies by donating biscuit, flour, and soap, and in addition, some chocolate, raisins, dried figs, and maize. All that was lacking was a congregation, but the Indians remained out of sight, doubtlessly frightened by the thundering noises from the muskets.

That evening, despite the constant pain in his infected foot and leg, Serra with Portolá and Father de la Campa walked over the area and up the arroyo to find where a dam for irrigation might easily be constructed. The situation appeared excellent for getting a new mission underway except for the lack of poles and timbers, which, they hoped, might be found in the hills.

The pack mules arrived the next morning in time for the priests to have candles with which to celebrate Mass. Serra retired under one of the small jacals to rest after the services, but was soon summoned to greet a band of Indians who were approaching camp. He rushed out to see twelve male Indians, two of them young boys, all stark naked. Serra patted them on the head, gave them dried fruit, which they immediately began to eat, and through an interpreter made them understand that Father de la Campa was to remain as their friend and priest and for them not to be fearful. In turn the Indians gave the missionaries some roasted mescal and four fish which proved to be spoiled. Serra believed that the Indians comprehended what was said to them and that soon they would become converts. One, who appeared to act as chief of the Indians, Portolá said now would continue to be captain in the name of the King of Spain.

That same evening Serra bade farewell to De la Campa and his new charges and left with Portolá and the retinue going toward San Juan de Dios, reaching there on May 16. About this place Serra wrote, "It is agreeable, with plenty of water, and pastures, willows, tule and a glad sky. . . . One descends to this arroyo and spot by a pretty high hill; but as it is already well trodden and mended, the descent does not cause especial hardship." Here they found Sergeant Ortega and some soldiers, with part of the animals, which had to rest from the trail for a brief spell.

Serra welcomed the respite from the rigors of travel. His pain was growing constantly more severe and he could not find any relief, but he said Mass on May 17 and nearly fainted. Later in recalling the painful ordeal he wrote, "Although with the great hardship it cost me to hold myself on my feet, because of my left foot having become much inflamed; from which for about a year, or something more, I have been suffering; and now it has become very swollen to half way up my leg, and its wounds are inflamed. Wherefore the days that we were detained here I passed mostly at full length upon the bed, and feared that soon I would have to follow the expedition on a stretcher."

After a sleepless night, the pain was so intense he found he could not stand or even sit and had to lie prostrate upon his bed and was unable to officiate at Mass that morning. Portolá, busy with final arrangements for the expedition and overseeing the condition of the pack animals, noticed Father Serra's grievous condition and was deeply concerned. Practical soldier that he was, he knew sympathy was not enough and also that he could not run the risk of Serra's condition delaying the entire march. Despite the fact that he before had tried to reason with Serra and to persuade him to refrain from going on the trek and had met with failure, Portolá determined again to try and dissuade him now that his condition had worsened.

"Your Reverence well knows that you cannot accompany the expedition. We are only six leagues from the place from which we set out. If your Reverence will permit, they can carry you back to the first mission in order that you may there become well again, and we will go on our journey," said Portolá, trying to be reasonable and gentle at the same time.

Serra shook his head and then said, "Please do not speak to me further about the matter, because I trust in God who will give me strength to arrive in San Diego, as He has given me strength to come this far." Seeing that Portolá was about to interrupt, Serra continued, "In case this is not His good pleasure for me, I shall resign myself to His holy will. Even if I die on the road, I will not go back, but you can bury me here and I shall very gladly remain among these pagan people if such be the will of God."

Portolá, realizing that Serra was going to remain adamant about continuing, although unable to travel either on foot or on horseback, gave orders that a litter be made out of small branches, in order that the Father might lie down and be carried by the converted Indians who were accompanying the expedition as servants and laborers. From where he lay, Serra heard the determined voice of Portolá giving these instructions for the construction of the litter and he was much grieved about it because of the extra labor which it would cause the already overworked Indians. His humble spirit cringed at the thought of having to be served in this manner.

As he lay upon the small, collapsible bed, which was his only earthly possession and which he had brought from Majorca and took everywhere, Serra knew black despair. Always before he had, by determination and will power, been able to sublimate his pain and find consolation in it. Upon occasion when doctors had come to some of the settlements in Mexico where he had been stationed and offered to treat him he had replied to them, "Never mind, it is an old sore and would need a long treatment." Another time when one of his intimate companions had grown insistent he had replied, "I have never applied carnal medicine to my body." Prayer had always been his source of strength. Now in his bleakest hour, he turned to prayer again, and asked for some slight alleviation, in order to avoid having to put this added burden upon the Indians. He closed his eyes, feigning sleep and withdrew unto himself praying all the morning. He gradually regained his composure and his faith.

He heard the voices of the muleteers outside the jacal in which he rested and called Juan Antonio Coronel to his side and said, "My son, don't you know how to make a remedy for my foot and leg?"

The muleteer looked perplexed and answered, "Father, what do I know about remedies? Am I a surgeon? I am only a muleteer and I only know how to cure the galls on the backs of pack animals."

"Very well then, my son, take into account that I am one of your beasts of burden and that this sore is a gall sore from which has resulted the swollen leg. The pains are so great that I cannot sleep, so please make the remedy and apply it just as if I was one of your animals."

At this the muleteer laughed as he agreed, "I will do it, Father, in order to give you pleasure."

Juan Coronel, the muleteer, went into the fields and found some herbs close at hand which he ground between two stones and this he mixed with some tallow. Heating it thoroughly, he applied the ointment as a poultice upon the sore.

That night Serra got his first real sleep and rested well until daybreak when he awakened refreshed. The pain was so much better he was able to rise and take part in the Matins and Praise as usual, and then he said Mass to the astonishment of everyone. Serra, suddenly restored to health and being of such good cheer, the expedition two days later went on its way.

Serra was later to write Palóu concerning his illness, "At present my foot is entirely well, but from the ankle half way up the calf of the leg there is a bad sore like there formerly was on my foot, but there is no swelling nor do I have any pain, only an itching sensation at times which is not worth speaking of."

After offering Mass on Sunday, the feast of the Holy Trinity, Serra exhorted the members concerning the good conduct which they ought to observe on a "road whose principal end was the greater honor and glory of God." He then blessed them and the march was ordered begun. They headed toward the west, but came to a high mountain that forced them to turn to the north. From the height of a hill they could look down upon a great number of Indians and Serra sent two of the Indian converts to invite them to come to him. The strange

Indians went off, leaving a bow and a few arrows which were skillfully and delicately wrought.

The way now plunged into a leafy arroyo and the cavalcade paused here and came upon an old man, naked as all of them. They fed him and talked to him, and he told them that the members of his tribe had fled when on another occasion a priest and his retinue had passed by. Serra assumed that this must have been a Jesuit priest, from the description offered, and noted that they readily could perceive the old man's unconcern for anyone, "for while he was conversing with us in the middle of the circle, he squatted, and as there was no clothing to loosen he promptly satisfied his necessity, still conversing with us, and remained as serene as relieved." The old one seemed eager to become a Christian and insisted upon being baptized forthwith, but Serra arranged for him to return to Velicatá for instruction in catechism.

The next morning while the animals were being saddled and the cargo loaded, Serra took advantage of the time and wrote a lengthy letter of farewell to his priests and sent the commission to Palóu, who became president of the missions, now that Serra was undergoing "civil death," or was absenting himself beyond jurisdiction over them. He wrote also to Gálvez, and since the letters were to be of considerable length, he suggested that the expedition go on without him. He caught up with Portolá and the others who had stopped after two and a half hours for the day because from that point on they would have to leave the arroyo and take to the heights.

The following day the path led directly into the mountains in the direction of the Contra Costa (opposite coast). They had traveled only four hours, because climbing and descending over the rocky way was toilsome, when they reached high mesas and came to a spacious spot with running water and good pasture. This place they called Santiago. The next day was hot and uncomfortable as they marched through a dry, sandy arroyo with a few palms, then going on to reach "painful and ugly hills." Passing through the hills they came upon a plain with a single leafy palm and stopped under its shade, naming the spot Corpus Christi. They saw a few rabbits and caught two, but their nights were tormented by the roaring of a lion which apparently was following them. Illusive tracks of Indians were constantly being seen, but the shy creatures failed to materialize. The travelers continued following this same arroyo and then started toiling upward on a high mountain and from the heights looked down upon another large green arroyo with large cottonwood trees. They made the difficult descent into this green arroyo and traveling along came to an excellent spot with plenty of water and pasturage. There on a level stretch they came upon a little pueblo of about ten huts, but no Indians were in view. Serra was charmed by the beauty of this place and described it rather fully: "A little later our attention was called by a tree, very tall and leafy, a thing we had not seen until now, outside the Missions. And coming up to it, I saw it was an Alamo [cottonwood], a thing which still more caused me to admire; and we called the place Alamo Solo [lone cottonwood]. Thereafter the land began to be more smiling and gladsome than thus far, with trees tall and tufted (altho' not so much as the said Alamo) whose branches and leaves are altogether like the Cypress; and various other trees of like height, various little flowers—and in fine, appeared a new country." After the bleakness of the desert regions with their sparse and grotesquely-formed plants, Serra, always a lover of beauty in nature, welcomed the sight of greenery and flowers in bloom. They saw in the distance three Indians watching them from a hillock and Serra sent two of his converts to convince the strangers that it was safe for them to come to the camp, but the Indians fled.

The party remained in this comfortable location another day so that the animals might rest and be tended. When two of the Gentiles again became visible, Serra's servants were more cautious in their approach and succeeded in overpowering one of them and brought him badly bruised and bound by a cord. Serra tried to soothe the terrified man and took him into Portolá's tent. After giving him food and assurances of friendship, they succeeded in learning from the frightened Indian that he had been sent by his chief to spy upon the expedition in order that the several tribes, who had gathered behind some cliffs, could come forth and kill the priest and members of his party. They forgave him and sent him back to his people so that he could explain the friendship and love of the priests and that they should come to treat with them. "He went naked like all," wrote Serra, "with his bow and arrows, which were returned to him, his disheveled hair long and bound with a little cord of blue wool, very well made, the which we could not discover where he had got it."

They continued their way north, now following the route of 1766 which had been covered earlier by Jesuit Padre Link, whose diary Serra had with him. The marching was easier than any they had previously encountered, the way going over gentle hills "smiling with many flowers of various colors" until they came to a marshy meadow, or *ciénaga*, from where they planned to take another course from the one they had been following. All along the road, they kept seeing one Indian after another, but none came close to them.

The following day was a Sunday and just before Mass, a group of threatening Indians approached the camp and Serra's neophytes tried to take hold of them. A dreadful argument ensued and the more threatening the Indians became, the more peaceful Serra tried to talk. At last, since it was time for the Mass, the soldiers seized the Indians and formed a circle around them so they were captives and were forced to listen to the Mass. Then a group of more Indians came until there were about forty of them and they would not leave until the soldiers fired their muskets into the air toward them and they then fled.

One day after another passed as they traveled on always seeking the coast line. Serra noted that some days the way was easy and pleasant and on others it was marred by toilsome hills or ravines, making progress slow and wearisome. He took great joy in the ever-changing landscape, and his general good health was evidenced by the excitement and enthusiasm he revealed in his entries in the diary.

Each stopping place was analyzed as to the prospects it offered for a new mission site or for the numbers of Gentiles living there as possible converts. The numbers of Indians increased with each day's journey and Serra took special delight in them. However, when the way was through a narrow pass, Portolá had his soldiers put on their leather jackets and alerted them for any possible attack from hostiles.

Passing through a hilly region and making camp one evening on a wide plain, they were joined by a merry band of Indians who brought roasted mescal for the travelers and then entertained them by staging a mock battle. "They played all the roles, with so much liveliness and grace," wrote Serra, "that we had a good bit of recreation." Suddenly, in the midst of the merriment two women appeared and Serra was relieved to see that they were modestly dressed, but were talking "as rapidly and efficaciously as this sex knows how and is accustomed to do." One of them had a pancake type of dough upon her head and when Serra patted her, as was his custom, his hand was covered with the substance. By yelling loudly, the woman explained how this was eaten. The next day, this same group of Indians continued following the party, making such an uproar the animals were frightened. The Indians refused to depart until, in desperation, Portolá ordered musket shots to be fired into the air to chase them away. Serra wryly commented upon the incident: "They ceased, and the trouble was ended—altho' I already felt that with this demonstration we left them with some doubt of our love toward them."

On the day of their patron, St. Ferdinand, they rested in a pretty *enramada,* or brush shelter, which the soldiers had prepared beforehand, hung about with their quilts and well garnished, and here Serra celebrated Mass. The beauty of this spot greatly impressed him. There were wide green plains with ample pasturage, cottonwood groves making a leafy semicircle around a gentle hill upon which was an ideal site for a mission. Two days later found the expedition in a place abounding in grapevines so loaded with fruit that it was a "thing of wonder." The next day they passed a large barranca and came to the foothills and Serra wrote in wonderment, "It seems that the thorns and the stones of California are finished, as those so high mountains are almost pure earth. Flowers many, and beautiful as I have already noted before; and that there should be nothing lacking in this line, today on arriving at the camping place we have met the Queen of them, which is the Rose of Castile." He continued to note in his diary, "The branch of a rose bush is at this moment caressing the hand that is setting down these lines. It has three full-blown roses, some buds which are about to open, and six roses whose petals have fallen. I bless Thee, Lord, for having created the Rose of Castile!"* They remained in this Arroyo of the Roses, as he called it, for three days to rest the animals. Serra reconnoitered the area since it seemed to him that "an arroyo so beautiful would not be without benefit." He found it to be worthy of a future mission and named the place in honor of St. Andres del Agua. "If these arroyos decline, the Saint, as patron of the water, will make it rain, if his Mission be dedicated here," optimistically added Serra.

Several days later, as camp was being set up, some Indians were seen on a little hill nearby, and one came to them carrying in one hand a stick and in the other a rattle. They welcomed him and brought food to him which he refused to eat, explaining to them that he was the dancer of that country and that he could eat nothing without first having danced for it. The soldiers took turns bringing pieces of tortilla and meat, but he always resisted when they tried to force this into his mouth, indicating that they should put it on the pile collecting on the ground. After dancing, the Indian ate and then told them they were but four and a half days away from San Diego. The Indian related to them by means of the interpreter that he had seen the first contingent pass by and offered to accompany this division to show them the way, providing they would permit him to dance as he went along the road. They agreed to this with much pleasure and Serra had hopes of baptizing this Indian when suddenly something frightened him and he ran off, taking only his stick and rattle and leaving behind the food they had piled up for him.

Over each hill they climbed Serra hoped to catch a glimpse of the sea, but each day mountains blocked the path forcing them to march through barrancas and painful rises and descents. "These compel us

* This five-petaled rose with a delicate fragrance is botanically known as *rosa californica* and is so registered in the Royal Botanical Gardens in Madrid.

to many circuits, doubling much of the road, the reason why today we have mostly traveled towards the west, although always forcing towards the sea, that does not wish to let itself be seen," he wrote. By now the Indian converts who had joined them at Mission San Borja had run away and could not be traced. But still the weary band plodded on, passing through another place of such beauty Serra joyfully jotted in the diary, "There are many roses of Castile, the water is much, and there are a thousand beauties. Thanks to God." This place, he thought, was ideally suited for the establishment of a mission which would be a fine neighbor to San Diego.

On the sixteenth, six soldier scouts returning to the camp reported that from the top of a high hill they had caught a glimpse of the sea, which appeared to be but four leagues distant. Close as the distance may have seemed, the rough surface of the area, the many hills to be climbed, the arroyos to cross, all delayed their progress and it was not until the evening of the twentieth that they made camp along the shore in the place they recognized from their maps as being Ensenada de Todos Santos. Serra dedicated the site to "Most Holy Mary, my Mother and Saint, and because we are in the days of the visita or pilgrimage in the Mountains of Judea, I said that we should call this site the Visitation, or Nuestra Señora la Peregrina (Our Lady the Pilgrim)."

They rested the animals for two days and the men took time out for hunting and fishing, but without success. On the third day they resumed their march and soon came upon a band of Indians who presented them with gifts of fish. "Their beautiful figure, deportment, and affability and joyousness have enamored us all," he reported. Later the expedition came upon Indians of a very different nature. They were brazen, mischievous, and insolent. As the priests patted them upon the head, they imitated and patted the priests in a similar manner. The Indians tugged and pulled at the clothing and so eager were they to possess cloth goods, they importuned the soldiers to enjoy the services of their women in exchange. The Indians showed great curiosity over Serra's spectacles and when he took these off to show them, one of the Indians snatched the eyeglasses from his hand and ran off. It was with considerable difficulty that these were reclaimed and returned to a very troubled Serra.

Later that same day two new Indians appeared and since these were fully dressed, Serra hoped they were from San Diego and could tell them good news. So it was—they had come from San Diego and reported that they had seen two boats in the water and many Padres. The next day in the middle of the morning, a party on horseback loomed up on the horizon and soon a sergeant arrived with ten soldiers from the first division who had come by order of Rivera to welcome Portolá and his party. They brought with them fresh horses and letters from Fathers Crespí and Parrón to Serra. "We rejoiced," wrote Serra, "and we heard all that had passed on the boats, and the reason they were there, and the four Padres, and the rest that there was about everything; this news livening in us, as in all, desires for our arrival."

In the early morning hours of the twenty-ninth, Portolá, his servant, and eight soldiers pushed ahead to arrive that same day at the port of San Diego. Serra remained to recite Mass for the benefit of the Indians who surrounded the camp and then traveled for a few hours toward San Diego.

The next day, despite the end of the long journey seemingly so close at hand, the going was especially difficult. Countless gullies blocked the way and they no sooner had climbed over one when others appeared in an endless number. Serra's "heart came to be compressed much, seeing in each one the danger, and that at times on coming out of one it was to cross soon without rest another. . . . But as with all things, in this world," he added, "they came to an end."

Serra reached San Diego on the first of July. When the members of his section came in view of the harbor, they gave shouts of elation and fired shots from their guns. These were answered by corresponding shots from Rivera's men. Salvos of welcome were fired from the two ships in the harbor. Friends greeted friends with affectionate embraces and expressions of great joy at the success of the venture and in their safely reaching the destination toward which they had all been assigned.

"Thanks to God," Serra wrote to Palóu, "I arrived here at this port of San Diego the day before yesterday, the first day of the month. It is truly a beautiful port and well deserving of its fame. . . ."

CHAPTER XXI

SAN DIEGO, 1769–70

San Diego was indeed a beautiful port, but the situation Serra came upon there was one which would have crushed a less courageous person with utter hopelessness. Many were sick unto death, and a fourth of all who had started upon the sea voyage had lost their lives.

While Monterey was to be the ultimate destination for the sacred expedition, Gálvez had selected San Diego as the rendezvous for the ships and the land parties, thinking they would all arrive there about the same time. The *San Antonio,* though it started the journey more than a month after the *San Carlos,* was the first to arrive on April 11, after a voyage of fifty-five days. The *San Carlos* did not arrive until the twenty-ninth and was virtually a charnal ship, twenty-four of the crew having died of the scurvy, leaving but two alive. The voyage had taken 110 days.

The disastrous conditions aboard the *San Carlos* were the result of two misfortunes. First, their barrels of water had leaked and the crew, most of them already weak with sickness, had to land to obtain water. What they found was not potable and they worsened and some died. Secondly, they were the victims of miscalculations in navigation. Gálvez, believing the port to be at a latitude of 33 or 34 degrees north, commanded that the captain put well out to sea and to head for this degree and then make toward land for the port. In reality, the latitude proved to be only 32 degrees, 34 minutes, according to observations made by the captain, and the ship went too far north and the port could not be located. The voyage lengthened and the already sickened crew suffered from the extreme cold and had to continue drinking the impure water until they were in such a state they would háve all died had they not finally reached the port of San Diego. The crew was too weak to man the launch to go ashore in search of fresh water, or to manage the sails or hoist the anchor. When the *San Carlos* entered the harbor of San Diego where the *San Antonio* stood at anchor, the two ships displayed their colors and fired salutes as a greeting after their lengthy separation. So many of the men aboard the *San Antonio* were totally disabled, and the two priests were so busy taking care of them, little had been done about finding a landing place. First the dead had to be buried and then the shores explored for a good campsite. The stalwart Fages and Costansó, along with the mate Estorace, the missionary Fathers, and a few sailors and soldiers were ordered ashore for this purpose, and, after searching for a day, chose a site near the beach beside a stream of clear fresh water, and where a number of Indian families were living. The ships moved closer in to the shore, and after a crude barricade of limbs and branches from trees growing in the vicinity was constructed, tents were put inside the enclosure and the sick moved ashore. Cannon were brought from the ships for protection.

Dr. Pedro Prat, although suffering from the same malady, made every effort to give succor and relief to the ailing men. He searched the hillsides for herbs with healing powers, but despite his untiring efforts the men died one after the other. He had hoped that the benefits of fresh air and sunlight, after the miserable cramped dark quarters of the ship, would prove beneficial, and to some, of course, the move was helpful. Funerals were held practically every day.

Supplies were running alarmingly low and the two ship captains conferred on what their plans should be in case neither of the landing parties arrived. Pérez, despite the disabled crew, had been on the verge of sailing northward to Monterey when the San Carlos arrived, thinking the ship had gone on without waiting for him. The possibility and necessity of sending one of the ships back for supplies and to make a report to Gálvez was considered, but there were not enough men in the combined crews who were physically capable of manning even the smaller vessel. On Wednesday, May 10, Costansó reported to Captain Vila, who was himself by this time unable to walk, that only eight of the men on shore were able to work and that Captain Pérez and Father Parrón were also ill. The situation appeared almost hopeless.

Desperately and anxiously all eyes turned toward the south, watching for the land divisions. Scouts went out daily to make unsuccessful attempts to find the overland parties and question the Indians. On May 14 the Indians reported that strangers were approaching from the south. In great rejoicing, the soldiers, who were able to do so, grabbed guns in their painfully swollen hands and fired a volley, which was immediately answered by Rivera's men.

He had arrived after traveling fifty-one days and covering a distance of over four hundred miles from Velicatá to San Diego. They had fared quite well except for occasional lack of water, although some of his Indians had died and others had deserted along the way.

Portolá's party, with Father Serra, arrived on July 1, having been on the way forty-eight days with no lives lost except for some of the

Indians. Thirty-two of the forty-four Indians who had started failed to reach San Diego. They had either died or deserted.

While the situation at San Diego was discouraging, Portolá, disciplined soldier that he was, began making preparations for continuing his part of the expedition northward to Monterey. He was determined to do his duty and carry out the orders which had been given him. He agreed with the ship captains that one of the vessels should be sent back for relief.

The *San Antonio* started on the return trip on July 9. Pérez, still weak from his illness, had only eight sailors as a crew instead of the twenty-eight who had made the original voyage with him. Since this might be the last opportunity for some time for sending letters, Serra hastily penned a note to Palóu and another to Andrés at San Fernando. He asked for two things: for his personal needs, he requested that his underthings be replaced, for despite his efforts to mend it along the road, his tunic had grown very worn and ragged. He then wrote to his superior at the college making the following request: "Above all, let those who are to come here as missionaries not imagine that they are coming for any other purpose but to endure hardships for the love of God and for the salvation of souls, for in far-off places such as these, where there is no way for the old missions to help the new ones because of the great distance between them, the presence of pagans, and the lack of communication by sea, it will be necessary in the beginning to suffer many real privations. However, all things are sweet to a lover. But these, my poor creatures [the Indians], have cost incomparably more to my Lord Jesus Christ."

The other part of the plan was that the *San Carlos* would sail for Monterey as soon as enough of her sailors recovered sufficiently. After doing everything in his power to ease the suffering of the sick, Portolá made preparations for his northward journey. The camp had been moved back from the shore about a league to the right bank of the river and placed upon the slight rise of a hill. He was eager to get started as soon as possible because he was fearful that the snows upon the mountains might impede their progress. Since the region through which they must pass was unknown, he felt the necessity of an immediate departure was imperative. Leaving enough soldiers to guard the fortified enclosure and Padres Junípero, Parrón, and Viscaíno to administer to the sick under Dr. Prat's guidance, Portolá set forth on July 14. That Friday morning Mass was celebrated in honor of St. Joseph, patron of the expedition. As he stated some years later in recalling the journey, "I gathered the small portion of food which had not been spoiled in the ships and went on by land to Monterey with that small company of persons, or rather say skeletons, who had been spared by scurvy, hunger, and thirst." They departed about four o'clock in the afternoon.

Once again, eager as he was to accompany the exploration party, it was Serra's lot to remain behind because of devotion to duty and to watch the colorful parade depart. Portolá rode at the head of the column, accompanied by Lieutenant Fages, and by Ensign Costansó, the two priests and the six regular soldiers following. The Indians who had accompanied the land parties from the start, carrying spades, axes, mattocks, and crowbars to clear the way, build bridges, and set up camps, came next. Long pack trains, divided into four divisions, each with a number of muleteers and a guard of soldiers, followed, with Rivera and the rest of the soldiers and Indians bringing up the rear. In addition, Captain Ortega commanded a party of scouts who were to move ahead one day in advance to select the safest routes, locate camping places provided with adequate water and forage for the animals, and wood for fires.

In this party accompanying Portolá were some of the names that were to gain fame and to go down in the annals of California history. Among the personnel were: "Portolá, the first governor; Rivera, commandante of California from 1773–77; killed in the Yuma revolt on the Colorado in 1781; Fages, first commandante of California, 1769–73; governor 1782–90; Ortega, pathfinder, explorer, discoverer of the Golden Gate and of Carquinez Strait; lieutenant and brevet captain, commandante of the presidio of San Diego, of Santa Barbara, and of Monterey; founder of the presidio of Santa Barbara and the missions of San Juan Capistrano and San Buenaventura. Among the rank and file were men whose names were not less known: Pedro Amador, who gave his name to Amador County; Juan Bautista Alvarado, grandfather of Governor Alvarado; José Raimudo Carrillo, later Alferez, lieutenant, and captain, commandante of the presidio of Monterey, of Santa Barbara, and of San Diego, and founder of the great Carrillo family; José Antonio Yorba, a sergeant of the Catalonian volunteers, founder of the family of that name, and grandee of the Rancho Santiago de Santa Ana; Pablo de Cota, José Ignacio Olivera, José María Soberanes, and others."*

The long train of the exploration party had scarcely wound over the first hill and disappeared from sight, when Serra turned to the immediate task at hand. "That ardent zeal," wrote Palóu, "which ever burned and consumed the heart of our Venerable Father Fr. Junípero did not permit him to forget the principal object of his coming."

* The March of Portolá and the Discovery of the Bay of San Francisco. Zoeth S. Eldredge. The California Promotion Committee. San Francisco, 1909.

Thus it was, that two days after Portolá's departure, Serra began efforts to establish a mission.

Unfortunately, Serra was so preoccupied with the duties of administering to the sick and dying, while at the same time laying plans for founding the mission, he made no further entries into his diary, consequently there is no written record of this event. However, since there are records of the procedure followed in the establishment of subsequent missions, it is undoubtedly safe to assume that the same took place on this occasion.

Serra would have busied himself directing the selection of trees to be felled for lumber out of which the Cross, sacred symbol of Christianity, was to be constructed. The Cross would have been blessed and the ground upon which it was to be placed sprinkled with holy water and sanctified. Serra, assisted by Father Parrón, and garbed in appropriate religious robes, would have then raised the Holy Cross in the spot which seemed to him most appropriate for the building of the future city and within sight of the harbor. The Mass would have been chanted, following which Serra would have preached a sermon. The soldiers who were able, probably fired their muskets in lieu of music and incense and then all would have joined in an effort to chant the "Te Deum." Serra had chosen Sunday, July 16, for this auspicious event, for this was the day of Our Lady of Mount Carmel, and also that of the Triumph of the Holy Cross—the anniversary of the great victory won by the Spaniards over the Moors in 1212.

The few men, who were well enough and had the strength, began building little shacks out of logs and thatched with tules. One of these was set apart as a chapel and the missionaries then redoubled their efforts to attract the Indians to the place, but the natives remained suspicious and fearful of all advances made toward them. They accepted gifts of beads and other trinkets but refused every gift of food, even sugar which they spat out when it was put into the mouths of some of the children. Possibly the Indians, noticing the bloated faces and hands of the strangers lying so ill upon their pallets, suspected that the food in some manner was harmful or poisonous. They were equally adamant against accepting Baptism.

The Indians in the area were bold and not as appealing in appearance as those Serra had encountered along the trek from Baja California. Not satisfied with the slight gifts proffered them, they began pilfering and growing more aggressive, started annoying the sick and stealing the blankets from their beds. They seemed to be mostly interested in cloth and one night they went out in their canoes and were caught trying to cut the sails off the *San Carlos*. It was necessary to place guards everywhere to keep off the marauding Indians. The main difficulty the missionaries faced was that of communication. The many tribes in the San Diego vicinity spoke a different language from the Indians who had served so well as interpreters.

One Indian, a boy of about fifteen, began visiting the mission. Since he did not steal and accepted food from them, the missionaries hoped that some progress could be made through this boy. But they were to be disheartened again when the Indians, growing restless, attacked, and armed force by the soldiers was required to subdue them. The Indians had watched the activities of the priests and soon learned that on Holy Days it was necessary for one of the Fathers to go aboard the ship to celebrate Mass, taking with him two of the soldiers and thus reducing the strength of the little encampment. On the night of August 15 the Indians swarmed down in great numbers and began to steal everything they could find. The four soldiers on duty quickly armed themselves and they were aided by the carpenter and by the blacksmith, Chacón. That morning Chacón had received Holy Communion and ran about without a leather jacket to protect him. As Palóu noted, "For without doubt the Holy Communion he had just received filled him with extraordinary courage and though he had no leather jacket to protect him he went about among the houses and shacks crying out, 'Long live the Faith of our Lord Jesus Christ, and let these dogs of enemies die the death,' firing at the same time upon the pagan."

During the altercation, Father Serra and his assistant knelt within the tiny chapel and prayed, commending all to God and that there might be no deaths among the men, and also praying for the lives of the Indians to be spared that they might not die without benefit of Baptism. Father Viscaíno raised the curtain slightly to peer out and check upon the progress of events and immediately had his hand pierced by an arrow. Although the wound later healed, the hand remained crippled.

As the battle continued, the servant José María Vergerano, who had attended to the priests since coming from the region of Guadalajara, rushed in and falling down at Serra's feet cried out in pain, "Father, absolve me, for the Indians have killed me." They administered Absolution and "helped him to die well," but the little hut was a "sea of blood." "All during this time," Serra was to write a friend later, "the exchange of shots from the firearms and the arrows continued. Only four of our group fired while more than twenty of theirs shot arrows. I continued to stay with the departed one, thinking over the imminent probability of following myself, yet I kept begging God to give victory to our Holy Catholic Faith without the loss of a single soul." Besides the injured priest, a Christian Indian from San Ignacio and Chacón, the blacksmith, were wounded, but these all recovered.

The Indians carried away their wounded and their dead and cremated them to the wailing of the grieving women. The Indians, realizing that the weapons of the Spaniards were so fierce they were defenseless against them, became docile. To the surprise of the Spaniards, the savages returned with their wounded, asking for medical assistance which Dr. Prat administered to them until they were healed. While the battle, which was the first in the conquest of California, seemed to have brought about a change in the attitude of the Indians, the soldiers, nevertheless, built a stockade of poles enclosing the camp and chapel, and the Indians were prohibited from entering. A guard was always on duty both on the ship and on shore until the exploring party returned.

While the Indians were willing to accept the medical ministrations, they continued their resistance to conversion and an entire year passed without a single Baptism, although the Padres continued their efforts to gain the good will and interest of the natives. Finally the youth once again started coming every day to the mission and ate whatever was offered to him. He began to learn enough Spanish so Serra could make the boy understand that he wished for him to bring a baby, with the consent of its parents, for Baptism. Serra explained that he wanted to put water on the child's head and in that way he would become a child of God and would receive gifts of clothing so he could go dressed as were the Spaniards. The youth understood and in a few days returned with one of the Indian men carrying a child in his arms. The man indicated willingness to have the child baptized. Serra was overjoyed and gave him some cloth with which to cover the naked child and assembled the soldiers and asked the corporal to act as sponsor at this first Baptism. The Indians watched with interest and crowded about the priest. Serra had almost finished the ceremony and was about to pour water upon the child when the father snatched it away from the corporal and ran away to the Indian village, leaving the Padre standing with the shell in his hand. The soldiers wanted to avenge the insult, but Serra restrained them. This was such a moment of sadness and disappointment to Serra that never again in his life could he mention the incident without tears springing to his eyes. At that sorrowful time he could not know that because of his labors, 1046 Indians, counting children and adults, would some day in the future be baptized at the Mission San Diego.

The days were long and dragged wearily by as Serra and his

assistant watched from the hill for the relief vessel to return bringing replenishment for the supplies which were growing dangerously low. The *San Antonio* had not returned, and in vain did they expect the *San José*, whose fate as yet was unknown to them. The *San Carlos* rode idly in the harbor for there were not enough sailors to man her either for a return trip to San Blas or to make the effort to find Monterey.

All the years of sacrifice and discipline had given Serra an inner strength and resiliency. He could find solace only in prayer. His tenacity never permitted his hopes to weaken and he believed that all would be well. He tried to comfort the men about him who were frightened and disheartened and cut completely off from the rest of the world. There is no record of the way in which the Christmas season was celebrated. Serra, remembering in his heart the joyous observances of his childhood in Petra, and of the happy torchlight processions and the little playlets the Indian children acted in Jalpan, undoubtedly tried to make some observation of the Nativity, but his heart surely must have ached over the frustration of not having brought about a single conversion during the six and a half months that Portolá was on the expedition to Monterey.

It was not until the noon hour on January 24, 1770, that Portolá and his band of weary, hungry, and dispirited men were sighted staggering through the mouth of the canyon below. Shots were fired in jubilation that all had survived the difficult journey and warm *abrazos* were given with friends pounding each other on the back in happiness. The men brought with them a terrible stench. For, as Portolá wrote, "In order that we might not die, I ordered that at the end of each day's march, one of the weak old mules which carried our baggage and ourselves, should be killed. The flesh we roasted or half fried in a fire made in a hole in the ground. The mule being thus prepared, without a grain of salt or other seasoning—for we had none—we shut our eyes and fell on that scaly mule (what misery!) like hungry lions. We ate twelve in as many days, obtaining from them perforce all our sustenance, all our appetite, all our delectation. At last we entered San Diego, smelling frightfully of mules."

They recounted their adventures and held their audience spellbound. They had marched through land which had never known a Christian and had traversed over one thousand leagues. They told of how they came to a region of gently rolling hills and entered a canyon when they were but a few days out upon their trek. There in the shelter of a large boulder by a spring they chanced upon two Indian mothers holding critically sick children in their arms. Gently and tenderly, by means of sign language, the friars persuaded the grieving women to permit them to christen the babies and name them María Magdalena and Margarita. In this manner occurred the first Baptisms in Alta California, and when the little girls died, the soldiers buried them and marked their graves. The spot was officially entered into the records of the Portolá expedition as San Apolinario, but Costansó, the engineer of the expedition, noted in his diary that the name of the place was Cañada del Bautismo (Canyon of the Baptism). The affectionate name the soldiers used was to be the one which would persist—and the ravine fed by the waters from the spring of Agua de la Piedra would henceforth be known as Los Cristianitos (Little Christians).

Having completed his report, it became apparent to Serra that Portolá had found the Bay of San Francisco, but had completely missed Monterey. In dismay and disbelief Serra incredulously cried out, "You come from Rome without having seen the Pope." He knew that Monterey actually existed and that it was a certainty it would be found sooner or later. How Portolá had failed to locate the port was incomprehensible to Serra.

Immediately upon his return Portolá realized that the situation facing him as commander was serious indeed. Supplies were limited and would surely vanish rapidly with the addition of his seventy-four men to feed. He looked around and saw that very little had been accomplished during his absence. The usually reliant Serra, having made no converts, could not draw upon the natives for a labor force with which to construct a permanent church, and the remaining men of his own party, for many more had died, were still too weak to perform heavy labor. Serra had hopefully looked to assistance from Portolá in getting the mission building underway as soon as the governor returned. When he made a request for help, Portolá, who had always been co-operative and interested, now showed complete indifference. His men were exhausted from the long frustrating expedition and he was anxious over the failure of the *San Antonio* to arrive with supplies and replacements for the crews. He felt that it was not the propitious time to undertake new projects. His anxiety increased as the days passed and no ship arrived.

Portolá wrote to a friend: "We remained at San Diego nine months waiting for the *San Antonio*, subsisting for that long period on geese and the fish and other food which the Indians brought us in exchange for clothing. Some of the soldiers were left with barely enough clothing to cover their backs, having given up the rest to avoid perishing from want. We planted a small quantity of corn in the best soil, but, although it grew well, the birds ate the best of it while it was yet soft, leaving us disappointed and bereft of the hope we had cherished of eating the grain which our hands had sown."

Holding out until what he considered to be the last possible moment, Portolá finally told Serra that they could not hold out indefinitely, and that San Diego would probably have to be abandoned if they were to save the men from starvation. He set the deadline of March 19, the feast of St. Joseph, the patron of the expedition, and said that if no ship had arrived by that date, he and his men would begin the return march the next morning.

Portolá began making prudent plans. Rivera, with most of the soldiers who were able to make the trip, was sent to Velicatá to round up the cattle which had been left there and to bring back any other supplies which they might be able to gather. If a relief vessel should arrive in the interval, these supplies he brought would be added to the general stores. If a ship did not come and a retreat by land was necessary, Portolá would intercept Rivera's party on the way back. Portolá had taken an inventory of the supplies on hand, and after setting aside a portion for the return trip, found that there would barely be enough food to last to the middle of March, thus confirming the wisdom of his decision to leave on the twentieth of that month.

The announcement for the abandonment of San Diego came as an almost mortal blow to Serra. The very thought of forfeiting the long dreary hours, the pain, and the sacrifices so many people had given to the effort, was beyond endurance. Concerning this Palóu wrote, "All these rumors and plans were as so many arrows which penetrated the fervent heart of our Venerable Father President, who unceasingly laid this matter before God in his prayers, asking Him to grant the arrival of the ship before the date assigned for the retreat in order that the opportunity might not be lost of converting to God the great host of Gentile souls which were at hand and which, if it were not then accomplished, might be forever impossible, or at least be deferred for many years. It should be remembered that the number of Spaniards who had come to this port by sea only and who had passed from sight reached the number of one hundred and seventy-six and if now, it should be abandoned, many centuries would pass before another such effort could be made."

In his agony Serra as always turned to prayer. It was the time of his Gethsemane. The thought of the thousands of savages being denied the blessings of the Church roused his apostolic zeal to a fervent conviction. He would remain. The others could retreat to safety, but he had directed every moment of his life toward this place and the conversion of these Indians. He sought out Father Crespí and told him of his determination. Crespí agreed to remain behind with him, in the event that a ship failed to arrive and Portolá began the retreat.

In his troubled frame of mind, Serra wrote to Palóu and lamented the lack of converts saying, "The slow steps with which everything moves and the fears we have that there will not be so great a harvest, although it seems to me it could not be more ready for the cutting and for us to thrust forth our hands for its gathering, as all can see and feel in view of so many things which have happened around us. Beloved Brother, for the love of God try from where you are to use all the influence you have that this work may go on."

Later in the same letter when writing of the possible abandonment of San Diego, he added, "Four of us remain here, Fathers Juan Crespí, Fr. Fernando Parrón, Fr. Francisco Gómez and myself, to see if, in case the ships should arrive, we may be able to found a second Mission. If we see the provisions are exhausted and also our hope, then I shall remain with only Fr. Juan to endure up to the very last. May God give us of His Holy Grace. Please commend us to God that so it may be."

Serra appealed to Captain Vila to permit the two friars to board the *San Carlos* and remain in the harbor until the arrival of the relief ship in the event Portolá and the others departed, while he and Crespí remained ashore. The captain agreed and thus, Serra and Crespí, if all else failed, could also find refuge aboard the *San Carlos*.

Once again Serra turned to prayer. He proposed to Portolá that the entire settlement join in a novena of prayers to St. Joseph. Daily during the nine days of prayer, the soldiers and sailors joined in observing Mass and daily Serra anxiously scanned the ocean for sight of the relief ship. On the morning of March 19, the day of the feast of St. Joseph and the last day of grace before the retreat was scheduled, Serra celebrated High Mass and preached.

About three o'clock that afternoon shouts went out from the observers watching high on the hill. The sails of a ship were sighted.

It was the long-awaited *San Antonio*. The march south was delayed by Portolá despite the fact that the ship did not enter the harbor but continued northward. She was heading for Monterey, but upon reaching the vicinity of Santa Barbara lost an anchor. The sailors learned from the Indians when they went ashore for fresh water that the Portolá party had returned to the south. The *San Antonio* turned south and reached San Diego four days later.

To the joy of both Portolá and Junípero Serra, San Diego and California were saved. Portolá would now resume his northward search for Monterey and claim California for Spain. Serra could move steadily toward the realization of his life's dream—a chain of beautiful missions and thousands of Indian converts. As long as he lived, Serra was to recall the benefaction of God in permitting the arrival of the *San Antonio* and celebrated a High Mass on the nineteenth of every month of the year in remembrance.

CHAPTER XXII

MONTEREY, 1773–84

Portolá read the letters from Visitador-General Gálvez which the *San Antonio* had brought and then, checking over the supplies, made the immediate decision to seek Monterey once again. This was the assignment Gálvez gave him and this was his goal, dutiful soldier that he was. He ordered that some of the provisions be unloaded from the ship and left with Fathers Parrón and Gómez who were remaining at San Diego with eight soldiers, a muletcer, and twelve neophyte Indians under the charge of Sergeant José Francisco Ortega.

Junípero boarded the *San Antonio* along with Costansó and Dr. Prat the day before Easter, the ship sailing from San Diego after the celebration of Easter services. The voyage was perilous and slow due to contrary winds which pushed them southward and off course, so that it took forty-six days of sailing to reach Monterey.

Portolá set out with the land party of thirty men. The thirteen Catalán volunteers were once again commanded by Fages, with Crespí, as usual, serving as diarist. The overland party traveled over familiar terrain and arrived a week before the ship.

While the pack train was being unloaded so that camp could be set up Portolá, Father Crespí, and Lieutenant Fages went to the site of the Cross, which they put up on their previous unsuccessful trip, and found that Indians had placed fish and foodstuffs at its base, because they believed it had magical powers. As the three were returning to the bay to see if the *San Antonio* might have hoved into sight, they observed that the sea in the whole immense bay was so calm that it resembled a large lake. In it were swimming and barking innumerable sea wolves, and near the shore there were two large whale cubs not farther than five yards from the land, a clear indication that there was a good depth. They traveled a short distance along the same beach and soon perceived that the bay was locked by points Año Nuevo and Pinos, in such a manner that the great bay resembled a round lake like an "o." Upon seeing this the three broke out with one voice: "This is the port of Monterey that we were seeking, for this is the letter described by Sebastian Vizcaíno and Cabrera Bueno."

A week later, on the afternoon of May 31, they sighted the

San Antonio, and Portolá ordered three signal fires be lighted, the prearranged signal to let them know the land expedition had arrived. The ship immediately acknowledged the signals by firing the cannon, and then following charts drawn by Cabrera in 1603, without departing from the descriptions he gave, the vessel entered the harbor until it reached a point just beyond the Point Pinos and dropped anchor in six fathoms. Monterey had indeed been found.

They fixed June 3 as the day for the taking of formal possession and built a small arbor on the same spot under the stalwart oak where Mass had been celebrated by the Viscaíno expedition long ago. A table formed the altar and bells were hung and with their pealing the festival began.

Serra, dressed in alb and stole, with all of the assemblage kneeling, conducted the solemn services and afterward they all joined in erecting the large wooden Cross that had been prepared for this purpose. The Mass was chanted before the image of Our Lady, which had been loaned to the expedition by Gálvez, after Serra had sprinkled all the fields and beach of the harbor with holy water to frighten away any lurking infernal enemies. Cannon salvos and shots from handguns and other firearms served in place of music.

The religious services having been completed, Portolá as commander, started the civil ceremonies whereby he took possession of the land in the name of Don Carlos III, King of Spain, and the royal standard was raised. The customary acts of taking possession such as pulling up grass and throwing of stones then were performed. "From this day," wrote Palóu, "Divine worship began and the famous port of Monterey came under the dominion and lordship of our King." Afterward the members of the land and sea parties joined together and had a picnic on the shore of the harbor. On that June 3, 1770, the Presidio and the Mission of Monterey were formally inaugurated.

"To God alone can be given all the honor and the glory," Serra wrote Palóu, telling him of the recent happenings. He then added wryly, "As regards the fact that this port could not be found by the members of the other expedition and that they had given out that it no longer existed, I have nothing to say, nor is it incumbent upon me to judge in the matter."

Portolá assisted in the rapid construction of a few huts and one, which was slightly larger than the others, was dedicated as the chapel and a wooden stockade was built to enclose all of the structures for defense against the Indians. Few of the natives had been seen as they doubtless had been frightened by the gunfire, and it would be quite a lengthy time until their fright was overcome by the priests who offered them trinkets to win their confidence. The first Baptism did not take place until December 26, when a six-year-old boy was christened Bernardino de Jesús.

Governor Portolá turned over the military command of the Presidio to Lieutenant Fages as soon as the Corpus Christi celebrations were over. He felt that he had fulfilled his responsibilities and had carried out Gálvez's orders by locating Monterey and claiming it for the crown of Spain. Accompanied by Dr. Prat and Costansó, Portolá boarded the *San Antonio* on July 9 and sailed for Mexico after having dispatched messengers overland to carry the triumphant news to the Viceroy and to Gálvez. Portolá landed at San Blas and sped the good news on to Mexico City. His messages arrived there before the soldiers coming overland.

The news of the founding of the two missions and the establishment of a Presidio in Monterey was joyously received by De Croix and especially Gálvez, who had been somewhat in disrepute since the period immediately following the departure of the "Sacred Expedition" from Loreto into Alta California. He had immediately embroiled himself in the military campaigns against the Indians in Sonora, actually serving in the thick of the battles. It was shortly after this that his health broke and his mind was deranged by persistent fevers. During this period of mental and physical colllapse, Gálvez had irrational delusions of paranoidal self-aggrandizement and alternately thought himself to be various saintly figures as well as the King himself. In maniacal frenzies, Gálvez dashed off numerous reports and on one of the papers he wrote, in a flash of pathetic rationality, "Joseph de Gálvez, insane for this unhappy world; pray God for him that he may be happy in the next."

He tried desperately to carry on his duties when he recovered sufficiently to return to Mexico City, but he was constantly troubled by his recurring illness. Thus it was that he was exceedingly pleased, after over a year's silence, to receive Serra's message which Portolá had forwarded to him telling of the success of the project. He ordered a ringing of bells at the Cathedral and other churches in the capital of Mexico "proclaiming with this glad peal the joy that he felt in his heart, on account of the importance of that port to the crown of our King," wrote Palóu, "and as an act of thanksgiving for the happy outcome of the expedition, and the extension by them of the dominions of our sovereign with more than three hundred leagues of good lands well populated with heathen, who little by little would be reduced to our Holy Catholic faith." Spain was in control of the California shores as far north as the 38th parallel. A special Mass was held which was attended by both De Croix and Gálvez along with all of the other public officials. A lengthy proclamation was printed and widely circulated, telling of the successful venture. At Serra's request, his name was not mentioned in connection with the success of the venture and Gálvez modestly refrained from mentioning himself or of claiming credit for being the innovator of the idea, but he and De Croix were widely congratulated. Gálvez's fame was certain and to him would go the credit for conceiving the daring plan of making secure the over 450 miles of coast land of Alta California for Spain. He would return to Spain two years later, in 1772, physically and mentally ill, without ever having stepped upon the soil of the fabled land which had been the lodestar of his life.

Junípero, in his report to the father guardian of the college, had asked that two more friars be sent so that the Mission San Buenaventura might be founded. The Viceroy ordered thirty to be sent, ten of them to go to Upper California and the others to be stationed in Baja California. With a renewed burst of enthusiasm toward getting the new missions founded, he assigned 10,000 pesos for this purpose, and 400 pesos to defray the traveling cost of each friar who was also promised an annual salary of 375 pesos. The supply of agricultural implements and the new vestments which Serra had also requisitioned were readied and shipped, along with the newly arrived priests from Spain, on board the *San Carlos* and the *San Antonio*. A full cargo of provisions was also sent. Rivera returned from San Diego with 80 mules loaded with supplies and driving a small herd of cattle a short time earlier. With the ample supplies and the extra priests Serra was elated and he felt certain that the future of his charges and his missions was assured.

His optimism was to be short-lived.

The last fourteen years of Serra's life were mostly to be spent in the region of Monterey. These would be the most challenging, frustrating, and difficult years he had ever experienced. He was to endure abuse, ridicule, chastisement from his superiors, as well as great disappointment, and would have to undergo the fears of seeing his missions threatened and faced with extinction. He would continue to grieve over the failure, despite all efforts, of the friars to convert more than a handful of the natives. He was to face starvation and, what was worse, the horror of seeing his charges go hungry—after they had trustingly placed themselves in the care of the missions—when crops failed to yield a sufficient supply of food and when supply vessels failed to arrive from San Blas. He would have to struggle against the constant vexatious delaying tactics of obdurate military commanders whose enmity he could not overcome, and whose actions prevented the founding of the missions he was so eager to establish. As his frail, tired, aging body yielded to the advances of age, he would be forced to make the long, exhausting journey to Mexico City to confer with his superior at the Colegio de San Fernando. As his illness and physical pain taxed his strength, his religious fervor burned brighter than ever. He would not, could not, succumb to the vicissitudes which assailed him from all sides.

During those long, toilsome years nine missions were founded and had it not been for the friction between Serra and the three governors, he might have added to his "ladder of missions," as he liked to refer to them. In order of their founding the missions were: San Diego, July 16, 1769; San Carlos de Monterey, June 3, 1770; San Antonio de Padua, July 14, 1771; San Gabriel, September 8, 1771; San Luis Obispo, September 1, 1772; San Francisco (Dolores), October 9, 1776; San Juan Capistrano, November 1, 1776; Santa Clara, January 18, 1777; San Buenaventura, March 31, 1782. Two of the missions, San Diego and San Juan Capistrano, would be destroyed and patiently had to be reconstructed. The sites chosen for placing the missions were fully noted in the diary Crespí wrote on the first journey toward Monterey made by the Portolá expedition in 1769.

Serra had the final approval, and the choice was with but one exception unerringly good. "Walking barefoot over those thorny miles, possessed with a burning desire to baptize, longing only to preach the everlasting gospel, one of the most devoted men who has ever followed in the footsteps of the founder of the Christian faith; yet he [Serra] knew where the land was good, where the wild grapes grew, where there were roses which reminded him of those that in his youth he had seen in the braids of the maids of old Castile."*

While the sites were carefully chosen with consideration as to their potentiality in supporting and feeding the hoped for neophytes, beauty surely must also have entered into the plan. Without an exception, each mission is located in a spot of rare beauty. Just so was it with the construction of the buildings. Utility was the prime concern, but relying entirely upon native labor and the materials close at hand, the Padres built structures of architectural grace which blended naturally into the landscape. They built of the earth, grass, water, and out of these basic elements created building blocks. Using roughhewn timbers, which sometimes had to be hauled many miles, the missions became a blending of the Old World of Spain and also assumed a distinctly individualistic appearance. "There is a tradition that adobe is more lasting than stone, and that rawhide will endure

* James Steele. *Old California Days*. Chicago, 1893.

longer than either, and these buildings were of the sun-dried bricks, whose permanency surprises every stranger."*

Both Serra and Crespí were dissatisfied with the present site chosen for the mission at Monterey and nothing much had been accomplished about the conversion of the Indians. Serra, therefore, asked for and received permission from the Viceroy to move the mission to the lovely Carmelo Valley where there were numerous natives and the land and water more suitable for stock raising and the growing of foodstuffs. It would be at this Mission San Carlos that Serra would have his "home" for the next thirteen years and it would be this place he loved so dearly that he would return to die.

The moment Serra saw that Indians had the construction of shelters well underway at Carmel, he and Father Pieras, with an escort of soldiers, set off up the Salinas valley to select a site for the next mission to be founded. They chose a lovely dell nearly sixty miles from Monterey and a five days' march, which Junípero named Valley of the Oaks or Cañada de los Robles. Nearby was a stream which he called the San Antonio. The mules were unloaded and the bells hung from a venerable old oak tree standing upon an imposing stretch of level ground. Serra began to ring the bells mightily and called out loudly, "Come, Gentiles, come to the Holy Church. Come and receive the faith of Jesus Christ!" There was not a native within sight and Father Pieras gently reproved Serra for wasting energies upon such a fruitless demonstration and suggested that it would be better if they got down to work. Thus was the Mission San Antonio de Padua founded on July 14, 1771.

*　　*　　*

When the affable Portolá departed Alta California in July 1770, Pedro Fages succeeded him and immediately Serra and he clashed in a dispute over divided authority. The basis for Fages being called governor was vague. Actually Portolá, while in Upper California, had been succeeded as governor by Matías de Armona, then by Felipe Barry, who arrived in 1771, and who in turn was succeeded by Felipe de Neve. None of these governors had any influence during this period beyond Baja California.

The main cause of the difficulty between Serra and Fages arose from this uncertainty and lack of understanding as to just where Fages's powers began and ended. He claimed that he had succeeded to all the powers Portolá had held and, therefore, believed that he had the authority to select the time and place of founding new mis-

* James Steele. *Old California Days*. Chicago, 1893.

sions. Since he had the responsibility of defending and provisioning these missions, he claimed that, because his staff and resources were limited, all plans regarding these must have his full approval. Serra, as president of the missions, was insistent that Fages had no authority over the friars or the missions, except for the few soldiers guarding them, and that Fages was merely the presidial commander. Neither would yield to the other, and while each pursued his duties assiduously and they maintained an outward agreeable relationship, the differences between them deepened as time went on. The situation was compounded by the jealousy of Rivera, who learned of Fages's appointment by Portolá when he returned from the peninsula where he had gone for supplies. He refused to follow orders and march on to Monterey and remained in San Diego, returning to Baja early the next year.

Pedro Fages was, indeed, a surprising selection for Gálvez to make. A man of brutish instincts, he proved to be everything that was contrary to the advancement of the cause the Visitador-General favored. He was generally despised by his soldiers, one of noncommissioned men reporting to the Viceroy: "At Monterey, starting from July 1770, he used to beat us, the men and ourselves, with cudgels; he would force us to buy from him, at three times their value, the figs and raisins in which he was trading; he would make sick men go and cut down trees in the rain, and would deprive them of their supper if they protested; he would put us all on half rations even though food might be rotting in the storehouse. We had to live on rats, coyotes, vipers, crows, and generally every creature that moved on the earth, except beetles, to keep from starvation. We almost all became herbivorous, eating raw grass like our horses. How many times we have wished we were six feet under ground!" Serra wrote of Fages, "In all fields, he strove to make trouble for us. . . . But what does suffering matter," he added, "if we finally succeed in accomplishing our spiritual ministry? That is the only thing that counts, after all!"

Fages had the entire responsibility of defending the territory of over four hundred miles from San Diego to Monterey with forty-three soldiers in 1770. He was able to increase this number to sixty-one in 1773 and with this insignificant number had to hold back thousands of Indians, many of whom were hostile to the Spaniards. Outbreaks occurred constantly, the most serious at San Gabriel shortly after the mission was founded.

The soldiers were for the most part a rough and reluctant military force, of lonely unschooled half-breeds who often molested the Indian women. They sometimes pretended to go out hunting, but their prey frequently was native women and these they roped and lassoed before making crude advances. This happened at San Gabriel to the wife of the Indian chief, who angrily shot an arrow which glanced off the leather shield of the guilty soldier. The Indian was killed in the uproar which followed, and his head cut off and impaled upon a pole to warn the other Indians. The natives were completely subdued and the priests comforted them and won back their confidence until the son of the slain chief was the first to come forth for Baptism.

Fages rushed six additional soldiers to San Gabriel from San Diego and announced that his remaining force was so limited he could not supply the necessary guard to protect San Buenaventura Mission. He thus delayed the founding of this mission which had been so long uppermost in Serra's mind.

The boyhood dreams Serra had on the hill of Bon Any so long ago of bringing thousands of infidels under the blessings of the Faith were slow in coming to realization. His heart was tortured and his religious zeal was as ardent as ever, but still the number of converts won remained very small. An entire year passed at San Diego before the first Baptism, and six months passed before a convert was made at San Carlos Borromeo. San Antonio and San Gabriel, founded in 1771, and San Luis Obispo in 1772, met with the same results. The Indians of the northern regions were more friendly than those in the south, but the Spaniards had few trinkets to give them and the Indians, for the most part, remained indifferent to any spiritual attractions. Rafael Verger, Father Superior of the Colegio de San Fernando in Mexico, wrote that he believed the missions of Alta California hardly warranted the name of mission. He frequently stated in his memorials of 1771 that he had never looked with favor upon the establishment of these missions and that he had acquiesced because of Gálvez's insistence. He predicted their ultimate failure and, somewhat impatient with Serra's sanguine reports, claimed that "it was necessary to moderate somewhat his ardent zeal." Rumors were rampant that the whole Alta California mission project was to be abandoned.

The year 1772 proved to be most crucial. Famine raged throughout the province. The supply ships had failed to arrive. Serra had the heartbreak of seeing his old, trusted friend Juan Crespí fail mentally and physically and go off to leave Serra alone for five months at Carmel. He had the satisfaction of having Mission San Luis Obispo established but was completely frustrated by Fages in getting San Buenaventura underway, the mission that had loomed so importantly in his mind since the very first days of the expedition northward. When Fages refused to assign soldiers for the protection of the friars,

Serra, in desperation, sailed from San Diego to present his case to Viceroy Bucareli who had succeeded De Croix.

Arriving at Tepic on November 7, he learned that the Dominicans had requested and received permission to take charge of the missions in Baja California, thus releasing Palóu and the remaining Fernandinos for service in Alta California. Journeying on to Guadalajara, Serra became seriously ill with a raging fever and while there was given Extreme Unction. He recovered sufficiently to travel on to Querétaro where he underwent a relapse and was delayed until the following month, finally reaching San Fernando barely alive on February 6, 1773. Serra presented his case to Viceroy Bucareli on February 13, and the new administrator was able to have before him a clear picture of conditions as they actually existed in Alta California.

Chevalier Antonio María Bucareli, Viceroy from September 1771 to April 1779, was understanding and sympathetic to Serra's presentation and suggested that he prepare a memoranda, which the critically ill Serra undertook and drew up six. The first contained thirty-two points for presentation to the Junta. He asked that the Port of San Blas not be abandoned, but at the same time that a new supply route be explored, so that supplies could be brought overland. He listed the various abuses of Fages and these ultimately resulted in the governor's dismissal. Serra asked for doctors, farmers, artisans of all sorts—such as blacksmiths and carpenters—to be sent along with settlers to colonize the territory. Among the other requests was one pleading that the cows, which Fages would not relinquish to the missions, forthwith be delivered to each of them.

It is to Bucareli's everlasting glory that he listened and was able to obtain most of Serra's demands in the petition, and he continued from that time to take an active interest in the welfare and development of Alta California.

Serra began the long, tiresome return trip to Monterey and learned that during May of 1773, Palóu had signed the official papers relinquishing the missions of Baja California to the Dominicans and began the long march northward accompanied by a few settlers, mules laden with church supplies, and the remaining priests. At a point about thirty miles below San Diego, he placed the royal banner in the cleft of a large boulder to announce for all the world the dividing line of authority between the two religious sects. While he and Serra were not destined to remain at the same mission, just having his old trusted friend within traveling distance was to be a never-ending comfort to Serra.

Serra sailed from San Blas and after landing at San Diego continued his journey northward toward Carmel, encountering the intrepid Juan

Bautista de Anza just south of San Luis Obispo. Anza had followed the trail first explored by Father Garces earlier and had succeeded in connecting Sonora with Alta California, establishing the badly needed overland supply route Serra had urged. Serra and Anza conferred for a brief time on April 27, 1774.

Immediately upon arriving at Monterey, Serra presented the orders to Fages informing him that he was being replaced by Rivera as governor. Fages, evidently shattered by this disciplinary action, became more amenable and Serra later wrote a letter to his superiors asking for leniency for the difficult soldier and stating that he, personally, forgave him for his actions.

Serra had been forced to secure the dismissal of Fages but Rivera, about whose appointment he was dubious from the start, proved to be more trying than the former governor. Fages functioned as governor from 1770 to 1774 and Rivera from 1774 to 1777. Rivera, the exact opposite of Fages, refused to act. He procrastinated in all matters, driving the energetic Serra to exasperation. Rivera resented suggestions coming from anyone but himself and delayed contrarily, often for months at a time, before taking any steps for advancing the spiritual and temporal causes in the province. While foodstuffs were plentiful in the warehouse, he delayed distribution of supplies so that hunger was still rampant. Serra, perforce, had to resume his letters of complaints to the superiors in Mexico.

The year 1775 was to be especially difficult for Serra. Realizing time was racing by and that the channel missions were no nearer being founded than when Fages was governor, he pleaded and harangued with the recalcitrant Rivera over the number of soldiers needed to protect the priests and little bands of Indian workers during the time of construction.

The arrival of his old friend Father Lasuén from Baja was a welcome relief to the harassed little Padre. Soon, however, he was to become puzzled by the actions of his friend, whose company he so cherished that he had stopped several days on the long, tiresome trek from Loreto to San Diego just to enjoy his conversation. Lasuén, seemingly affable enough, immediately resumed his friendship with Rivera, whom he had known while stationed in Lower California. The two became inseparable even to sharing the same quarters.

Serra, knowing full well that the Viceroy keenly wanted those channel missions built, requested the customary twelve or thirteen soldiers which he claimed could easily be spared. Rivera remained adamant and insisted that only six could be mustered for this task. Day by day the conversations grew more heated until in exasperation Serra pounded upon the table and spoke to Rivera in a loud voice.

Whereupon Rivera produced a letter from the Viceroy in which it was stated that six soldiers were to be supplied. Somehow, Serra had misread the illegible handwriting and thought that it stated thirteen. He had to admit his error and withdraw all demands for the building of the missions along the channel.

Because the Indians farther south were more tractable, it was agreed to start construction on Mission San Juan Capistrano. Serra, half apologetically and in vexation, turned to Lasuén, who had witnessed every encounter, and offered him the administration of this mission. Lasuén, despite his constant importunings for Serra to give him a mission, now considered this an insult. He looked upon Capistrano as a less favorable spot than one of the missions farther north. He wrote lengthy letters to the guardian at San Fernando stating that it was becoming increasingly more difficult to work with Serra because of his irascibility.

Lasuén would soon become disenchanted with Rivera and would realize his mistake in writing the denigrating letters. He would go on to make San Juan Capistrano one of the most successful missions in the entire chain, but as for the moment, the harm had been done and the action was to result in Serra's receiving a severe reprimand from the headquarters in San Fernando.

It was Anza who delivered the letter from headquarters castigating Serra for his actions in seeming to go around the authority of the college by writing reports to the Viceroy. The License, which was signed by every member of the descritory, deprived Serra of much of his authority, but he bowed his head and with humility accepted the rebuke and refused to give way to injured pride. His lengthy response resulted in the License being revoked, but the damage had been done.

It was during this same bleak month of March 1776 that Rivera, insensitive as always to the sanctity of the Church, refused to heed the pleas of the friars and rushed in to seize a culprit who had sought sanctuary within the Church. For this act, Rivera was excommunicated and from that time forward ate alone and was treated as a spiritual leper. He did, however, follow orders and, with Palóu, and Crespí, explored the San Francisco area and at last the mission in honor of St. Francis was founded on October 9, 1776. Serra, busily occupied in re-establishing San Juan Capistrano, had to forego the joy of being present when this long dreamed of mission in honor of the Seraphic Founder of his Order was begun. It was at San Francisco that Palóu remained and wrote his voluminous *Noticias de la Nueva California,* his almost daily historical record of the coming of the Fernandinos to replace the Jesuits in Baja California and their coming on into New California.

Another disappointment for Serra was to come during the latter part of that fateful year of 1776 when the jurisdiction of the two Californias was removed from the Viceroy and placed under that of the commandant with headquarters at Arispe, Sonora. Monterey replaced Loreto as the capital of both Californias, Felipe de Neve established himself as governor in the Presidio of Monterey, and Rivera returned to Mexico—all at the instructions of Bucareli.

De Neve, later to become one of the ablest of California governors, immediately showed his animosity toward Serra and entered into a persistent vindictive form of persecution which caused constant torment to the aging priest. The first conflict was over the amount of supplies which were to be granted to the friars at the new missions. Later De Neve challenged Serra's cherished authority to administer the rite of Confirmation to Christian converts.

Serra long had hoped to have the authority to administer the sacrament of Confirmation which usually is reserved in principle to the bishops of the Church, but in rare instances when no bishop is available, is sometimes given to priests. The prefect general of Mexico, Father García, had requested this privilege for Father Serra and it was granted by Pope Clement XIV on July 10, 1774. The papal brief arrived in Mexico in 1776, but it was not until June 10, 1778, that the authenticated certificate and copy of the instructions were received by Serra in far-off California. The "Faculty," as this was called, was for the duration of a ten-year period. Four of the precious years had slipped away due to the vast distances involved before delivery could be made. Serra immediately put into effect this most precious right of Confirmation, whereby "the Christian regenerated by Baptism" is bestowed the "energies and faculties which will permit him henceforth to live in Christ."

Within ten days Junípero had confirmed ninety children at Carmel. Two months later he sailed for a tour of Confirmations among the southern missions and confirmed 1897 by the time he returned to Carmel on Christmas Eve. He requested military escort from De Neve later the next year to go to the missions to the north and carry on his holy task of Confirmation. De Neve, not only refused the escort, but challenged Serra's right to confirm. This resulted in a bitter struggle in which Serra was finally triumphant. De Neve demanded that he discontinue the rite of Confirmation, but Serra defied this order, and performed the rites at San Francisco.

The death of his old friend, Juan Crespí, struck another cruel wound into the heart of the aging and infirm Padre. A wound from which, it is said, he never fully recovered. One ray of light came into his troubled waning life and that was the long awaited and dreamed of founding of the Mission San Buenaventura on March 31, 1782.

It was in June of the following year that the rumor of the possible danger to his missions reached Serra. He learned that there was a possibility that the Franciscans faced expulsion as had the Jesuits in 1767 and that the Dominicans might supplant them and take over the missions in Alta California.

The most serious conflict, next to the matter of the Confirmations, was De Neve's *reglamento,* ordering the establishment of a chain of new missions to be located fifteen or twenty leagues farther inland and which were to be merely a church and residence for the priests. The governmental and economic phase of the customary mission plan was to be abandoned and instead of two priests, only one was to be at each mission, and they were to be limited to religious instruction. Serra refused to put this plan into action and on this basis, in support of Serra's stand, the Colegio de San Fernando refused to send additional friars to man the missions.

Calamity followed calamity and the force of their impact took its toll upon the frail body of Junípero Serra. He resolved to sail on August 15, 1783, for San Diego and begin his last round of Confirmations. The thought of hundreds of his children being denied the comfort of this sacred rite gave him the courage to make this last trip. He prayed that strength would be granted him.

CHAPTER XXIII

THE FINAL DAYS OF JUNÍPERO SERRA

For the first time in his life, Serra's sanguine hopefulness gave way to despair. Physically exhausted with constant battling to keep his missions intact and functioning and anxious over the approaching date of expiration of his Faculty, whereby he was granted permission to bestow Confirmation, made him aware of the swift passage of time. The Faculty was to expire on July 16, 1784, and no mention of its being renewed had been made. Weary from all the internal and political struggles of the recent years, Serra knew that a new adversary had entered the race against time—Death.

His infirmities, aggravated by increasing age and ceaseless toil, had become sources of constant pain. It had become almost impossible for him to walk, and a painful respiratory malady weakened him. Whether this difficulty in catching each rasping breath was the result of those days as a walking friar, when in religious fervor he had beat upon his bare breast with stones or held lighted tapers against the flesh, as Palóu believed, or was caused by a chronic asthmatic condition, is a matter of conjecture, and there is no recorded information to rely upon for a clue.

Throughout the years Serra ignored this trouble, as he did his injured foot and leg, and refused medication saying, "Never mind, we might make it worse; I shall get along somehow." Whatever the cause of the illness, Junípero suffered constantly from "a certain heaviness of the chest, from which he was relieved only when he had discharged or vomitted certain phlegms." As his physical condition worsened, his spiritual determination increased. The thought of all the hundreds of neophytes not receiving the blessings of Confirmation was more than he could endure. He determined once again to visit the missions to the south.

He announced his plans to take a boat that was going to sail for San Blas and in a few days his friends lifted him upon a mule and he started for Monterey, leaving them with heavy hearts and fearful that his worsening condition would keep him from sailing, much less from returning by foot up the mission trail. Serra must have thought the same for he wrote to Palóu on the day of his sailing, charging him with the particular duties of his office and bidding him farewell. He closed the letter by stating, "I am very seriously ill. Commend me to God."

Arriving in San Diego and seeing the prosperous condition of the mission which had suffered so many vicissitudes and caused him such heartbreak during the first dreary months after its founding, he appeared momentarily to improve in health. Where he originally found indifferent dirty and naked savages he now saw a well-constructed church with a congregation of nearly seven hundred Indians. The mission had 1000 sheep, 500 goats, more than 200 horses, and many milk cows. On September 13 he had the great joy of entering the 606th Confirmation in the records of Mission San Diego.

Serra remained at San Diego until the second of October, reviving memories of good departed friends—Father Crespí, companion since days in Palma; his little page José María, who died in his arms; valiant Juan Pérez, pilot of the *San Antonio,* whose body was committed to the sea. Many of the Indians remembered him and brought happiness to his fervent heart. The night before leaving San Diego, Junípero baptized a six-year-old Indian boy named José Setemerp and recorded this as the 984th Baptism at San Diego.

He made his way northward visiting each mission as he traversed the 175 leagues to Monterey. Despite his worsening physical condition, Serra strove to make certain that not a single Christian was left without Confirmation. He found San Juan Capistrano prospering in the capable hands of Father Lasuén. In Mission San Gabriel his illness made it impossible for him to offer Mass, but he confirmed the little Indian boys who assisted at the altar. The pains in his chest were so severe, the Fathers thought he would die before leaving there. The altar boys wept as they saw his pain and said to the priests, "The Old Father [for so they called him] wants to die." All despaired of his living long enough to reach Mission San Buenaventura, which he had founded the year previous. The joy Serra felt at seeing the hosts of Indians awaiting his Confirmation seemed to relieve his maladies and he was able to leave much better in regard to the choking sensation in his chest.

His heart was overcome with sorrow as he passed through the beautiful regions of the Channel of Santa Barbara where for so long his dreams of founding a mission there had been thwarted by lack of interest and a sufficient supply of friars. He visited missions San Antonio and San Luis Obispo and returned to San Carlos in January of 1784 to the surprise and joy of all those who had thought they would never see him again when he left for San Diego.

Lenten season was upon him again and he performed all the responsibilities of this holy season so dear to his heart. Then without allowing time for rest, he set off to visit the missions to the north. He left his mission the latter part of April, going directly to San Francisco, bypassing Santa Clara, which he intended to visit on his return trip in time for the dedicatory services in the middle of May. Palóu was overjoyed at seeing his master and teacher and hoped to have the pleasure of his companionship for a few days, but fate intervened when word came that Father Murguía was seriously ill. Palóu hastened to the bedside of Father Murguía and found him seriously ill and with a high fever. He administered the Holy Sacraments to this faithful friend and companion of twenty-six years of missionary service among the Pames of the Sierra Gorda. Murguía, one of the original band of friars accompanying Serra when he first assumed supervision of the missions on Baja California at the time of the expulsion of the Jesuits, had remained there even after the departure of Palóu, to deliver these same missions into the hands of the Dominicans. It was then that he came to rejoin his friends and to found Mission Santa Clara, building a large stone church. His death, coming quickly after the administrations of Palóu, was a sad blow to Junípero Serra.

It was a grieving Serra who arrived at Santa Clara for the blessing of the Church and who preached an eloquent and fervent sermon despite his sorrow over the death of his friend. Once the dedicatory ceremonies were over, Palóu expecting to return immediately to San Francisco, was surprised when Serra detained him saying that he "wished to prepare himself for death, as it might be," recalled Palóu in the diary, "that we would not see each other again, and as he felt so seriously ill that it could not now be very long before the end would come." The two old friends spent days in spiritual exercises, making their Confessions to each other. "I feared," wrote Palóu, "that this would be the last time that I should see him, as it could not be what both of us so much desired, viz., that we should die together, or at least, that one should be able to accompany the other in his last moments, and as his Reverence was looking forward to going back to his Mission and I to mine, making a distance of forty-two leagues all inhabited by pagans, it would not be easy for us to enjoy this privilege."

Even though preoccupied with his preparations for death, Serra continued baptizing a few Indians and even went out into the countryside to those who were unable because of sickness to come to the mission. Immediately upon returning to San Carlos, Serra feverishly resumed his apostolic labors of instructing all those who had not received Confirmation. He was rushing against time for his Faculty had not been renewed and was up for expiration on July 16. By the time this happened, Serra had confirmed 5307 persons and it was on that same day he received the sad news which was a death blow to his frail body. A vessel arrived from San Blas carrying supplies and a letter which dashed all Serra's hopes for future expansion of the missions which he had hoped to found before his death. The Reverend Father Guardian had written to say that no more friars would be coming since the ranks of those at San Fernando had been decreased by infirmity and death and the failure of new recruits to arrive from Spain.

According to Palóu this information was a hard blow to the fervent heart of the venerable Father Serra, because he saw his desires frustrated. When he read the letter it was as though he also read in it the announcement of his own death. Serra wrote the missionaries in the south, telling them of the arrival of this vessel and the letter and then bade them farewell for eternity. He then wrote the Fathers of the nearby missions of San Antonio and San Luis Obispo and requested that one representative from each come and receive the supplies brought by the ship, and he expressed the desire to speak with them and bid them good-by. He wrote to Palóu and asked him to come to him by land or sea in whichever manner seemed better.

In the *Vida*, or biography, Palóu later wrote about his friend, giving a day by day and almost hourly account of Serra's approaching death. This is one of literature's most poignant accounts of death's relentless onslaught and the helplessness of the bystander to comfort the victim. In simple words Palóu tells the story in stark dramatic form. He tells us that he hastened overland and arrived at Mission San Carlos on the eighteenth of August to find his friend very weakened and suffering acutely with the heaviness in his chest, but withal, attending daily services and singing Mass in his usual melodious voice. Palóu, cheered by the sight of his friend attending church, said to a soldier standing nearby, "The Father President does not seem to be so very sick."

The soldier who had been with Serra since the early days in Mexico responded sadly, "Father, we must not be too confident; he is sick, but this Saintly Father, when it comes to praying and singing, is always well; but he is almost finished."

The next day Serra was too ill to sing the Mass in honor of St. Joseph as he was accustomed to do every month and asked Palóu to act in his stead. Serra took his place in the choir. After the service, the two old friends conversed quietly and discussed all the points Serra had in mind. Whenever Palóu went into the small cell Serra occupied, he found him very much absorbed in quiet prayer. Five days after Palóu's arrival a packet boat arrived in port and the royal surgeon called and applied medication to Serra's chest. Serra permitted the poultice to be applied and then went about cutting bolts of material which had arrived on the vessel into lengths to be given to the Indians to clothe themselves.

The morning of August 26 Junípero was exhausted and told Palóu that he wished to make disposition of himself in order that God might dispose of him. He withdrew into himself and spent the entire day in silent meditation and that night, after making his complete Confession once again to Palóu, he managed to drink a cup of broth and then lay down saying that he wished to be completely alone.

The next day he asked Palóu to consecrate a Host and to keep it in reserve. Palóu did this and after Mass went to tell his friend that such was in readiness. Serra insisted, in spite of all Palóu's pleadings, that since he could walk, he would go to church and into the presence of his Lord to receive the Most Divine Viaticum. Serra walked the hundred yards to the church accompanied by the commander of the garrison and the Indians of the village who wept with sorrow as they looked upon their Padre with extreme tenderness and affection.

Serra knelt at a little table prepared for this service and then after receiving the Holy Viaticum withdrew into his cell and seating himself in a chair fell into deep abstraction while Palóu stood guard outside and would not let anyone enter. The carpenter came and said that Serra had sent for him to come and measure for the coffin and insisted upon seeing the ailing priest. Palóu remained firm and would not permit Serra's profound silence and reflection to be interrupted, finally saying to the carpenter to "make the coffin just as you made the one for Father Crespí."

That night Serra's condition worsened and he asked for and received the Holy Sacrament while seated upon a small stool made of rushes. Serra spent a sleepless night kneeling with his aching breast pressed against the boards of his bed or against the body of one of the Indian converts who had crowded into the cell to be with him during the long night. It was in this manner that he was able to obtain some relief. Palóu, seeing his friend so exhausted and leaning upon the Indians, inquired of the surgeon how he thought Serra was. The surgeon replied, "It appears to me that the Venerable Father is anxious to die upon the floor."

Serra asked for and received Absolution and the application of Plenary Indulgence and seemed to be greatly comforted by this. The next day was August 28, the day of St. Augustine, and he spent the entire day seated upon the little stool leaning against the bed. This plain little bed, Serra's only material possession in this world, is described by Palóu in the following manner: "This consisted of a few hard boards roughly hewn and covered with only a blanket, which he used rather to cover himself with than to soften his couch for resting, and he did not even have a sheep skin as is the custom of the College. He always slept this way when on the road, stretching out on the ground a blanket, and a pillow and lying down upon them to get the necessary rest, sleeping always with a Cross upon his breast which he held in his arms. It was about a foot in length and he had carried it since he lived in the novitiate of the College and had never left it behind, but always took it with him on his journeys together with the blanket and the pillow. In the Mission, and in other places where he stopped, as soon as he arose from the bed he would put the Cross upon the pillow."

About midmorning of St. Augustine's Day two officers from the frigate called upon Serra and he greeted them affectionately and despite his weakened condition ordered the mission bells rung in their honor. The two old friends—one, Captain and Commander Don José Cañizares, whom Serra had known since the days of 1769 and the time of the first expedition, and the other, the royal chaplain, Don Christóbal Díaz, whom Serra had known since 1779—told him of their adventures and of the voyages they had made to Peru since the last time he had seen them. He listened with interest.

When they finished, Serra said to them, "Well, sirs, I am thankful that after so long a time in which we have not seen one another and in which you have made so long a voyage that you have been able to come to this far distant port in order to place a little earth upon my body."

The guests protested and cried out, "No, Father, we trust in God that you may yet recover and continue your work of conversion." Serra, knowing that his time was drawing near spoke gently to them, "Please do me this charity and work of mercy of throwing a little earth over me and I shall be thankful to you." Then turning to Palóu he said, "I wish you to bury me in the church next to Father Juan Crespí, for the present, and when the stone church is built, you may place me where you will."

Palóu, scarcely able to check the flow of tears enough to speak, promised to do what he asked and then implored Serra to "offer adoration in my name when you arrive in the presence of the Holy Trinity, and that you will not forget me nor to pray for all those who dwell in these establishments."

"I promise," Serra said, "that if the Lord in His infinite mercy shall grant me this everlasting felicity which I in no wise deserve on account of my faults, that I will do so for all, and that He may grant the conversion of all these pagan people whom I am leaving unconverted."

He then lapsed into deep contemplation for a while and then roused up to request that Palóu sprinkle the room with holy water. Overcome by the realization that the moment of physical death was near at hand, Junípero suddenly cried out in fright, "I have come under the shadow of a great fear. I am very much afraid. Read to me the Recommendation for the Soul and please speak loud that I may hear it."

Palóu read the Recommendation for the Soul, to which the dying man made the responses as if he were well, sitting on his little stool, and moving their hearts to tenderness. All the officers from the frigate, as well as the other priests of the mission, were in attendance.

"Thanks be to God! Thanks be to God!" cried Serra joyously, "He has quite taken away my fear! Thanks be to God, there is no fear now, and so let us go outside."

In amazement at his seeming revival of strength, the crowd followed Serra into another small room where he again sat and began reading the Divine Office and reciting the prayers. When the captain of the ship said to him, "Father President, you see what my Patron Saint, San Antonio, can do. I have asked him to make you well and I expect that he will do it," Serra smiled gently and all present understood without his making any reply, that he did not think he would recover. Once again he began reading and reciting his prayers. Palóu reminded him that the hour was well past noon and asked if he wouldn't like a cup of broth. When he brought it to him, Serra quietly drank it and then said, "Let us now go to rest." He walked into his cell and taking off only his mantle lay down upon the bed of boards and holding the Cross to his chest closed his eyes. They all left the room thinking him asleep, but Palóu, growing uneasy, returned to find that Serra had gently slipped away and was "sleeping with the Lord."

There was an expression of peace and contentment upon the tired old face and the great crucifix, which always accompanied him, was upon his breast. Death came early in the afternoon of August 28, 1784. Serra lived to reach the age of seventy years, nine months and four days, after spending fifty-four of them as a religious and thirty-five in the missionary field.

He was tenderly and lovingly prepared for burial by his grieving friends. Divested of his sandals and hair shirt, clad only in his homespun Franciscan habit with the thrice-tied rope about his waist, they laid him in a plain coffin. For the brief hours of mourning they placed the coffin in the church, near the steps of the sanctuary, opposite the altar. Soldiers stood at guard as the weeping Indians came all during the night to recite the Rosary and to cover Junípero's body with flowers.

Visiting dignitaries and humble folk crowded the church to pay homage to their spiritual guardian during the funeral on August 29. Cannon from the nearby fort thundered every half hour as did the broadsides from the frigate in the harbor.

They took Junípero Serra on a final tour of his most cherished mission for the last time as four crews of the King's officers bore the casket upon their shoulders. Clad in their black copes, priests slowly walked before the bier, and following it marched soldiers and sailors carrying lighted torches in their hands. Last of all came the settlers and the Indians. The procession returned to the church for the singing of lauds. They lowered him into his tomb during the last response and laid him close to the grave of his friend, Father Juan Crespí. The service ended with the singing of the "Responsorio," the wailing, sobbing voices of the mourners almost drowning out the voices of the singers. "His children," Palóu was to write, "were mourning the death of their Father, who had left his own old father and mother in his native land and had come this long distance for no other purpose than to make these his children and the children of God through Holy Baptism. The flock was lamenting the death of its Shepherd who had labored so assiduously to provide them with spiritual food and who had delivered them from the claws of the infernal wolf. His faithful subjects were mourning the loss of their Prelate, the wise, the prudent, the courteous, the diligent, and the model leader, as they all recognized how greatly he would be missed in the development of these Spiritual Conquests."

When the funeral services were over, the congregation pressed Palóu for some remembrance, some little thing which had belonged to Serra. Because of his poverty, Serra owned nothing and so Palóu took the tunic, which he was not wearing at the time of his death and which had newly been washed, and gave it to the commander of the vessel, telling him to divide it among the crew. He instructed them to make these fragments into scapulars which he in turn would bless seven days hence during the memorial services for the departed presidente. To the others, he gave the little holy medals Serra kept for this purpose.

Immediately, claims of miraculous cures began coming in to Palóu, who discounted any such supernatural virtue in the objects, but rather that it may have been in each case the result of natural causes or simple coincidence. The people continued to believe in the mystical qualities of the fragments and coveted them as mementos of the man who had served them in such an exemplary manner for so many years.

The memorial services were held a week later and all of the governmental and religious dignitaries who were unable to reach Carmel at the time of Serra's death were there. Palóu blessed the scapulars the sailors had made and they were greatly comforted by them.

Immediately upon receiving word of Serra's death, the Indians came in great numbers to all of the missions for Baptism. This was the result, believed Palóu, of the little Padre remembering his dying promise to intercede on their behalf when he stood before the Lord. His apostolic zeal was being carried on, for, as Palóu wrote, "His memory will not be blotted out because the works which he did while alive have been stamped upon the inhabitants of this New California who, in spite of the devouring element of time, will perpetuate it to all generations."

CHAPTER XXIV

A VERY BURDENSOME SAINT

Had the weary, suffering, and heartbroken Serra but realized that most of his fears for his missions were groundless, he could have been spared hours of anguish. He would have rejoiced to know that it was the intercession of his old friend, Joseph de Gálvez, which was to prevent the missions from falling into the hands of the Dominicans. The Franciscans were to continue their labor for fifty years.

The burden of building new missions was to fall upon the sturdy, reliable shoulders of capable Father Fermín Lasuén, who served as prefect from 1785 to 1803. Twelve more missions were to be founded: Santa Barbara in 1786; La Purísima Concepción in 1787; Santa Cruz and Soledad in 1791; San José, San Juan Bautista, San Miguel and San Fernando in 1797; and San Luis Rey in 1798. Continuing into the nineteenth century Father Tapis founded Santa Inés in 1804; San Rafael in 1817 by Father Sarria; and San Francisco Solano in 1823 by Father Altamira.

These missions were interspersed between the original nine in such a manner as to form Christian communities within a day's journey from each other. There was renewed interest taken by the College of San Fernando and friars sent in sufficient numbers so that two could be located at each mission. Days of plenty came to the missions and an era of tranquillity and prosperity blessed the land of California—for a period of time.

Palóu, failing in health, determined to write the life of his venerable lector so that all would recall his many virtues and saintly accomplishments upon this earth. Not satisfied with writing a biography, he felt impelled to add supplementary information on "the virtues" as an aid to future postulators of the cause for Serra's glorification and elevation to sainthood, all the while modestly claiming that such was not his intention and declaring his personal unworthiness for the task of recording the life of one whom he had followed in nearly all of his pilgrimages upon earth. "It is true," wrote Palóu, "that since the year 1740 up to the year 1784, in which death separated us, I had enjoyed his very special affection and that we had mutually loved each other more than do those who are brothers by ties of blood." Palóu began the last chapter of his remarkable literary effort with the following words: "If the preceding history of the Life and Apostolic Labors of the Venerable Father Fr. Junípero has been read with any degree of reflection, the reader will have discovered that his laborious and exemplary life was like a beautiful and charming field, carpeted with every variety of flowers, which are his excellent virtues."

In an honest effort to appear as objective as his fervent admiration for his subject of the diary would permit, Palóu frankly admitted, "As it was apparent to all that Father Junípero had a special genius of founding new Missions there were not lacking persons in authority and of rank who said of him: 'This Father Junípero is a holy man, but in this matter of asking for help for the founding of Missions he is a very burdensome saint.'"

Days of calamity were to fall upon the missions, secularization and then abandonment would come; walls crumbled and the work done by the Padres held in disrepute, but through all the long period of distress, the reputation of Father Junípero Serra remained unsullied. His apostolic zeal, his physical courage, and the very human characteristics of obstinacy and occasional bluntness of speech, made his nobility shine forth in an indifferent world.

The "burdensome saint" left his impression upon the people of the state of California and his influence grows steadily.

The California State Board of Education requires that each fourth-grade class in every school must have a study unit on the missions so that school children will know about Father Serra. Schools and colleges have been named for him. A section of highway in San Mateo County is called the Serra Freeway. The mission influence carried over into the realms of architecture, furniture, and even landscaping.

The mission Fathers enriched the agriculture of the state for it was they who introduced subtropical fruits such as the orange. They brought seeds and cuttings of plants. They introduced apples, peaches, plums, and the pomegranate. Their extensive vineyards were the start of the great wine industry in California while cattle, sheep, and horses, all brought so toilsomely across the rough terrain of Baja, soon roamed wild across the hills.

But, despite all this rich heritage, it is to the gentle priest, Father Junípero Serra, that Californians turn to for real inspiration. And yet so very little is known about the man. History records his accomplishments and deeds, but of the real Serra, virtually nothing is known. His innate modesty, shyness, and reticence made Junípero Serra an enigma even to his lifelong friend and Father Confessor. Palóu would not write about these inner qualities.

What did he look like, this dauntless apostle from Majorca, this spiritual giant who settled California and converted thousands of heathen in the name of God and the King of Spain as he founded a chain of missions with practically nothing but his faith to sustain him?

Although the ever-faithful Palóu tells us very little about his teacher's appearance, we do have some indications of his traits. Serra's voice was described as melodic and powerful. Palóu tells us that the inborn gentleness and modesty of the "Venerable Father" led him to turn away from earthly hurtful speech and to change any conversation, which was bordering upon the ugly side of life, into loftier channels. We learn that in his evangelical zeal he forgot one of the precepts of his order—to sermonize always briefly—and sometimes exhorted congregations too long and too forcefully.

He walked with a painful limp on a festering leg. He denied himself sleep, considering slumber an indulgence except for his afternoon siesta. He ate sparingly and with total disregard for what was served. We know from his infrequent letters that he suffered from loneliness and from the lack of intellectual companionship, for he constantly asked that news of fellow priests be sent to him so that he could pray for them.

But what did he look like? There is so little to go on, no one actually knows. A reverent scientific investigation was conducted at his final resting place at Carmel and his mortal remains examined by Dr. Theodore McCown of the University of California and by Dr. Mark R. Harrington of the Southwest Museum in 1943. Serra's height was determined as having been five feet two or three inches, as a maximum. A pair of rope sandals, tattered and frayed with long wear, indicate his feet were no larger than those of a young boy.

Statues honoring Fray Junípero Serra are numerous. One stands in a dark corridor of the church of San Fernando in Mexico City and another in the gardens outside the national shrine of Guadalupe. His likeness stands in the Statuary Hall in the Capitol building in Washington, the overwhelming choice of the people of California for his place in its history. There is another in Golden Gate Park, San Francisco, and one in the midst of the swirling traffic of downtown Los Angeles.

In all probability, none of these captures the essence of the venerable Padre. All are based upon a poorly painted picture done by an inadequate artist who, following the custom of the times, purposely sought to be flattering rather than historically accurate. This familiar portrait of Serra, the only picture we have of him, fails to portray him as he must surely have been that day in Mexico City when Father Rafael Verger, a friend of many years standing insisted that the "indomitable old lion," as one friend called him, pose for a painting so that his features should be preserved forever. Serra, then in his late sixties, had come to report to Viceroy Bucareli and to seek his continued support for the California missions. A month previous, Serra had nearly died from raging fevers in Guadalajara, but had somehow summoned the strength to journey on to Mexico City.

It was, therefore, a desperately ill man the portraitist seated in an armchair, and then proceeded to paint the flaccid, vapid, almost jovial face of a man in full health of the middle forties. The stubborn strength, the spirituality, the marks of physical pain long endured, the signs of a lifetime of self-immolation are ignored, and instead we gaze upon a very dull, commonplace face.

The records made in 1749 by officials of the Board of Trade in Cádiz, and which are now in the Archivo de Indias at Seville, tell a different story: "Father Junípero Serra, lector of theology, native of Petra, thirty-five years old, of medium height, swarthy, dark eyes and hair, scant beard."

The painter failed to portray the small wiry frame and the sinewy arms and hands, made so by hard physical work, and the skin of leathery texture from exposure to the intense California sun. Nor did he capture the etched lines of physical pain, the fatigue, and compassion for his fellow creatures and the ardent love of God, which must have shown in those dark eyes and been imprinted upon the weary face.

The real Serra was indeed a remarkable man. Already at an advanced age when he came to Alta California, he nevertheless possessed the traits which were most needed in the pioneer. He was an enthusiastic, battling, almost quarrelsome, fearless, keen-witted, fervidly devout, unselfish, single-minded missionary. He subordinated everything, and himself most of all, to the demands of his evangelical task as he understood it.*

We know, from Palóu, that Serra gave comfort and encouragement to every one of the priests under his charge. His letters and physical presence, although infrequent, literally provided the "shade of the Juniper tree," which sustained them and assisted them to continue and refreshed them at times of frustration and despair.

As long ago as 1910 American Catholics began to take an interest in obtaining Junípero's beatification. A Friends of Father Serra organization was started. In 1949 Father Maynard Geiger gathered together all of the documentary evidence for formal presentation of

* Charles Edward Chapman. *History of California: The Spanish Period.* New York, 1921.

the Serra Cause. Today the process of compassing the "position" or actual presentation of the Serra case to the Sacred Congregation of Rites is underway. Once the authorities of this Congregation have received and approved the position, Fr. Junípero Serra will then be eligible for presentation to the Holy Father for the declaration of "Venerable." This is the most difficult phase and the most arduous portion of the world's "most complicated legal process," as Canonization has been described. What the outcome will be, of course, no one knows. It is doubtful if the matter will be decided in our lifetimes.

In 1963 the Philadelphia Mint was authorized by an Act of Congress to strike a unique national medal commemorating the 250th anniversary of the birth of Serra on November 24, 1713. This was the first national medal to honor the life of a Catholic priest.

By special concession five medals were struck in gold for presentation to the President of the United States, Pope Paul VI, Generalissimo Franco, Serra International, and for loan to California museums. On October 16, 1963, President John F. Kennedy signed the authorizing Act of Congress into law. On the date of the actual 250th anniversary of Junípero Serra's birth, the martyred President Kennedy's body lay in state in the Capitol building not far from the statue of Serra.

One side of the medal reproduces that same statue in relief. The reverse shows California with its first ten missions: San Francisco (Dolores), 1776; Santa Clara, 1777; San Carlos Borromeo (Carmel), 1770; San Antonio, 1771; San Luis Obispo, 1772; Santa Barbara, 1786; San Buenaventura, 1782; San Gabriel Archangel, 1771; San Juan Capistrano, 1776; and San Diego de Alcala, 1769. Serra's motto encircles the outline of the state:

Always Go Forward and Never Turn Back

EPILOGUE

THE QUEST FOR SERRA

BY KATHERINE AINSWORTH

This book is the result of a thirty-year-long friendship with a man we never saw or knew. How did it come about that two Protestants took such an interest in the Catholic missionary who left his indelible mark upon the New World and the Californias?

My first acquaintance with the Serra legend came during early childhood when my parents took me on the hurtling, big red cars of the interurban Pacific electric railway to the small town of San Gabriel for the matinee performance of the *Mission Play,* a romanticized story authored by John Steven McGroaty, poet laureate of California.

Ed came from Texas as an eighteen-year-old youth, fell in love with the state of California, and immediately began to read omnivorously about its history. He went to work for the Los Angeles *Times* and after a few years became the state editor and wrote a column called "Along El Camino Real." He became the interpreter of the news events happening in the hinterlands of Southern California to the readers of the metropolitan daily and related these developments to the historical past.

One of our earliest involvements with Serra material came as a result of Ed's writing about the now famous return of the swallows to Mission San Juan Capistrano each St. Joseph's Day, March 19. His stories resulted in nationwide publicity that was warmly welcomed by our good friend, Father Arthur J. Hutchinson since it was most helpful in his difficult program to restore the mission at least partially to its former beauty. In appreciation, Father Hutchinson opened the safe at the mission and allowed us to handle and read the ancient registry books bound in soft cowhide. The once jet black ink had faded to a light brown color, but the exquisite script done with a quill pen by Serra in 1776 as he wrote the title pages in the books of Marriages, Baptisms, and Deaths is still plainly legible. As he was to so many places in Spain, Mexico, Baja California, and throughout the mission chain, Father Junípero Serra became a fascinating, almost living inspiration to us, as we later retraced the indomitable little friar's travels.

Through the years this sense of knowing Serra increased for no matter how demanding the duties of journalism and the authoring of plays and books, Ed continued to gain new information and insights through reading and making explorations about a man and an epoch that fascinated us both. Hardly second to this fascination with Serra was our love for Mexico. No matter how far we traveled, the year we failed to get to Mexico was a year that was lost in Ed's thinking. He looked upon it as his second home.

It was on such a trip in 1963 that perhaps his deepest communion with Serra was achieved. We had driven down the west coast of Mexico stopping briefly at Guaymas, then on through Navojoa, Los Mochis, and stopping at Mazatlán. Continuing south the next day I was surprised when Ed turned off the main highway and took the road through the jungle to the ocean at San Blas. The harbor of San Blas, so important in earlier centuries is no more. The tides have choked it off with sand and the sawmills at Matanchel are gone. High on a bluff overlooking the village stands the unpretentious ruins of the old church. We slithered and jolted up over the slippery rocks on the almost obliterated dirt tracks up to the lovely ruins where Serra had preached during those anxious days while all was being readied for the journey that changed the course of history.

Ed walked around the ruin. He touched the walls. He sat on a fallen fragment and stared pensively out over the cobalt sea. He made copious notes—a thing most unusual for him—while I swatted away the mosquitoes, which never seemed to attack him.

Suddenly he stood and after taking one last look about, walked with me to the car and we drove on to Tepic.

After dinner that evening he wrote for a long time on his portable typewriter, having explained that it was his annual piece on Serra that had become a tradition in the Los Angeles *Times*. Finished at last, Ed gathered the pages up and still perhaps deep in thoughts of another time, silently gave them to me.

I was profoundly affected by what I read. It was as though Ed had written a tribute to a personal friend rather than a historical personage and it glowed with understanding and compassion. Although I had no foreknowledge of it at the time, this essay was directly responsible for an involvement with our beloved Serra beyond any we had dreamed of.

After centuries of indifference and neglect of Fray Junípero Serra, the Spanish government in a surprise action decided to commemorate the 250th anniversary of his birth "with all due honors." Among the events were several literary competitions. Soon after the appearance of Ed's piece, George M. Straszer, assistant to the editor of the *Times*, wrote to the Spanish authorities as follows:

> I have the honor to enclose three copies of the tribute to Fra. Junípero Serra, written by Ed Ainsworth, staff member of the Los Angeles *Times*, and published by this paper on Sunday, Sept. 15, 1963. We offer this exhibit as an entry in the journalistic contest honoring the 250th anniversary celebration of the birth of Fra. Serra, conducted by the Spanish Ministry of Tourism in Madrid and your Spanish Tourist Office.
>
> The Los Angeles *Times* is particularly pleased to submit this entry because it is the product of the writing skill of a distinguished historian of California, who has himself contributed greatly toward the public's knowledge of the revered Serra.

Ed told me nothing about this contest or his entry. I was thus quite astonished by his excited telephone call some two months later with the news that his entry had won the nationwide contest. I could scarcely tell him how proud and pleased I was before he was happily explaining that all of this meant a trip to Spain as guests of the Spanish government and participation in the commemorative events in Madrid and Majorca.

This all became a reality some time later and after the formalities of our visit were attended to, we had ample time in our quest for Serra for following his footsteps from the birthplace in Petra to Cádiz, the port from whence he sailed to the New World in May of 1749.

Our final adventures along El Camino Real took place soon after Ed's retirement that completed forty-three years on the *Times*. Characteristically, we were off for Mexico almost before the happy sounds of his memorable retirement party in Temecula had died away. We began as Serra and Palóu had in Vera Cruz and managed to experience each location of their labors and studies. Although we could not follow the overland trek up the Baja peninsula, we picked up the trail once again in San Diego and have visited in addition to the missions founded by Serra and the Franciscans all the others in California.

Retracing the odyssey of the indomitable and courageous little man of God, reaching from a tiny house in Petra in the Mediterranean to Carmel on the Pacific, after decades of study and curiosity about the man was profoundly gratifying to Ed. Those who knew my husband may perceive, as I do, certain similarities between Ed and his hero revealed in the lines of the commemorative tribute that brings this book to a close.

"Across the barren lands under the glaring sun the holy man with the glowing eyes and the lame leg trudged to his terrestrial goal and then on to the Throne of God.

"He founded a new land but his thoughts were ever upon saving heathen souls.

"He immortalized his own name but he forgot himself for others.

"He scourged his own flesh but he laid gentle hands upon the sick and the blind.

"He is synonymous with California.

"Yet the very name by which we know him was won as a missionary, so that it transcended the one with which he was christened in the fabled isles of the Hesperides.

"Now, in this year of 1963 the world joins to acclaim Fr. Junípero Serra a quarter of a millennium after he was born and christened Miguel José Serre, according to the spelling of the Island of Majorca, on Nov. 24, 1713. The 'Junípero' was chosen later at the time of his ordination.

"Eventually he typified both the names he emblazoned across the pages of 18th century achievement: the hardiness and resilience of the Junípero (Juniper) tree, undaunted by any winds of adversity; and forever, as long as breath lasted him, wielding a persistent Serra (Saw) to cut down all the works of the Devil.

"Here was a man so steeped in Christian faith that he prayed in his sleep and, following the example of the Saviour, washed the feet of humble Indians. He was capable of walking 1,000 miles with an ulcerated leg. He outdistanced the hardy 'Leather Jacket' soldiers with whom he marched. He lived on little, but his strength was great. It was so great that he was willing to go halfway around the world to redeem naked savages. It was so great that he went forth dauntlessly into the wilderness to challenge idolatry and preach the gospel.

"This missionary ardor amid the rigors of hostile jungles and menacing deserts in the mainland Mexico and the two Californias— Baja and the new colony at Alta—was made doubly impressive because of the Eden-like land of his birth which Serra left for the service of the Lord. In Majorca, amid the blue and purple seas, surrounded by pomegranates, figs, plums, melons, olives and oranges he grew up where life was easy and contentment was a way of life. Still, there was no contentment in the material sense for him. He was driven by the flagellations of an inner faith to renounce ease and comfort and home and parents to go forth into the heathen for Jesus' sake.

"From birth, he was close to animals and the soil.

"The Serra house in Petra was Biblical in its primitiveness. The donkey and the chickens and goats were part of the household. A crawling baby, looking up, could see the udders or the friendly eyes of a cow. Nearby, were fields where plots of soil were tilled by the Mallorquin natives, like Serra's father, who preferred to live in villages rather than in isolated houses.

"On the natural tree trunk beams of the Serra house the smoke of innumerable winter fires had performed their mellowing function. The house was dim, like a cloister, with most of the light coming down the big chimney rather than from the one small window.

"Parental piety was infused into the son. The Serra home radiated religion. The boy said his catechism as naturally as he ate the blood sausage of the island and made his devotions quite as matter-of-factly as he took the cattle to pasture or carried water home from the pump. Still, very early, he began formal studies which indicated his tendency toward the priesthood. And, when he was only 16, he was invested with the Franciscan habit at the Convento de Jesus September 14, 1730. Then began his religious duties in Palma, the magnificent seaside city of Majorca. Here he took the name 'Junípero.'

"Now, more than two centuries later, his name is being considered for sainthood as a result of his Christian zeal in his native land, in Mexico and in Baja and Alta California.

"Here in modern California we are perhaps too prone to evaluate Junípero Serra on his accomplishments in setting up a colony amid savages in a new land and building nine missions with faith and his bare hands. When he arrived at the site of what was to be San Diego July 1, 1769, he was 55 years of age, and most of his life was gone. He spent the ensuing 15 years, until his death Aug. 28, 1784, in Herculean efforts to Christianize the Indians, clothe their bodies and feed their bellies.

"But what stupendous qualities of mind and soul had this small man built into his character during the almost 40 years from that moment when he became a Franciscan until he stood by the Pacific shore to found the colony of Alta California? How had he endured the physical travail? Whence came the qualities which won the confidence of Spanish administrators and caused Fr. Serra to be chosen for one of the most crucial expeditions in Spanish history?

"How did the slight youth amid the farm animals of Petra come to have the resonant voice of an apostolic evangelist, the skill of an engineer, the courage of a gladiator, the stoicism of a Greek philosopher, the enduring religious ardor of a mystic and the compassion of a St. Francis?

"Only one answer seems possible: An inner flame nurtured throughout life by an abiding faith in God.

"When Junípero Serra, after determining to become a missionary, arrived in Mexico at the age of 36 and started the weary walk through the jungle toward Mexico City, he was setting forth on an upward trail that was to last, spiritually, until death closed his eyes. This was in effect, a novitiate upon a novitiate; a mature man, building upon humility in an alien land, the postgraduate qualities of bravery and persistence which were to be his only temporal salvation later amid the unparalleled rigors of California.

"To the New World with him had come two of his friends from Palma, Fr. Francisco Palóu, later to become Serra's chronicler; and Fr. Juan Crespí, later immortalized as the diarist of the Juan Bautista de Anza expedition to found the Presidio of San Francisco in 1776.

"It was typical of Serra that he determined to walk from Vera Cruz to Mexico City. On the way he incurred an injury that plagued him all the rest of his life. His leg became infected from a bite—probably from a mosquito, although a snake has been mentioned, too—and never healed. He limped in pain from then on.

"Arriving in Mexico City, he reported to the fathers at the College of San Fernando. Soon he was appointed to a difficult missionary post.

"In the frightening forests amid the massive mountains of the Sierra Gorda, 200 miles northeast of Mexico, in the State of Querétero, where fiery opals flashed in the rich earth, Fr. Serra was sent in 1750 to attempt to convert the unpredictable Pame Indians. Until he was given this assignment he had been carrying on his religious work at the college in Mexico City. His fervor had been almost terrifying to the sophisticated residents of the capital. Here was a zealot who publicly scourged himself with chains, applied flames to his naked flesh to epitomize the horrors of hell fire to his hearers. It was slightly shocking to the gay social set drinking their chocolate all day and dancing all night.

"With the Pames, Fr. Serra did not have to combat mere social sins. Theirs was a pagan idolatry. He was compelled to ferret out great idols hidden on mountain tops and in the forest. He was constantly striving to convince his Indian parishioners to work in the fields or aid in the construction of the missions.

"In Jalpan, one of the communities within his territory, he began his architectural career. A creditable church was built with the aid of the Indians, forerunner of the nine missions of earth and stone to emerge later upon the soil of distant California.

"After several years of toil in the Sierra Gorda, Fr. Serra returned once more to the College of San Fernando in Mexico City.

"Not yet was his time. But it was approaching. World events almost beyond his ken were fashioning the future pattern of his life.

"Spain had been complacent for a long time about her colonial empire. She was glutted and surfeited with gold and silver and spices and silk from Mexico, Peru and the Philippines. Now, though, just after midcentury in the 1700s an ominous shadow, elongated by the Northern Lights, was cast down from the North along the Pacific shores of North America. It was that of the Russian bear.

"Spain suddenly realized that she might lose the entire Pacific Coast to the Russians and, even though it was unexplored and uninhabited, the prospect of it being swallowed up was unthinkable. The King of Spain at this juncture sent to Mexico a remarkable administrator with virtually dictatorial powers—José de Gálvez, visitador general. From Gálvez stemmed the appointment of Serra as the spiritual leader of the expedition in 1769 to settle the wilderness of Alta California and forestall the Russians.

"All this was happening in the late 1760s just after the expulsion of the Jesuits in 1767–68, in one of the great secret coups of international history, from all of Mexico including Baja California.

"Fr. Junípero Serra was appointed president of Baja California missions to succeed the Jesuits. He took up his post in Loreto just before Easter of 1768, still unaware of his impending role to the north.

"He had sailed from San Blas, the jungle port on the West Coast on the Mexican mainland after coming down the long dangerous trail, dragging his injured leg, from Mexico City to Tepic. At San Blas he had stood on the hill and looked out over the vast green jungle and the blue Pacific toward distant Baja. Did he have any premonition even yet of the role in store for him?

"It is probable he did not. He seems never to have speculated on personal advancement. His critics have accused him of being phlegmatic, commonplace, unimaginative. Yet in the day-to-day conduct of affairs, in the infinitely-important matter of getting things done, in his devotion to duty he was unexcelled. His record was so solid in its accomplishments that it was brought to the attention of Visitador General Gálvez.

"Then came Serra's appointment. He was put in charge of the missionary facet of Spanish expansion to Alta California; Capt. Gaspar de Portolá, commandant at Loreto, in charge of the military.

Ships were sent to San Diego to rendezvous with Serra and Capt. Portolá and the land expedition which was to travel up the Peninsula almost 1,000 miles and then settle San Diego and Monterey.

"Only the incredible personal courage of Serra brought him to San Diego. His infected leg was much worse on the march. At times he was unable to stand. Finally, when it appeared he must give up and remain behind, he induced a muleteer to treat him with the herb ointment used on the gall sores of the animals. Immediately a transformation was wrought. Serra was able to proceed and to finish the march, although his leg troubled him all the remainder of his days and he was never without pain.

"He arrived in San Diego July 1, 1769, and founded the mission July 16.

"Alta California was the supreme challenge. While the soldiers were away hunting the port of Monterey, the Indians attacked the rude brush huts of the Spaniards, the food ran out, the San Blas supply ship was agonizingly late, abandonment of the new San Diego mission was imminent. But through it all Serra, with his calm faith, remained resolute and determined. Nothing daunted him.

"When supplies did finally arrive, Serra went forth by ship, taking weeks for the short voyage to Monterey.

"On the shores of the fabled port, Serra built the second—and his personal favorite—of the missions, San Carlos. From here, during his remaining days he directed or participated in the founding of seven other missions, a total of nine of the eventual 21. Included was his beloved San Juan Capistrano with its stone church, founded in 1776, the year of the American Revolution on the opposite shore of America.

"Serra's labors were titanic. He walked thousands of miles despite his injured leg. He kept in touch with Mexico City. He pleaded for church supplies; never for anything for himself. He quelled military troubles as well as spiritual rebellions. He worked for political rule in California on a plane equal to church administration.

"All the while he slept on the rough boards, brought from distant idyllic Palma, which constituted his bed for 50 years. He prayed by day. His prayers continued in his sleep at night. He saw naked Indians saved. He sought always to extend the Kingdom of God, forgetful of himself and his ills.

"So his days went.

"At last he knew his labors were nearing an end.

"On St. Augustine's Day, Aug. 28, 1784, he lay down on his rude bed in San Carlos Mission, beside the blue Bay of Monterey. There he spoke quietly to God, closed his eyes, went to sleep, and never awoke again. His faithful friend, Fr. Palóu, found him lying there, at rest.

"He was buried in the mission garden, far from the terrestrial isles of the Hesperides, but certainly very near to the celestial Throne of God."

*   *   *

BIBLIOGRAPHY

Altamira, Rafael. *History of Spain from the Beginnings to the Present Day*. New York, 1949.

Aschmann, Homer. *The Central Desert of Baja California: Demography and Ecology*. Riverside, Calif., 1967.

Baegert, Johann Jakob, S.J. *Observations in Lower California*. Tr. by M. M. Brandenburg and C. L. Caumann. Berkeley, 1952.

Bancroft, Hubert Howe. *History of California*. 7 Vols. San Francisco, 1886.

Bancroft, Hubert Howe. *History of Mexico, 1600–1803*. Vols. III, VIII. San Francisco, 1883.

Bolton, Herbert F. *Rim of Christendom*. New York, 1936.

Briggs, Laurence Palmer. *A Pilgrimage to the Home of Joseph de Gálvez, the Father of California*. Oakland, Calif., 1942.

Cambridge Modern History, Vol. VI, "The Eighteenth Century." New York, 1909.

Chapman, Charles Edward. *Founding of Spanish California: The Northwest Expansion of New Spain*. New York, 1916.

Chapman, Charles Edward. *History of California: The Spanish Period*. New York, 1921.

Clavigero, Francisco Javier. *The History of (Lower) California*. Tr. from the Italian and ed. by Sara E. Lake and A. A. Gray. Stanford, 1937.

Clinch, Bryan J. *California and Its Missions*. 2 Vols. San Francisco, 1904.

Costansó, Alferez Don Miguel. "Dairy of the Expeditions of 1769." *Land of Sunshine*, Vol. XIV, No. 6, June 1901. *Land of Sunshine*, Vol. XV, No. 1, July 1901.

Diez del Corral, Luis. *Majorca*. Adapted from the Spanish by Michael C. Byrne. London, 1962.

Dunne, Peter Masten. *Black Robes in Lower California*. Berkeley, 1952.

Dunne, Peter Masten. "Expulsion of the Jesuits from New Spain, 1767." *Mid-America*, Vol. XIX, No. 1; New Series, Vol. VIII. Jan. 1937.

Eldredge, Zeoth Skinner, ed. *History of California*. 5 Vols. New York, 1915.

Ellis, Havelock. *The Soul of Spain*. London, 1911.

Engelbert, Omer. *The Last of the Conquistadors: Junípero Serra (1713–1784)*. Tr. from the French by Katherine Woods. New York, 1956.

Engelhardt, Fr. Zephrin. *The Missions and Missionaries of California*. San Francisco, 1908.

Fülöp-Miller, Rene. *The Power and Secret of the Jesuits*. Tr. by F. S. Flint and D. F. Tait. New York, 1930.

Geiger, Maynard. *Life and Times of Fray Junípero Serra*. 2 Vols. Washington, D.C., 1959.

Geiger, Maynard. *Palóu's Life of Fray Junípero Serra with Critical Notes and Annotations.* Washington, D.C., 1955.

Gerhard, Peter and Gulich, Howard E. *Lower California Guidebook.* Glendale, Calif., 1962.

Gibson, Charles. *Spain in America.* (New American Nation Series, ed. by Henry Steele Commager and Richard B. Morris.) New York, 1966.

Hittell, Theodore H. *History of California.* San Francisco, 1885.

Ingold, Ernest. *The House in Mallorca.* San Francisco, 1950.

Jackson, Helen Hunt. *Father Junípero and the Mission Indians of California.* Boston, 1902.

Madariaga, Salvador de. *The Rise of the Spanish American Empire.* New York, 1947.

Palóu, Francisco. *Life of Fray Junípero Serra.* Tr. and annotated by Maynard J. Geiger, Washington, D.C., 1955.

Palóu, Francisco. *Noticias de la Nueva California.* Herbert Eugene Bolton, ed. New York, 1966.

Palóu, Francisco. *Relación Histórica de la Vida . . . del V.P. Fray Junípero Serra.* Mexico City, 1787.

Parkes, Henry Bamford. *A History of Mexico.* 3rd ed. Boston, 1960.

Paulin, Arturo Dominguez. *Integración Histórica, Política, Social y Económica del Estado de Querétaro.* Querétaro, Mexico, 1966.

Paulin, Arturo Dominguez. *Querétaro en la Conquista de las Californias.* Querétaro, Mexico, 1966.

Pesman, M. Walter. *Meet Flora Mexicana.* Globe, Ariz., 1962.

Pradeau, Alberto Francisco. *La Expulsión de los Jesuítas de las Provincias de Sonora, Ostimuri y Sinoloa en 1767.* Mexico City, 1959.

Priestly, Herbert Ingram. *José de Gálvez Visitador-General of New Spain (1765–1771).* Berkeley, 1916.

Priestly, Herbert Ingram. *The Mexican Nation, A History.* New York, 1924.

Richman, Irving Berdine. *California under Spain and Mexico (1535–1847).* Boston, 1911.

Serra, Junípero. "Dairy, March 28–June 30, 1769." Tr. by C. F. Lummis. *Out West,* Vol. XVI, Jan.–June 1902. Vol. XVII, July–Dec. 1902.

Smith, Donald Eugene. *The Viceroy of New Spain.* Berkeley, 1913.

Steele, James. *Old California Days.* Chicago, 1893.

Thurman, Michael E. *The Naval Department of San Blas: New Spain's Bastion for Alta California and Nootka 1767 to 1798.* Glendale, Calif., 1967.

Tibesar, Antoine. *Writings of Junípero Serra.* 3 Vols. Washington, D.C., 1955.

INDEX

DATE DUE